ATLA BIBLIOGRAPHY SERIES
edited by Dr. Kenneth E. Rowe

A Scholar's Guide to Academic Journals in Religion

by

JAMES DAWSEY

ATLA Bibliography Series, No. 23

The Scarecrow Press, Inc.
Metuchen, N.J., & London
1988

British Library Cataloguing-in-Publication data available

Library of Congress Cataloging-in-Publication Data

Dawsey, James M.
  A scholar's guide to academic journals in religion /
by James Dawsey.
      p.   cm. -- (ATLA bibliography series : no. 23)
  Includes index.
  ISBN 0-8108-2135-4
  1. Religion--Periodicals--Bibliography. 2. Religious
literature--Authorship. 3. Theology--Periodicals--
Bibliography. 4. Christian literature--Authorship. I.
Title. II. Series.
Z7751.D33   1988
[BL48]
016.2'005--dc19   88-18104

To my good friends

Elsie Reynolds and Richard Penaskovic

CONTENTS

LIST OF ABBREVIATIONS

A.I.P.P.   Annual Index to Poetry in Periodicals

A.S.&T.Ind.   Applied Science & Technology Index

Abstr.Anthropol.   Abstracts in Anthropology

Abstr.Engl.Stud.   Abstracts in English Studies

Abstr.Musl.Rel.   European Muslims and Christian-Muslim Rela-
                            tions. Abstracts. (Ceased)

Abstrax   Abstrax

Access   Access: the Supplementary Index to Periodicals

Adol.Ment.Hlth
   Abstr.   Adolescent Mental Health Abstracts

Alt.Press Ind.   Alternative Press Index

Amer.Bibl.Slavic.   American Bibliography of Slavic and East
   &E.Eur.Stud.   European Studies

Amer.Hist.&Life   America: History & Life (Parts A, B, C)

Amer.Hum.Ind.   American Humanities Index

Art Ind.   Art Index

Arts&Hum.Cit.Ind.   Arts & Humanities Citation Index

Aus.Educ.Ind.   Australian Education Index

Aus.P.A.I.S.   Australian Public Affairs Information Service
                            (Now: APAIS: Australian Public Affairs
                            Information Service)

Bibl.Engl.Lang.&   Bibliography of English Language and Litera-
   Lit.   ture (Now: Annual Bibliography of English
                            Language and Literature)

Biog.Ind.   Biography Index

Biol.Abstr.   Biological Abstracts

Bk.Rev.Dig.   Book Review Digest

Bk.Rev.Ind.   Book Review Index

Bk.Rev.Mo.   Book Reviews of the Month

Br.Educ.Ind.   British Education Index

Br.Hum.Ind.   British Humanities Index

Bull.Signal   Bulletin Signaletique (Now: PASCAL Explore,
                       PASCAL Folio, PASCAL Therma) (Programme
                       Applique a la Selection et la Compilation
                       Automatique de la Literature)

CERDIC   Bulletin du CERDIC (Centre des Recherche et
                       de Documentation des Institutions Chre-
                       tiennes) (Ceased)

C.I.J.E.   Current Index to Journals in Education

CINAHL (also   Cumulative Index to Nursing and Applied
   C.I.N.I.)   Health Literature

C.L.I.   Current Law Index

CLOA   Current Literature on Aging

Can.Ind.   Canadian Periodical Index

Canon Law Abstr.   Canon Law Abstracts

Cath.Ind.   Catholic Perodical & Literature Index (Formerly:
                       Catholic Periodical Index)

Chem.Abstr.   Chemical Abstracts

Chr.Per.Ind.   Christian Periodical Index

Commun.Abstr.   Communication Abstracts

Curr.Bk.Rev.Cit.   Current Book Review Citations (Ceased)

Curr.Cont.   Current Contents

ERIC   Eric Clearinghouse (See: C.I.J.E.)

Educ.Admin.Abstr.	Educational Administration Abstracts
Educ.Inc.	Education Index
Eng.Ind.	Engineering Index (Now: Engineering Index Monthly and Author Index)
Excerp.Med.	Excerpta Medica
Film Lit.Ind.	Film Literature Index
G.Indian Per.Lit.	Guide to Indian Periodical Literature
G.Soc.Sci.&Rel. Per.Lit.	Guide to Social Science and Religion in Periodical Literature
Gdlns.	Guidelines
Geneal.Per.Ind.	Genealogical Periodical Annual Index
Hist.Abstr.	Historical Abstracts
Hum.Ind.	Humanities Index
I.C.U.I.S.Abstr.	ICUIS Abstracts Service (Institute on the Church in Urban Industrial Society) (Now: ICUIS Justice Ministries)
Ind.Heb.Per.	Index to Hebrew Periodicals
Ind.India	Index India
Ind.Islam.	Index Islamicus
Ind.Jew.Per.	Index to Jewish Periodicals
Ind.Med.	Index Medicus
Ind.S.A.Per.	Index to South African Periodicals
Ind.Sel.Per.	Index to Selected Periodicals (Now: Index to Periodical Articles by & about Blacks)
Ind.U.S.Gov.Per.	Index to U.S. Government Periodicals
Int.Nurs.Ind.	International Nursing Index (Now: International Nursing Index, including Nursing Citation Index)
Int.Z.Bibelwiss.	Internationale Zeitschriften fuer Bibelwissenschaft und Grenzgebiete

LCR   Literary Criticism Register

LISA   Library & Information Science Abstracts

L.R.I.   Legal Resource Index

Lang.&Lang.   Language and Language Behaviour Abstracts
  Behav.Abstr.   (Now: LLBA Linguistics and Language Be-
                              havior Abstracts)

Leg.Per.   Index to Legal Periodicals

M.L.A.   MLA Abstracts of Articles in Scholarly Journals
                              (Ceased)

Mag.Ind.   Magazine Index

Media Rev.Dig.   Media Review Digest

Meth.Per.Ind.   Methodist Periodical Index (Now: United
                              Methodist Periodical Index) (Ceased)

Music Artic.Guide   Music Article Guide

Music Ind.   Music Index

New Per.Ind.   New Periodicals Index (Ceased)

New Test.Abstr.   New Testament Abstracts

Old Test.Abstr.   Old Testament Abstracts

P.A.I.S.   PAIS Bulletin (Public Affairs Information Ser-
                              vice)

PMR   Popular Magazine Review

Past.Care&Couns.   Pastoral Care & Counseling Abstracts (Now:
  Abstr.   Abstracts of Research in Pastoral Care and
                              Counseling)

Phil.Ind.   Philosopher's Index

Psychol.Abstr.   Psychological Abstracts

Pt.de Rep.   Point de Repere (Formed by the merger of:
                              Periodex and RADAR)

R.G.   Readers' Guide to Periodical Literature

RILA   RILA (International Repertory of the Literature
                              of Art)

Rel. & Theol. Abstr.	Religious & Theological Abstracts
Rel. Ind. One	Religion Index One: Periodicals
Rel. Ind. Two	Religion Index Two: Multi-Author Works
Rel. Per.	Index to Religious Periodical Literature (Now: Religion Index One: Periodicals & Religion Index Two: Multi-Author Works)
Rural Recreat. Tour. Abstr.	Rural Recreation and Tourism Abstracts (Now: Leisure, Recreation and Tourism Abstracts)
SSCI	Social Science Citation Index
Soc. Sci. Ind.	Social Science Index
Sociol. Abstr.	Sociological Abstracts
South. Bap. Per. Ind.	Southern Baptist Periodical Index (Ceased)
Vert. File Ind.	Vertical File Index
World Agri. Econ. & Rural Sociol. Abstr.	World Agricultural Economics & Rural Sociology Abstracts

EDITOR'S FOREWORD

The American Theological Library Association Bibliography
Series is designed to stimulate and encourage the preparation of reliable bibliographies and guides to the literature of religious studies
in all of its scope and variety. Compilers are free to define their
field, make their own selections, and work out internal organization
as the unique demands of the subject indicate. We are pleased to
publish James Dawsey's <u>Scholar's Guide to Academic Journals in Re-
ligion</u> as number twenty-three in our series.

Following undergraduate studies in liberal arts at Florida
Southern College, James M. Dawsey studied theology at Emory University and in 1983 completed a doctorate in religious studies at
Emory. He currently serves as Associate Professor in the Department
of Religion at Auburn University in Auburn, Alabama. Mr. Dawsey's
guide grows out of his own rich experience as the author of two
books and numerous scholarly articles.

Kenneth E. Rowe
Series Editor
Drew University Library
Madison, NJ   07940

INTRODUCTION

How does a writer get published? This is an important question in present-day academics. Most of us wish to take part in our discipline's discourse and express our ideas before the public. Writing satisfies an inner longing. It goes hand and glove with learning and teaching, for it hones the mind. Moreover, there are other practical reasons for wishing to be published. Finding a job in a competitive market often depends on one's list of publications. Tenure, promotion, higher salaries, better working conditions, prestige, and a host of other benefits come to those who are most successful at getting into print.

Unfortunately, there are many good articles, essays and reviews that remain forever in manuscript form, buried in dusty files. It is difficult to get published. A Ph.D. helps the scholar get to the door, but no further. One has to "break into print." The quality of the author's research and thoughts, the clearness of the writer's expression, and knowing the journal market count more than does an introduction to an editor.

Publishing is like giving birth. Beyond the work of love, there is labor. The purpose of this book is to ease the post-composition parting by offering in accessible form the information that you as a writer need to choose the right journal to which to submit your work. Before seeing your name in print, you must send your article or review to an appropriate journal.

Writers will find that this book provides information that is not otherwise so easily available. For instance: Which academic journals publish articles in Scripture? In Religious Education? In Social Justice? What types of articles does a specific journal normally accept, and what types does it not publish? What are the manuscript requirements--the style, the length, the language--of a journal? To whom should an article be addressed? Are the editors looking for a specific kind of submission? Will the submission be refereed? How long does it take for a particular journal to respond to a submission? What approximate proportion of submissions does it accept?

Besides describing the journal market, this book also provides information concerning subscriptions and advertisements. Thus, editors and publishers will perhaps also find the work helpful. It

xiii

xiv / Academic Journals in Religion

should reduce the number of inappropriate submissions while increasing the number of those that speak to the subject of the journal; also, the editors and publishers should find that it brings their publication to the attention of new readers, subscribers, and advertisers.

Most of the material contained in this book was provided by editors who responded to a questionnaire requesting information concerning their journals. The editors were asked to describe the subject matter of their journals and to indicate the type(s) of articles being sought, naming, if possible, topics or areas of special interest. They were asked to identify the audience of the journal and whether their journals accepted unsolicited articles and reviews, dot-matrix printing, simultaneous submissions, research notes, review articles, and advertising. They were asked to describe the style of the journal, the language(s) of submissions, length requirements, and number of copies of manuscripts required. They were also asked to describe the selection process, to indicate the length of time that it generally takes them to respond to a submission, and to indicate the approximate proportion of submissions accepted for publication. Finally, the editors were asked to provide correct mailing addresses and information concerning subscription costs and the number of issues published each year. Many respondents also included helpful comments about their journals, which sometimes found their place in this book.

Additional information was sometimes garnered from the written instructions that appear on the inside cover or the first page of some journals. The information concerning indexing and abstracting comes from Ulrich's International Periodicals Directory. Also, when available, the name of the parent organization of the journals is given. That too comes from Ulrich's.

Over 500 journals that publish academic articles in religion are included in this book. I have organized the journals themselves into categories that I hope will be useful to writers. I have also included a cross-listing at the end of each section (except Section 1). An Appendix listing full bibliographical information for style manuals appears at the back, followed by an index. There are a number of journals that do not seem to be specific to any subdiscipline, but instead publish equally in several areas of religious studies. These I have grouped together at the beginning of the book, cross-referencing them at the end of each section to which they most apply.

This project could not have been undertaken without the support and assistance of Auburn University. The book would not have been completed without the support of the many editors with whom I have corresponded. Also, Cynthia Runyon from the Pitts Theology Library at Emory University and Glenn Anderson from the Ralph Brown Draughon Library at Auburn have provided much assistance. I thank all of those involved. The constraints of this project to be comprehensive--giving as much information as possible, yet doing so in a timely fashion--have surely taken their toll on accuracy. I trust that the value of the book will outweigh its limitations. My sweet Dixie did much of the work. Thank you, Jenny, and thank you, Ciro.

J. D.

ON TAMING YOUR MUSE

Richard Penaskovic
Auburn University

You already know all about writing scholarly articles in the area of religion. As Red Smith says, "There's nothing to writing. All you do is sit down at the typewriter and open a vein."

I like to think of writing scholarly articles in religion as a two-stage process: 1) doing the research and 2) putting words down on paper.

With regard to the research part, I try to be thorough in finding out what has been done on the subject during the last five years at least. I would say that the biggest reason for the nonacceptance of a scholarly book or article in religion may be chalked up to inadequate research. Thus, extensive and exhaustive research is the first step toward scholarly publication.

I spent six months doing the research for an article on the Augsburg Confession for Theological Studies. I did not put all of my eggs into this one article. This half year allowed me to find other material on the same subject for two other related articles, one on the "Ecclesiology of the Augsburg Confession" for The Heythrop Journal and one on the Roman Catholic-Lutheran Dialogue for The Ecumenist.

There are no shortcuts through stage two, putting words down on paper. Books and articles are written one word at a time, just as the Great Pyramids were raised stone by stone. As someone once said, writing is like "digging ditches with a spoon." I like to think of it as manual labor of the mind.

Here are some of the hints that help me be productive:

1) Stick to a schedule. I close the door to my office every morning between 8 and 9 a.m., and I write when I'm fresh. To those who say they have no time to write, I retort that other matters are more important to you than writing by your own choice. It's a question of setting priorities. We always find time to do the things we

consider essential. I prefer the early mornings for writing and the afternoons for research in the library.

I keep a special table in my office for writing. When I'm at the table writing in the morning, it's all business. I know that if I flitter away the hour, that's it for the day. I'll come up empty. By having your own writing time, your muse will know when to visit.

2) Read widely with a writer's eye to get ideas for books and scholarly articles. I recommend reading the best scholars in the field to see what topics are hot and also to find out what writing techniques they use. Read widely, then, in order to get the wheel turning in your own mind in terms of generating new and exciting ideas. By doing this I find more ideas than I can pursue in a life-time.

A word of caution: Reading should not be used as an excuse for writing. At a certain point in your research, writing must commence. As James Joyce once said, "In the writing the good things will come." Not everything I write is of high quality. We all write drivel at times. Over time, I find that the cream floats to the top.

3) Begin to keep a journal. I believe that a journal is a writer's best friend. A journal serves many functions. I use it to record the progress of a manuscript, and for writing notes to myself as to what I accomplished each day and what I have to do tomorrow. This is particularly helpful for those who write in bits and snatches.

A journal is to writing what warm-ups are to jogging. It serves to get the ink flowing, the blood of writing. Write something in your journal daily. As the writer Don Reed said, "Daily writing helps you develop conscious control; when lightning does strike, you can convert it to usable electricity." Both Henry James and John Henry Newman kept journals in the last century. This venerable nineteenth-century tradition should not be lost today even if this means keeping a log on one's computer.

I also record bibliographic references in my journal. I jot down in the journal ideas for future articles, titles for books, all future writing plans, even though I may not actually use them for years. My journal contains a title for a book or article on the sacraments, which I got fifteen years ago from George McCauley, S.J. He suggested a title, "Touch of a God," which I really liked.

4) Write to express yourself, not to impress others. The more complex the subject, the clearer your writing must be. For starters, sum up the main point of your book or article in one thesis sentence. If you're unable to do this, you are not ready to submit your material for publication.

5) Be creative. Try to find a fresh angle on a subject. Editors of first-rate journals do not want a simple rehashing of the literature. What they do look for is this: articles that advance the discussion along new paths. Write your article in such a way that others want to read it.

6) Keep on trucking. Some of the most brilliant writing will die a natural death in a desk drawer. Talent alone doth not a writer make. You must persevere; that is, you must finish your manuscript before a publishing decision can be made. There comes a point in writing a book when one inwardly feels that one will complete the work. After that moment of truth, the writing just seems to flow.

This does not mean from that point on, it's all fun and games. There's always the iceberg effect. Above the water there's little to see. Beneath the surface there's the long search for the right metaphor, the agony and the sweat and the screaming at a computer which has just devoured one's bon mot.

To write means to participate, in an infinitely small way, in the creativity of God. I have given you only some hints in taming your muse. Now it's up to you.

ENTERING THE HOLY OF HOLIES: FIRST GETTING PUBLISHED

Rick Nutt
·Muskingum College

Having one's work published is a satisfying achievement. It brings one into dialogue with the community of scholars and provides the opportunity to put one's ideas in the public domain--not to mention helping academicians face the dilemma of publishing or perishing. For those who have never published, however, it may seem a difficult and a rare attainment reserved only for the few--a type of holy of holies one enters by grace alone. It need not be. Let me mention some factors that have helped me, at the beginning of my career, get some of my work into print.

First, choose a topic that does something new. You do not have to delineate a brilliant thesis which will alter the course of study in your field. In fact, it might be best to save your most radical ideas for later in your career when they stand a better chance of getting a fair hearing. But editorial boards do look for at least a different angle on a topic or an essay which asks new questions about previously argued theses. Originality in some aspect of your work will help catch an editor's eye.

Do not just write--rewrite. Vince Lombardi once said, "Practice doesn't make perfect. Perfect practice makes perfect." Just writing does not make good writing, either--I have learned that the hard way. If you are not facing a deadline, write a draft and put it aside a few days. Then, come back to your paper so that you might read it with fresh eyes. You will detect sections with poor syntax and be able to see whether or not the paper flows well. Simple grammatical errors should jump off the page (split infinitives are my downfall). Let someone else read the piece and make suggestions. Proofreading and rewriting are the polish which makes good research shine.

Make contacts. Your professors may help here; they have published and may know editorial staff members. Will they study your work and recommend it be given a reading? A contact cannot get you published, but it may get you serious consideration by an editor. Another good idea is to read papers at meetings. That forces you to write, and you may find that someone who hears it will consider it for publication. I once had a request for an article from an editor on the basis of reading the abstract of a paper he had not heard.

Do not limit your list of publications. Rare is the person who publishes in the top journal in her or his field the first time. What are the secondary and tertiary publications in your area? Might your work be of interest to a journal in another, related field? A corollary to this point is being aware of your audience and the audience of a journal. Yet another corollary is not confining yourself to articles; you might break into print with a book review.

Finally, if you have a specific journal in mind, gear your article to it. Do not send a twenty-page manuscript to a small magazine which uses essays ten pages long; the editor will hardly open the envelope before sending it back. Does this publication require footnotes or endnotes? Does it accept unsolicited material? I have found it helpful to write a letter to the editor in which I describe my research and the thesis I am proposing; would the editor be interested in seeing a manuscript? If so, how long should it be and are there any particular points of style to observe? If the editor declines, time and money have been saved; if the response is favorable, the editor will appreciate your inquiry and be open to the work you submit. (Do not be discouraged by work that is not accepted. It happens to everyone, the comments may lead to a stronger piece, and the comments are not personal.)

These ideas have proven helpful to me, but you will surely be able to add to the list. Some good advice is to seek advice. Talk to your colleagues and find out what has worked for them. Then try it. This book by Professor Dawsey can serve as a valuable tool to those who write. Best wishes to the beginning writer for joy in research, pleasure in writing, and in the end the satisfaction of publishing.

WRITING BOOK REVIEWS

Bill Pitts
Baylor University

A. PURPOSE

1. The purpose of a book review is to acquaint a reader with the book.

2. It is essential that the contents of the book be described clearly.

3. It is also expected that the reviewer will use knowledge of an area and critical skills to evaluate the book.

B. PREPARATION

1. A very helpful exercise is to read regularly good quality reviews such as those found in The New York Times Book Review and major scholarly journals.

2. Another useful exercise is to assign students (under-graduate and/or graduate) to review books and to evaluate the strengths and weaknesses of the reviews. This helps the reviewer develop an understanding of what should be addressed in a review.

3. Most journals do not accept unsolicited book reviews. However, many journals need reviewers. It is therefore appropriate to write journals which publish reviews in your area of speciality and ask to be added to their reviewer list. Provide a curriculum vitae, a description of your dissertation research, and a sample review. Many younger scholars begin their publishing careers with book reviews.

C. MECHANICS

1. The book review is a formal report which should be prepared in proper essay form.

2. It should be submitted in double-spaced typewritten form.

3. Book reviews are usually 500 words (plus or minus 100 words) in length.

4. Book notes are usually 250 words (plus or minus 50 words) in length. They tend to be descriptive rather than analytical.

5. Book review editors usually have more books on hand than can be reviewed in their journals. It is therefore fairly common practice to review two books on the same subject at once. This approach invites comparisons helpful to the readers.

6. Book reviews have very short life. The journal's function is to keep readers current. Therefore, many journals will not publish a review of a book which is over two years old. This means it must be reviewed within a year or so of publication in order to be printed in a timely fashion.

D. CONTENT

1. Include full bibliographic data: authors, title, place of publication, publisher, year of publication, pages. Some journals publish other features, such as cost, bibliography, indexes, illustration, etc. Simply consult the journal for which you are reviewing for desired format.

2. In one or two sentences answer succinctly the question, "What is this book about?" or "What is the author's purpose in writing this book?" This provides an appropriate introduction to your review.

3. Give a brief statement about the author if such information is available. Biographical and academic data are usually included on the dust jacket of the book, in Who's Who, Current Biography, Current Authors, Directory of American Scholars, and so forth. Note the author's professional position and the titles of other pertinent publications. Occasionally it may be useful to describe the author's academic training and how work and experience have prepared or failed to prepare him or her to write this book.

4. Describe the sources used by the author, and assess how

well they have been used. Does the author rely on primary sources (letters, diaries, books written by the person being studied, official documents, etc.) or does the book rely only on secondary works (books written by others)? Is the author aware of current research?

5. Explain the content of the book and comment on its organization. Do not merely list or restate chapter titles. This technique is seldom helpful, and almost always dreadfully boring. Summarize the contents so the reader will know what can be found in this book. You can help the reader decide whether to read the book or simply be informed of its content by your review. This part of the review may be combined with item 2 above, which also focuses on content and purpose.

6. Give a careful incisive evaluation of the work. This is the heart of the review. In this section attempt to think creatively about the book. Describe themes presented. What is the leitmotif of the book? Explain how the author developed major ideas, including presuppositions, arguments, and conclusions. Explain at what points the arguments are weak and can be challenged. Are there errors of fact or interpretation? Read the book actively; dialogue with the author. Make comments in the margin or on a sheet of paper to which you can refer readily; this procedure will help your remarks to be specific rather than general and vague. Cite strengths of the book. Evaluate the purpose of the book and whether the author achieved it. Were you convinced by the argument? Is the author biased? If so, in what way? Does the author present both sides of debated issues? Is the interpretation fairly standard or does it suggest important new lines of thought? What did you learn from the book?

7. The review should have a brief conclusion. It is appropriate to state for whom this publication would be most useful and how it relates to contemporary scholarship. Also helpful are suggestions of other books pertinent to the area of research discussed. Close with a sentence summary of your impression of the value of the book.

1. GENERAL THEOLOGICAL JOURNALS

1. AMERICAN BAPTIST QUARTERLY
   Dr. William R. Millar, Ed.
   Linfield College
   McMinnville, OR 97128

   Subscription--4/yr.--$15, U.S.; $20, overseas. Description of
   subject matter of journal--Usually issues are oriented toward a theme.
   Recommendations to the Board regarding future themes are welcome.
   Publishes articles in Scripture, Ethics, Church History, Theology,
   Evangelism, Church Administration, Pastoral Counseling, Missions,
   Religious Education, and Baptist Studies. Submissions must be in
   English. For: professors, students, laypersons, and Baptist clergy.
   Seeks articles that enlighten the reader on some aspect of Baptist
   studies written from a historical, biblical, theological, or professional
   perspective. Requires 3 copies of manuscript. Selection process--
   Editorial Board makes a decision based on the recommendation of as-
   signed readers. Indexed: Hist.Abstr., Rel.Per., Amer.Hist.&Life,
   Rel.&Theol.Abstr., Rel.Ind.One.

2. ANDREWS UNIVERSITY SEMINARY STUDIES
   Kenneth A. Strand, Ed.
   Andrews University Press
   Berrien Springs, MI 49104

   Subscription--3/yr.--$12, individuals: $15, libraries. Description
   of subject matter of journal--Biblical and Theological. Publishes
   articles in Scripture, Ethics, Church History, Theology, Philosophy
   of Religion, Biblical Archaeology, Biblical Linguistics: its Cognates,
   and Ancient History. For: professors, students, and laypersons.
   Submissions must be in English, German, or French (occasionally).
   Accepts unsolicited articles, simultaneous submissions; does not accept unsolicited reviews, dot-matrix printing; publishes research
   notes and review-articles; does not accept advertising. Seeks
   articles of a scholarly nature. Seeking articles--new insights. Style
   of journal--style guide available. Requires 2 copies of manuscript.
   Length requirements--maximum, 26 pages; minimum, 10 pages. Selection process--refereed by three professors at the seminary. Responds in 1-6 months. Approximate proportion of submissions accepted for publication--20 percent. Indexed: Rel.Per., New Test.

Abstr., Old Test.Abstr., Rel.&Theol.Abstr., Rel.Ind.One. Parent Organization: The Journal of the Seventh-day Adventist Theological Seminary.

3. ANGELICUM
   Jordan Aumann, Ed.
   Raimondo Spiazzi, Ed.
   Pontificia Università S. Tommaso d'Aquino
   Largo Angelicum 1
   00184 Rome, Italy

   Subscription--4/yr.--$25. Publishes articles in Scripture, Theology, and Philosophy. For: professors. Submissions must be in French, German, Spanish, English, or Italian. Does not accept unsolicited articles, unsolicited reviews, dot-matrix printing, simultaneous submissions; does not publish research notes or review-articles; does not accept advertising. Articles are scholarly. Indexed: New Test.Abstr., Old Test.Abstr., Rel.&Theol.Abstr.

4. ANGLICAN THEOLOGICAL REVIEW
   James Dunkly, Ed.
   Episcopal Divinity School
   99 Brattle St.
   Cambridge, MA 02138

   Subscription--4/yr.--$15, individuals; $18, institutions. Description of subject matter of journal--Anglican Theological Review is a general theological journal in which the problems and implications of one area of study are related to those of others. Publishes articles in Scripture, Ethics, Church History, Theology, Psychology of Religion, Sociology of Religion, World Religions, Philosophy of Religion, Language Studies, and the Human Sciences. For: professors, students, and laypersons. Submissions must be in English. Accepts unsolicited articles; sometimes accepts unsolicited reviews; accepts advertising. Encourages articles written by specialists in a wide variety of fields that show to those outside those fields the difference their investigations make in shaping Christian life and ministry. Style of journal--University of Chicago. Manuscript should be double-spaced; footnotes should be double-spaced. Requires 2 copies of manuscript. Selection process--Editor makes a decision on the recommendation of assigned readers. Responds to a submission in 3-6 months. Indexed: Bull.Signal, Rel.Per., New Test.Abstr., Old Test.Abstr., Rel.&Theol.Abstr., Rel.Ind.One.

5. ASBURY THEOLOGICAL JOURNAL
   Laurence W. Wood, Ed.
   Asbury Theological Seminary
   204 N. Lexington Ave.
   Wilmore, KY 40390

Subscription--2/yr.--$8. Subject matter of journal--discusses in a scholarly manner all religious issues across the curriculum as they relate to Christian thought. Publishes articles in Scripture, Ethics, Church History, Theology, Evangelism, Pastoral Counseling, Missions, Psychology of Religion, Sociology of Religion, World Religions, Philosophy of Religion, Judaism, and Religious Education. For: professors, students, scholarly community. Submissions must be in English. Accepts unsolicited articles, unsolicited reviews, dot-matrix printing, simultaneous submissions; publishes research notes, review-articles; does not accept advertising. Seeks articles that particularly address recent and contemporary issues as they relate to Christian thought and practice. Style of journal--Campbell's. Requires one copy of manuscript. Selection process--Editorial Review and an outside critical evaluation. Parent Organization--Asbury Theological Seminary. Indexed: Chr.Per.Ind., Rel.&Theol.Abstr.

6. BANNER
   Rev. Andrew Kuyvenhoven, Ed.
   Rosemary Van Allsburg, Ed. Assist.
   Christian Reformed Church of North America
   CRC Publications
   2850 Kalamazoo Ave., S.E.
   Grand Rapids, MI 49560

Subscription--46/yr.--$20.50. Subject matter of journal--whatever the editor deems of interest to members of the Christian Reformed Church, including Scripture, Ethics, Church History, Theology, Evangelism, Church Administration, Pastoral Counseling, Missions, Psychology of Religion, Sociology of Religion, World Religions, Philosophy of Religion, Judaism, Islam, Hinduism, Buddhism, Eastern Religions, Religious Education. For: professors, students, laypersons, and ministers. Submissions must be in English. Sometimes accepts unsolicited articles, unsolicited reviews; accepts dot-matrix printing; does not accept simultaneous submissions; does not publish research notes; publishes review-articles. Seeks articles that have a clear thesis and focus, based on Reformed theology, which are interesting, educational, inspirational, helpful, or challenging to our readers. Style of journal--style sheet may be obtained from journal. Selection process--Editorial-Committee. Responds to a submission in 6 weeks. Approximate proportion of submissions accepted for publication--90 percent of the submissions are requested by journal's editorial committee from writers who have proved themselves to be able to meet the requirements of the journal. Comments: Because of our denominational, Reformed, Calvinistic requirements we discourage any submissions that are not consciously based on our stipulations. Indexed: G.Soc.Sci.&Rel.Per.Lit.

7. BERLINER THEOLOGISCHE ZEITSCHRIFT
   Prof. Dr. Peter von der Osten-Sacken, Ed.

Leuchtenburgstrasse 39-41
D-1000 Berlin 37,
West Germany (B.R.D.)

Subscription--2/yr.--38 DM. Subject matter of journal--Scripture, Ethics, Church History, Theology, Evangelism, Church Administration, Psychology of Religion, Sociology of Religion, and Religious Education. Submissions must be in German.

8. BIBLIOTHECA SACRA
   Roy B. Zuck, Ed.
   Dallas Theological Seminary
   3909 Swiss Ave.
   Dallas, TX 75204

Subscription--4/yr.--$12. Description of subject matter--Biblical and theological studies from a conservative evangelical perspective. Publishes articles in Scripture, Theology, Evangelism, Church Administration, Pastoral Counseling, and Missions. For: professors, students, laypersons, and pastors. Submissions must be in English. Sometimes accepts unsolicited articles; does not accept unsolicited reviews, dot-matrix printing, or simultaneous submissions; does not publish research notes; publishes review-articles; does not accept advertising. Style of journal--Chicago Manual of Style with some adaptations. Length requirements--maximum, 25 pages; minimum, 10 pages. Selection process--We select articles which have content relevant to our purpose and standards; clear, cogent writing; balance with other articles. Responds in 2-3 weeks. Approximately 30 percent of all submissions are accepted for publication. Indexed: Old Test.Abstr., Rel.Per., Chr.Per.Ind., Int.Z.Bibelwiss., New Test. Abstr., Rel.Ind.One.

9. BIJDRAGEN
   International Journal in Philosophy & Theology
   Stichting Bijdragen
   Keizersgracht 105
   1015 CH Amsterdam, Netherlands

Subscription--4/yr.--95 fl; 25 fl for students. Subject matter of journal--Scripture, Ethics, Church History, Theology, Psychology of Religion, Sociology of Religion, World Religions, Philosophy of Religion, and Judaism. For: professors and students. Submissions must be in French, German, English, or Dutch. Accepts unsolicited articles; sometimes accepts unsolicited reviews; does not accept dot-matrix printing; publishes research notes, review-articles; does not accept advertising. Style of journal--academic. Requires 3 copies of manuscript. Selection process--Editorial Selection Committee. Responds to a submission--min. 3 months. Approximate proportion of submissions accepted for publication--75 percent.

Parent Organization--Nederlandse Organisatie voor Zuiver-Weten-
schappelijk Onderzoek. Indexed: Old Test.Abstr., Int.Z.Bibelwiss.,
New Test.Abstr., Rel.&Theol.Abstr., Rel.Ind.One.

10. BURGENSE
    Nicolas Lopez, Ed.
    Editorial Aldecoa
    Martinez del Compo 7
    Burgos, Spain

    Subscription--Sept.-April--$15. Publishes articles in Scripture,
Ethics, Church History, Theology, Psychology of Religion, Sociology
of Religion, Philosophy of Religion, Judaism, Islam, Patristics, Mysticism, Dogmatic Theology, Spirituality, Philosophy. Submissions
must be in French, German, Spanish, English, or Italian. Most
articles are in Spanish, but occasionally an article is published in
English. Accepts unsolicited articles and unsolicited reviews. Parent Organization--Facultad de Teologie de Burgos. Indexed: Old
Test.Abstr., New Test.Abstr.

11. CALVIN THEOLOGICAL JOURNAL
    John H. Stek
    Calvin Theological Seminary
    3233 Burton St., S.E.
    Grand Rapids, MI 49506

    Subscription--2/yr.--$8. Description of subject matter--Biblical,
theological, pastoral, ecclesiastical, and missions. Publishes articles
in Scripture, Ethics, Church History, Theology, Evangelism, Church
Administration, Pastoral Counseling, Missions, Philosophy of Religion,
Religious Education, History of Theology--especially Calvinism, Ecumenism. For: professors, students, and pastors. Submissions must
be in English. Sometimes accepts unsolicited articles; does not accept unsolicited reviews, simultaneous submissions; does not accept
dot-matrix printing; does not publish research notes; publishes
review-articles; does not accept advertising. Seeks articles that are
carefully argued, well documented, lucidly presented, addressed to
significant issues related to the areas specified above. Requires 2
copies of manuscript. Length requirements--maximum, 8000 words;
minimum, 5000 words. Selection process--Articles are refereed by
2-3 scholars familiar with the area/field of the essay's topic. Responds in 3-6 months. Approximately 25 percent of all submissions
are accepted for publication. Indexed: Old Test.Abstr., Rel.Per.,
Chr.Per.Ind., Int.Z.Bibelwiss., New Test.Abstr., Rel.&Theol.Abstr.,
Rel.Ind.One.

12. CATHOLICA
    Hans Joerg Urban, Ed.

Leostrasse 19a
4790 Paderborn,
West Germany (B.R.D.)

Subscription--4/yr.--DM 68. Subject matter of journal--Scripture, Church History, Theology, Liturgy, Church Doctrine, Ecumenism, and Ecclesiology. For: professors, students, and laypersons. Submissions must be in German. Accepts unsolicited articles; accepts advertising. Selection process--Editorial Board responds to evaluation of appointed readers. Parent Organization-- Johann Adam Moehler-Institut Paderborn. Indexed: Rel.Per., New Test.Abstr., Rel.Ind.One.

13. CERCLE ERNEST RENAN. CAHIERS
    Pierre Soisson, Secrétaire Général
    9 ter, rue Paul-Féval
    75018 Paris, France

Subscription--5/yr.--120 francs. Subject matter of journal-- Scripture, Church History, Theology, Psychology of Religion, Sociology of Religion, World Religions, Philosophy of Religion. Submissions must be in French. Indexed: Int.Z.Bibelwiss., New Test. Abstr.

14. CHURCH HERALD
    John Stapert, Ed.
    Church Herald Inc.
    1324 Lake Dr., SE
    Grand Rapids, MI 49506

Subscription--22/yr.--$10.25. Description of subject matter-- general interest--Reformed Christian American. Publishes articles in Scripture, Ethics, Theology, Evangelism, and Religious Education. For: laypersons and clergy. Submissions must be in English. Accepts unsolicited articles; does not accept unsolicited reviews; accepts dot-matrix (if near letter quality), simultaneous submissions; does not publish research notes; publishes review-articles; accepts advertising--any of interest to our audience. One copy of manuscript required. Length requirements--maximum, 2000 words; minimum, 1000 words. Selection process--Editors read all submissions, confer with each other before acceptance. Responds in 2-3 weeks. Approximately 5 percent of all submissions are accepted for publication. Indexed: G.Soc.Sci.&Rel.Per.Lit. Parent Organization--Reformed Church in America.

15. CHURCHMAN
    Reverend Dr. Gerald L. Bray, Ed.
    Church Society

186 Kennington Park Rd.
London SE11 4BT, England

Subscription--4/yr.--$20. Description of subject matter of
journal--Comparative Anglican theology from a Protestant reformed
and evangelical standpoint. Publishes articles in Scripture, Ethics,
Church History, Theology, Evangelism, Church Administration, Pastoral Counseling, Missions, Psychology of Religion, Sociology of Religion, World Religions, Philosophy of Religion, and Religious Education. For: professors, students, theologically literate laypeople.
Submissions must be in English. Seeks articles in hermeneutics,
doctrinal history, and topical theology. Accepts unsolicited articles,
dot-matrix printing, simultaneous submissions; sometimes accepts unsolicited reviews; publishes research notes and review-articles; accepts advertising--new books. Style of journal--graduate level. Requires two copies of manuscript. Selection process--Each article is
read by the Editor or a member of the Editorial Board with specific
knowledge of the particular subject matter. Publication decisions are
confirmed at Board meetings. Responds in 1-2 months. Approximate
proportion of submissions accepted for publication--30 percent. Com-
ments--Churchman was founded in 1878 and is of the highest reputa-
tion. Indexed: Br.Hum.Ind., Hist.Abstr., Rel.Per., Rel.Ind.Onc.,
Rel.&Theol.Abstr.

16. CHURCHMAN
     Edna Ruth Johnson, Ed.
     Churchman Co., Inc.
     1074 23rd Ave., N.
     St. Petersburg, FL 33704

Subscription--9/yr.--$10. Description of subject matter--hu-
manistic religion of all kinds. Publishes articles in Psychology of
Religion, Sociology of Religion, World Religions, Philosophy of Religion, and Humanism. For: professors, students, laypersons, and
clergy. Articles appear in English. Accepts unsolicited articles;
does not accept unsolicited reviews, dot-matrix printing, simultaneous
submissions. Does not publish research notes; publishes review-
articles. Accepts advertising--humanitarian flavored. Seeks controversial articles. Style journal follows--Forthright. Submit one manuscript. Length requirements--maximum, 1000 words; minimum, 100
words. Articles are chosen according to how relevant they are to
today's values. Approximately 25 percent of the submissions are accepted for publication. Indexed: Rel.Ind.One.

17. CITHARA
     John Mulryan, Ed.
     Franciscan Institute
     St. Bonaventure University
     Box BC
     St. Bonaventure, NY 14778

Subscription--2/yr.--$6. Publishes articles in Scripture, Ethics, Church History, Theology, Sociology of Religion, World Religions, Philosophy of Religion, and Literary Criticism. For: professors, students, and laypersons. Accepts unsolicited articles, unsolicited reviews; publishes review-articles. Seeks articles that relate to the problems of man in the light of his heritage and of his future. Especially seeking interdepartmental essays that state or imply a relationship to the Judaeo-Christian tradition. Style of journal--MLA. Requires 2 copies of manuscript. Selection process--An Editorial Board makes a decision informed by consultants. Indexed: Cath. Ind., Curr.Cont., Hist.Abstr., M.L.A., Arts&Hum.Cit.Ind., Hist. Abstr.&Life.

18. LA CIUDAD DE DIOS
    Miguel Angel Keller Perez-Herrero, Secretario
    Real Monasterio
    San Lorenzo del Escorial
    Madrid, Spain

Subscription--3/yr.--$25. Subject matter of journal--Scripture, Church History, Theology, Sociology of Religion, and Philosophy of Religion. Accepts unsolicited articles and unsolicited reviews. For: professors and students. Submissions must be in Spanish. Selection process--Editorial Board. Parent Organization--Real Monasterio del Escorial. Indexed: New Test.Abstr.

19. CIVILTA CATTOLICA
    Padre Gian Paolo Salvini S.I.
    Compagnia di Gesù
    Via di Porta Pinciana 1
    00187 Rome, Italy

Subscription--24 issues/yr.--$55. Publishes articles in Scripture, Ethics, Church History, Theology, Psychology of Religion, Sociology of Religion, World Religions, Philosophy of Religion, Judaism, Islam, Hinduism, Buddhism, Eastern Religions, Religious Education. For: professors, students, laypersons, priests, journalists. Does not accept unsolicited articles, unsolicited reviews, dot-matrix printing, simultaneous submissions; publishes research notes and review-articles; accepts advertising.

20. COLLOQUIUM: THE AUSTRALIAN AND NEW ZEALAND
    THEOLOGICAL REVIEW
    Rev. Dr. Brian J. Jackson, Ed.
    St. Francis Xavier Seminary
    101 Morialta Road
    Rostrevor, South Australia

Subscription--2/yr.--$25. Subject matter of journal--Scripture, Ethics, Church History, and Theology. Submissions must be in English. Style of journal--Authors are requested to follow the style of JBL, CBQ, HTR, etc. Accepts unsolicited articles. Indexed: Rel. Inc.One.: Periodicals.

21. COMMUNIO
Miguel de Burgos Núñez, O.P., Dir.
Dominicos de Andalucia
Studium Generale
Apdo. 820
41080-Seville, Spain

Subscription--3/yr.--Spain, 2000 ptas.; overseas, $30. Description of subject matter of journal--Holy Scripture, Theology and Ecclesiology. Publishes articles in Scripture, Ethics, Church History, and Theology. For: professors and students. Submissions must be in Spanish. Accepts unsolicited articles, unsolicited reviews, dot-matrix printing, simultaneous submissions; publishes research notes; does not publish review-articles; does not accept advertising. Style of journal--academic. Requires one copy of manuscript. Length requirements--maximum, 60 pages; minimum, 20 pages. Selection process--Editorial Board. Indexed: Old Test.Abstr., New Test.Abstr., Rel.&Theol.Abstr.

22. COMMUNIO
Dr. David L. Schindler, Ed.
P.O. Box 144
Notre Dame, IN 46556

Subscription--4/yr.--$18, individuals; $23, institutions. Description of subject matter--quarterly journal of Catholic reflection--theological and cultural (affiliated with 12 other national editions). Publishes articles in Scripture, Theology, Philosophy of Religion--In general, anything of substantial interest, theological/cultural, to educated Catholic audience (professors, laypersons, clergy). Submissions must be in any Western language. Style of journal--Chicago Manual. Requires 3 copies of manuscript. Length requirements--maximum, 30 typewritten pages; minimum, 5. Selection process--review by various consulting editors. Responds within 2 months. Approximate proportion of submissions that are accepted for publication--12 percent. Indexed: Cath.Ind., Old Test.Abstr., Rel.Ind.One., Rel.&Theol.Abstr.

23. CONCORDIA JOURNAL
Quentin Wesselschmidt, Ed.
Concordia Seminary
801 DeMun Ave.
St. Louis, MO 63105

Subscription--4/yr.--$10. Description of subject matter of journal--Theology--Exegetical, Historical, Systematic, Practical. For: professors, students, laypersons, clergy. Submissions must be in English. Accepts unsolicited articles, dot-matrix printing, simultaneous submissions; sometimes accepts unsolicited reviews; does not publish research notes; publishes review-articles; accepts advertising (very limited at present)--currently only from Concordia Publishing House. Seeks articles that are scholarly and are of practical value to pastors. Style of journal--Concordia's own style manual, but generally in keeping with Turabian and Chicago. Requires one copy of manuscript. Length requirements--maximum, 25 pages double-spaced; minimum, none as long as appropriate. Selection process--Articles are reviewed by Editorial Committee which makes its decisions in a regularly convened meeting. Responds in 1-3 months. Approximate proportion of submissions that are accepted for publication--50-60 percent. Indexed: Old Test.Abstr., Chr. Per.Ind., Int.Z.Bibelwiss., New Test.Abstr., Rel.Ind.One., Rel.& Theol.Abstr.

24. CONCORDIA THEOLOGICAL QUARTERLY
    David P. Scaer, Ed.
    Concordia Theological Seminary
    6600 N. Clinton St.
    Fort Wayne, IN 46825

Subscription--4/yr.--$5. Description of subject matter of journal--publishes articles, homiletical studies, and book reviews of interest to the Lutheran Church. For: professors, students, laypersons, ministers. Submissions must be in English. Publishes articles in Scripture, Ethics, Church History, and Theology. Does not accept unsolicited articles, unsolicited reviews; accepts advertising--new book releases. Comments: Almost all articles are prepared by the faculty of Concordia Theological Seminary. Indexed: Old Test.Abstr., Rel.Per., New Test.Abstr., Rel.Ind.One., Rel.& Theol.Abstr.

25. DIALOG
    Robert W. Jenson, Ed.
    Dialog, Inc.
    2375 Como Ave.
    St. Paul, MN 55108

Subscription--4/yr.--$14. Subject matter of journal--Scripture, Ethics, Church History, Theology, Missions, and Sociology of Religion. For: professors, students, laypersons, clergy. Submissions must be in English. Accepts unsolicited articles; publishes reviews. Length requirements for submissions--maximum, 10 pages. Selection process--Editorial Council. Indexed: Old Test.Abstr., Rel.Per., New Test.Abstr., Rel.Ind.One., Rel.&Theol.Abstr.

26. DOWNSIDE REVIEW
    Secretary
    Downside Abbey
    Stratton on the Fosse
    Bath BA3 4RH, England

Subscription--4/yr.--$24. Description of subject matter of
journal--The monks and friends of Downside endeavor to discuss new
and old problems with Catholic freedom and an awareness of the re-
sponsibility which that freedom involves and thus try to present a
less cut-and-dried way of thinking about religion. Publishes articles
in Scripture, Ethics, Church History, Theology, and Philosophy of
Religion. For: professors, students, and laypersons. Submissions
must be in English. Does not accept advertising. Indexed: Cath.
Ind., Rel.Per., New Test.Abstr., Old Test.Abstr., Rel.Ind.One.,
Rel.&Theol.Abstr.

27. THE DREW GATEWAY
    Dr. Darrell Doughty, Ed.
    Drew University
    The Theology School
    Madison, NJ   07940

Subscription--3/yr.--$9. The Drew Gateway is a journal of
theological scholarship and interpretation directed primarily to the
alumni and friends of the Theology School and Graduate Schools of
Drew University. Publishes articles in Scripture, Ethics, Church
History, Theology, Evangelism, Pastoral Counseling, Missions, Psychology of Religion, Sociology of Religion, and Religious Education.
For: professors, students, laypersons, Drew friends, and alumni.
Submissions must be in English. Accepts unsolicited articles; sometimes accepts unsolicited reviews; does not publish research notes;
publishes review-articles. Seeks articles of original and creative
scholarship directed to the concerns of church and ministry from the
perspectives of biblical, theological, and religious studies. Especially seeking articles that represent serious scholarship and that
may set theological trends and shape the life of the church. Style
of journal--Chicago Manual of Style. Requires 3 copies of manuscript. Selection process--Editorial Board. Indexed: Rel.Per.,
Rel.Ind.One.

28. DUKE DIVINITY SCHOOL REVIEW
    Charles Robinson, Ed.
    Duke University
    Divinity School
    Durham, NC   27706

Subscription--3/yr.--Free. Description of subject matter of
journal--A forum for the publication of invited lectures presented at

Duke Divinity School and for articles prepared by the faculty and
students of the Duke Divinity School. Publishes articles in Scripture, Ethics, Church History, Theology, Evangelism, Missions, Psychology of Religion, Sociology of Religion and Philosophy of Religion. For: professors, students, and alumni. Submissions must
be in English. Does not accept unsolicited articles, unsolicited reviews; does not accept advertising. Indexed: Rel.Per., New Test.
Abstr., Rel.Ind.One.

29. EGLISE ET THEOLOGIE
    Leo Laberge, Ed.
    Saint Paul University
    Faculty of Theology
    223 Main St.
    Ottawa K1S 1C4, Ontario, Canada

    Subscription--3/yr.--Canadian $30. Subject matter of journal--
Theology, Scripture, Ethics, Church History. For: professors.
Submissions must be in French or English. Accepts unsolicited
articles, dot-matrix printing; does not accept unsolicited reviews,
simultaneous submissions; publishes research notes and review-
articles. Seeking articles--scholarly contribution. Style of jour-
nal--Chicago Manual of Style. Requires 3 copies of manuscript.
Length requirements--maximum, 30 pages (in print). Selection pro-
cess--Editorial Board with readers who examine the articles and send
in their reports. Responds to a submission in more or less three
months. Approximate proportion of submissions accepted for publi-
cation--50 percent. Others, with suggestions and corrections. Text
in English and French. Indexed: Old Test.Abstr., Rel.Per., Canon
Law Abstr., New Test.Abstr., Rel.Ind.One., Rel.&Theol.Abstr.

30. EPIPHANY JOURNAL
    Philip Tolbert, Ed.
    Epiphany Press
    Box 14727
    San Francisco, CA 94114

    Subscription--4/yr.--$18.50/$24.50 foreign. Description of sub-
ject matter of journal--Seeks to re-establish an orthodox Christian
world-view and hierarchy of values. Writers should be patristically
oriented. Publishes articles in Scripture, Ethics, Church History,
Theology, Evangelism, Missions, Environmental Ethics, Literature,
Arts, and Cultural Trends. For: professors, students, and laypersons. Submissions must be in English. Sometimes (rarely) accepts unsolicited articles; sometimes accepts unsolicited reviews; accepts dot-matrix printing, simultaneous submissions; does not publish research notes; publishes review-articles; considers advertising,
especially--publishers. Seeks literary reviews and articles on child
education, sustainable culture, television, radio and film, the church.

Style of journal--Chicago. Requires one copy of manuscript. Length requirements--maximum, 2500 works; minimum, 500 words. Selection process for publishing an article--right perspective/clear and interesting style/no academic footnotes/explanation of technical language. Responds in less than 3 months (usually). Approximate proportion of submissions accepted for publication--one percent of unsolicited manuscripts. Comments--Writers should study the journal before submitting. Writers' guidelines available. Discount on first copy for writers: $6 postage included. Indexed: Rel.Ind.One.

31. ESTUDIOS ECLESIASTICOS
    Prof. Antonio Vargas-Machuca, S.J., Dir.
    Universidade Pontificia "Comillas"
    28049 Madrid, Spain

    Subscription--4/yr.--$39. Subject matter of journal-- Scripture, Church History, and Theology. Seeks well documented articles that make a significant contribution to our understanding of the Church. For: professors, students, and laypersons. Submissions must be in Spanish. Accepts unsolicited articles; sometimes accepts unsolicited reviews. Selection process--Editorial Board. Parent Organization--Compania de Jesus, Facultades de Teologia. Indexed: Old Test.Abstr., Canon Law Abstr., New Test.Abstr.

32. EVANGELICAL QUARTERLY
    I. Howard Marshall, Ed.
    Paternoster Press Ltd.
    Paternoster House
    3 Mount Radford Crescent
    Exeter EX1 4JW, England

    Subscription--4/yr.--$16.80. Description of subject matter of journal--An international review of Bible and theology in defense of the historic Christian faith. Publishes articles in Scripture, Ethics, Church History, Theology, and Evangelism. For: professors, students, laypersons, and clergymen. Submissions must be in English. Requires one copy of manuscript. Length requirements--maximum, 8000 words; minimum, 3000 words (but flexible). Selection process-- Editor's decision on quality and interest supplemented as necessary by verdict of editorial advisers. Responds in 2 months. Approximate proportion of submissions accepted for publication--50 percent. Indexed: Chr.Per.Ind., Old Test.Abstr., Rel.Per., New Test. Abstr., Rel.Ind.One., Rel.&Theol.Abstr.

33. EVANGELICAL THEOLOGICAL SOCIETY JOURNAL
    Dr. Ronald Youngblood, Ed.
    c/o Simon J. Kistemaker, Sec. Treas.
    Evangelical Theological Society

5422 Clinton Blvd.
Jackson, MS 39209

Subscription--4/yr.--$18. Publishes articles in Scripture, Eth-
ics, Church History, Theology, Missions, Philosophy of Religion.
For: professors, students, laypersons, pastors. Submissions must
be in English. Accepts unsolicited articles, unsolicited reviews, dot-
matrix printing; does not accept simultaneous submissions; publishes
research notes, review-articles; accepts advertising--publishers.
Style of journal--our "Instructions for Contributors" is identical to
that of CBQ and SBL. Requires one copy of manuscript. Selection
process--Editorial Committee. Responds--no more than 3 months.
Approximate proportion of submissions accepted for publication--25-
30 percent. Indexed: Old Test.Abstr., Chr.Per.Ind., New Test.
Abstr., Rel.Ind.One., Rel.&Theol.Abstr.

34. EVANGELISCHE THEOLOGIE
     Christian Kaiser Verlag
     Isabellastr. 20
     8000 Munich, West Germany (B.R.D.)

Subscription--6/yr.--57 DM. Publishes articles in Scripture,
Ethics, Church History, Theology, Evangelism, Sociology of Religion,
Missions, and Judaism. For: professors, students, and laypersons.
Submissions must be in English. Does not accept unsolicited articles,
unsolicited reviews, dot-matrix printing, simultaneous submissions;
publishes review-articles; accepts advertising. Style of journal--
historical academic theology, etc. Length requirements--maximum,
100 pages; minimum, 80 pages. Selection process--Editorial Board.
Indexed: Old Test.Abstr., Rel.Per., New Test.Abstr., Rel.&Theol.
Abstr., Rel.Ind.One.

35. FAITH AND MISSION
     Alan Neely, Ed.
     Southeastern Baptist Seminary
     Wake Forest, NC 27587

Subscription--2/yr.--$6. Description of subject matter--Four
articles on theme of the issue, two sermons, plus approximately 25
book reviews. Publishes articles in Scripture, Ethics, Church History, Theology, Evangelism, Church Administration, Pastoral Counseling, Missions, Psychology of Religion, Sociology of Religion, World
Religions, Philosophy of Religion, Judaism, Islam, Hinduism, Buddhism,
Eastern Religions, Religious Education. For: professors, students
and laypersons. Submissions are in English. Does not accept unsolicited articles, dot-matrix printing, simultaneous submissions;
sometimes accepts unsolicited reviews; does not publish research
notes; does not accept advertising. Major articles on the theme of
the issue are solicited. Style of journal--Turabian. Require one

copy of manuscript. Length requirements--maximum, 6000 words; minimum, 400 words. Articles are by invitation only. Responds in one month when articles are sent unrequested. Approximate proportion of submissions accepted for publication--none, unless requested. Indexed: Rel.Ind.One.

36. FRANCISCANUM
    Jairo Munoz M., Ed.
    Universidad de San Buenaventura
    Calle 73 No. 10-45
    Apdo. Aereo 52312
    Bogota 2, Colombia

Subscription--3/yr.--$15. Subject matter of journal--Systematic Theology, Modern Theology, Philosophy, Sociology of Religion, Scripture, Ethics, Philosophy of Religion, and Religious Education. For: professors and students. Submissions must be in Spanish (preferably), French, or English. Does not accept unsolicited articles, dot-matrix printing, simultaneous submissions; sometimes accepts unsolicited reviews; publishes research notes, review-articles; accepts advertising. Requires 2 copies of manuscript. Style of journal--academic. Length requirements--maximum, 40 pages; minimum, 20 pages. Selection process--1) Editorial Board; 2) selection and revision committee; 3) Editor. Indexed: Old Test.Abstr.

37. THE FURROW
    Ronan Drury, Ed.
    The Furrow Trust
    St. Patrick's College
    Maynooth, County Kildare, Ireland

Subscription--12/yr.--$25. Subject matter of journal--Scripture, Theology, Evangelism, Spirituality, Church Administration, Pastoral Counseling, Missions, Liturgy. For: professors, students, laypersons, priests, ministers. Submissions must be in English. Accepts unsolicited articles, dot-matrix printing; sometimes accepts unsolicited reviews; does not accept simultaneous submissions; does not publish research notes; publishes review-articles; accepts advertising. Description of article journal seeks--Intelligent reflective--intelligible to layman/non-professional. Requires one copy of manuscript. Length requirements--maximum, 5000 words; minimum, --. Selection process for choice of an article--Topicality; freshness of approach; absence of jargon. Responds in 3 weeks. Approximate proportion of submissions that are accepted for publication--25 percent. Indexed: Cath.Ind., Old Test.Abstr., Canon Law Abstr., New Test.Abstr.

38. GEREFORMEERD THEOLOGISCH TIJDSCHRIFT
    Dr. W. Bakker, Ed.

Theologische Faculteit van de Vrije Universiteit
Postbus 7161
1007 ML Amsterdam, Netherlands

Subscription--4/yr.--45 fl. Publishes articles in Scripture,
Ethics, Church History and Theology. Submissions must be in
Dutch. The journal is often organized around a common theme. In-
dexed: Old Test.Abstr., New Test.Abstr., Rel.&Theol.Abstr.

39. GRACE THEOLOGICAL JOURNAL
    John C. Whitcomb, Ed.
    D. Brent Sandy, Mng. Ed.
    Grace Theological Seminary
    200 Seminary Dr.
    Winona Lake, IN   46590

Subscription--2/yr.--$11.50. Description of subject matter--
articles reflecting sound exegesis that leads to thoughtful theology
of a conservative premillennial bent. Publishes articles in (primary)--
Scripture and Theology; (secondary) Ethics and Church History.
For: professors, students, and pastors. Accepts unsolicited articles, unsolicited reviews, dot-matrix printing; does not accept simultaneous submissions; publishes research notes and review-articles;
and does not accept advertising. Seeks articles that are well-
researched and well-documented and that address issues in the
Scriptures with which pastors and scholars are grappling. Journal
style--Turabian. Requires 2 copies of manuscript. Length require-
ments--maximum, 50 pages; minimum, 5 pages. Selection process--
Articles are referred to two faculty readers, neither of whom know
the identity of the author. The readers report independently to
the managing editor who then (unless both readers recommend outright rejection) takes the article to the editorial committee (5 members) for a decision on its status. Responds in one to six months.
Approximately 20 to 25 percent of the submissions are accepted. Indexed: Old Test.Abstr., Rel.&Theol.Abstr., Chr.Per.Ind., New
Test.Abstr., Rel.Ind.One.

40. GREEK ORTHODOX THEOLOGICAL REVIEW
    Rev. Dr. N. M. Vaporis, Ed.
    Holy Cross Orthodox Press
    50 Goddard Ave.
    Brookline, MA   02146

Subscription--4/yr.--$16, U.S.; $17.50, overseas. Description
of subject matter of journal--Publishes papers and reviews in the
fields of Theology, Biblical Studies, Church History, Byzantine History and related Classical, Archaeological, and Philosophical Studies.
Submissions must be in English. Accepts unsolicited articles, unsolicited reviews; does not accept simultaneous submissions; publishes

research notes; accepts advertising. Seeks articles that bridge the gap between the Church in the United States and the culture and language of the Greek world. Requires 2 copies of manuscript. The GOTR is usually organized around a central theme. Parent Organization--Holy Cross Greek Orthodox School of Theology, Hellenic College. Indexed: Hist.Abstr., Old Test.Abstr., Rel.Per., New Test.Abstr., Rel.Ind.One., Rel.&Theol.Abstr.

41. GREGORIOS HO PALAMAS
     Director, Prof. Ioannis E. Anastasiou
     Mitropolis Thessalonikes
     P.O. Box 335
     Salonika, Greece

Subscription--5/yr.--$20. Subject matter of journal--Scripture, Ethics, Church History, Theology, Pastoral Counseling, and Religious Education. For: students, laypersons, and clergymen. Submissions must be in Greek. Sometimes accepts unsolicited articles and unsolicited reviews; does not accept dot-matrix printing, simultaneous submissions, or advertising; publishes research notes and review-articles. Style of journal--Orthodox theology and tradition. Requires one copy of manuscript. Length requirements--maximum, 16 pages; minimum, 5 pages. Selection process--must conform to orthodox theology and tradition and be written in a scholarly way. Responds to a submission in 2-3 months. Indexed: M.L.A., CERDIC.

42. HARVARD THEOLOGICAL REVIEW
     Helmut Koester, Ed.
     Harvard Divinity School
     45 Francis Ave.
     Cambridge, MA 02138

Subscription--4/yr.--$25. Publishes articles in--Scripture, Ethics, Church History, Theology, Sociology of Religion, World Religions, Philosophy of Religion, Judaism, Islam, Hinduism, Buddhism, Eastern Religions. For: professors, students, and clergy. Articles appear in English. Accepts unsolicited articles and dot-matrix printing; does not accept unsolicited reviews or simultaneous submissions; publishes research notes; does not publish review-articles; and accepts advertising--from publishers. Seeks scholarly investigations of specific topics in religious studies. Style of journal--Chicago Manual, some modifications published in style sheet. Requires 2 copies of manuscript. Length requirements--maximum, 30+ notes; minimum,-- Selection process--1) preliminary reading in house; 2) second reading by consultant; and 3) editor, associate editors. Responds in 2-3 months. Accepts 10 percent of submissions for publication. Indexed: Curr.Cont., Hum.Ind., Old Test.Abstr., Rel.Per., Arts& Hum.Cit.Ind., New Test.Abstr., Rel.Ind.One., Rel.&Theol.Abstr.

43. ILIFF REVIEW
    Charles S. Milligan, Ed.
    Iliff School of Theology
    2201 S. University Blvd.
    Denver, CO   80210

Subscription--3/yr.--$4.00. Subject matter of journal--religious studies in the scholarly sense. Publishes articles in Ethics, Church History, Theology, Psychology of Religion, Sociology of Religion, World Religions, and Philosophy of Religion. For: professors and students. Submissions must be in English. Sometimes accepts unsolicited articles, unsolicited reviews; accepts dot-matrix printing; does not accept simultaneous submissions; does not publish research notes; publishes review articles; does not accept advertising. Seeks well focused articles that deal with a particular topic with competent academic knowledge. Style of journal--standard academic. Requires 2 copies of manuscript. Selection process--1) submit article to readers qualified in the subject; 2) preference given to articles in which the topic is fresh and the approach is original and interesting; 3) tend to avoid subjects currently being published elsewhere. Responds to a submission in 6 weeks. Approximate proportion of submissions accepted for publication--1/3. Indexed: Old Test.Abstr., Rel.Ind.One.

44. INTERNATIONALE KATHOLISCHE ZEITSCHRIFT
    Franz Greiner, Ed.
    Suertherstrasse 107
    5000 Koeln 50, West Germany (B.R.D.)

Subscription--DM 9--single issue. Subject matter of journal--Scripture, Church History, and Theology. For: professors, students, and laypersons. Submissions must be in German. Accepts advertising. Indexed: Old Test.Abstr., New Test.Abstr., Rel. Ind.One.

45. IRISH THEOLOGICAL QUARTERLY
    Patrick Hannon, Ed.
    St. Patrick's College
    Faculty of Theology
    Maynooth, County Kildare, Ireland

Subscription--4/yr. Subject matter of journal--Scripture, Ethics, Church History, Theology, Sociology of Religion, and Philosophy of Religion. For: professors, students, and laypersons. Submissions must be in English. Accepts unsolicited articles and unsolicited reviews. Does not accept advertising. Indexed: Old Test.Abstr., Canon Law Abstr., New Test.Abstr., Rel.&Theol.Abstr.

46. JOURNAL FOR THE SCIENTIFIC STUDY OF RELIGION
Donald Capps, Ed.
Princeton Theological Seminary
Princeton, NJ 08542

Subscription--4/yr.--$24; student and emeritus, $10. Subject matter of journal--Psychology of Religion, Sociology of Religion, Onthropology of Religion, Religion and Political Science. For: professors, students, denomination based researchers. Submissions must be in English. Accepts unsolicited articles, dot-matrix printing; does not accept unsolicited reviews, simultaneous submissions; publishes research notes; does not publish review-articles; accepts advertising--publications. Seeks articles that integrate theory and empirical data. (Articles lacking in one of these are usually rejected.) Style of journal--social-scientific format (described in JSSR, 1975, vo. 14, pages 65-66). Requires 3 copies of manuscript. Length requirements--maximum, 30 pages--officially (Some others exceed this length; articles still sent out for review but not if they exceed 45 pages.); minimum, none. Selection process--Article sent to two outside referees. Responds to a submission in 2 months or less. Approximate proportion of submissions accepted for publication--1 out of 7. Comments: Very few articles accepted outright; some articles accepted after other revises and resubmits. Indexed: Curr.Cont., Hum.Ind., Old Test.Abstr., Psychol.Abstr., Rel.Per., SSCI, Sociol. Abstr., Arts&Hum.Cit.Ind., G.Soc.Sci.&Rel.Per.Lit., Rel.Ind.One., Rel.&Theol.Abstr.

47. JOURNAL OF RELIGION
Anne E. Carr, Ed.
Robin W. Levin, Ed.
Anthony C. Yu, Ed.
Daniel W. Smith, Editorial Assist.
University of Chicago
1025 E. 58th St.
Chicago, IL 60637

Subscription--4/yr.--$22, individuals; $35, institutions. Description of subject matter--The journal seeks to promote critical systematic inquiry into religion. Publishes articles in Scripture, Ethics, Theology, Psychology of Religion, Sociology of Religion, World Religions, Philosophy of Religion, Judaism, Islam, Hinduism, Buddhism, Eastern Religions. For: professors, students. Submissions must be in English. Accepts unsolicited articles; sometimes accepts unsolicited reviews; does not accept dot-matrix printing, simultaneous submissions; does not publish research notes; publishes review-articles; accepts advertising. Articles that are sought--The editors welcome contributions from scholars in theology (biblical, historical, ethical, constructive) and in other types of religious studies (literary, social, psychological, and philosophical). Articles especially looking for--Articles which display a high quality of scholarship

and have significance for a wide readership in religious studies.
Style of journal--Submissions must be double-spaced throughout,
including endnotes, and should conform to the Chicago Manual of
Style (13th edition, revised). Requires three copies of manuscript.
Length requirements--maximum, 25 pages; minimum, 20 pages. Se-
lection process--Editorial review based on referee evaluations. Re-
sponds in 3-4 months. Approximate proportion of submissions ac-
cepted for publication--20 percent. Indexed: Curr.Cont., Hum.Ind.,
Old Test.Abstr., Rel.Per., SSCI, Arts&Hum.Cit.Ind., Bk.Rev.Dig.,
G.Soc.Sci.&Rel.Per.Lit., Int.Z.Bibelwiss., New Test.Abstr., Rel.
Ind.One, Rel.&Theol.Abstr.

48. JOURNAL OF RELIGIOUS STUDIES
    Dr. Derwood Smith, Ed.
    Cleveland State University
    Department of Religion
    Cleveland, OH 44115

Subscription--2/yr.--$6. Description of subject matter of jour-
nal--academic articles concerning any aspect of religion. Publishes
articles in Scripture, Ethics, Church History, Theology, Psychology
of Religion, Sociology of Religion, World Religions, Philosophy of Religion, Judaism, Islam, Hinduism, Buddhism, and Eastern Religions.
For: professors, students, laypersons. Submissions must be in
French, German, or English. Accepts unsolicited articles, unsolicited
reviews, dot-matrix printing; does not accept simultaneous submissions; publishes research notes, review-articles; does not accept
advertising. Requires one copy of manuscript. Length requirements--
none. Selection process--Final decision is Editor's. Advice is sought
from several readers. Responds to a submission--varies, 2 weeks
to 3 months. Indexed: Rel.Per., New Test.Abstr., Rel.Ind.One.

49. JOURNAL OF RELIGIOUS THOUGHT
    Cain H. Felder, Ed.
    Howard University Divinity School
    14th & Shepherd St. N.E.
    Washington, DC 20017

Subscription--2/yr.--individuals; $14, institutions. Description
of subject matter of journal--generally academically based research
on topics related to religion, especially as related to the Black Religious Experience across the world. Publishes articles in Black
church and religion, Scripture, Ethics, Church History, Theology,
Evangelism, Church Administration, Pastoral Counseling, Missions,
Psychology of Religion, Sociology of Religion, World Religions,
Philosophy of Religion, Religious Education, and Judaism, Islam,
Hinduism, Buddhism, and Eastern Religions as these are compared/
contrasted with Christianity. For: professors, students, laypersons.
Submissions must be in English. Accepts unsolicited articles,

unsolicited reviews; dot-matrix printing (letter quality); does not
accept simultaneous submissions; generally does not publish research notes; sometimes publishes review-articles; accepts adver-
tising--(JRT maintains right of refusal); books; publications; meetings; institutions. Style of journal--a feature article section, a
Pastor's Corner section, Books Received/Reviewed--(Indexed in #2
issue of each volume). Requires 3 copies of manuscript. Length
requirements--25-28 pages, double spaced, including footnotes. Selection process--try to select pertinent articles which address issues
frequently overlooked by other scholarly journals. Since the journal
is one of two consistently published journals which originate in Black
Theological Schools, Black involvement in religion is stressed (not
just in this hemisphere but worldwide). Responds to a submission--
initial acknowledgment within 2 weeks; final acceptance/rejection may
take longer. Approximate proportion of submissions accepted for
publication--There are generally 5 feature articles plus those which
are suitable for the Pastor's Corner, and then reviews/book notes.
Parent Organization--Howard University, Divinity School. Indexed:
Ind.Sel.Per. , Rel.Per. , New Test.Abstr. , Rel.Ind.One, Rel.&Theol.
Abstr.

50. JOURNAL OF THE AMERICAN ACADEMY OF RELIGION
    W. S. Green, Ed.
    Scholars Press
    P.O. Box 1608
    Decatur, GA   30031-1608

Subscription--4/yr.--$50. Publishes articles in Theology, Psy-
chology of Religion, World Religions, Philosophy of Religion, and
Eastern Religions. For: professors, students, and laypersons. Submissions must be in English. Accepts unsolicited articles, dot-matrix
printing; does not accept unsolicited reviews, simultaneous submissions; does not publish research notes; publishes review-articles;
accepts advertising--presses. Indexed: Curr.Cont. , Hum.Ind. ,
Rel.Per. , SSCI, New Test.Abstr. , Arts&Hum.Cit.Ind. , Old Test.
Abstr. , Rel.Ind.One, Rel.&Theol.Abstr.

51. THE JOURNAL OF THE INTERDENOMINATIONAL THEOLOGICAL
    CENTER
    John C. Diamond, Jr. , Ed.
    Interdenominational Theological Center
    671 Beckwith St.
    Atlanta, GA   30314

Subscription--2/yr.--$6, individuals; $8, institutions. Seek to
specialize in subject matter of interest to Blacks and persons interested in Black issues. Subject matter of journal--Scripture, Ethics,
Church History, Theology, Evangelism, Church Administration, Pastoral Counseling, Missions, Psychology of Religion, Sociology of

Religion, and Religious Education. For: professors, students, lay-persons. Submissions must be in Spanish or English. Accepts un-solicited articles, unsolicited reviews, dot-matrix printing, simul-taneous submissions; does not publish research notes; publishes review-articles; and does not accept advertising. Style of Journal--Turabian or Chicago Style Manual. Length requirements--maximum, 30 typed pages; minimum--none. One copy of manuscript required. Selection process--Committee (a group of readers) recommends "pub-lish or not publish" to editor who makes final decision. Responds in 60 days, usually. Approximately 20 percent of the submissions are accepted for publication. Indexed: Rel.&Theol.Abstr., Rel.Ind. One.

52. KERYGMA UND DOGMA
    Prof. Dr. R. Slenczka, Ed.
    Vandenhoeck und Ruprecht
    Theaterstrasse 13
    Postfach 37 53
    3400 Goettingen, West Germany (B.R.D.)

Subscription--4/yr.--DM 59. Publishes articles in Scripture, Church History, Theology, Church Doctrine, Ecclesiology, and Ecu-menism. Submissions must be in German. Accepts unsolicited articles; accepts advertising. Selection process--Editorial Board makes a decision after articles have been reviewed by readers. In-dexed: Old Test.Abstr., Rel.Per., New Test.Abstr., Rel.Ind.One, Rel.&Theol.Abstr.

53. LATERANUM
    Alessandro Galuzzí, Direttore
    Pontificia Università Lateranense
    Piazza S. Giovanni
    4 I-00120, Vatican City

Subscription--2/yr.--$24. Publishes articles in Scripture, Eth-ics, Church History, and Theology. Submissions must be in French, German, Spanish, English, or Italian. Indexed: Old Test.Abstr.

54. LAURENTIANUM
    David Covi, Ed.
    Collegio Internazionale S. Lorenzo da Brindisi
    G.R.A. Km 68,800
    00163 Rome, Italy

Subscription--3/yr.--$20. Subject matter of journal--Scripture, Ethics, Church History, Theology, Missions, Psychology of Religion, Sociology of Religion, Philosophy of Religion, and Religious Educa-tion. For: professors and students. Submissions must be in French,

German, Spanish, English, or Italian. Accepts unsolicited articles; does not accept unsolicited reviews, dot-matrix printing; publishes research notes and review-articles; does not accept advertising. Requires one copy of manuscript. Length requirements for a submission--maximum, 40 pages; minimum, 20 pages. Responds to a submission in 6-12 months. Selection process--Articles are chosen by the "Comitato Redazionale" in February. Parent Organization-- International College of the Capuchin Order. Indexed: Old Test. Abstr., Canon Law Abstr., New Test.Abstr.

55. LUMIERE ET VIE
    Michel Demaison, Ed.
    Association Lumière et Vie
    2 place Gailleton
    69002 Lyon, France

    Subscription--5/yr.--190 F (Etranger). Publishes articles in Scripture, Ethics, Theology, Psychology of Religion, Sociology of Religion, Judaism, and Ecumenism. For: professors, laypersons, and religious orders. Submissions must be in French, German, or English. Does not accept unsolicited articles, unsolicited reviews, simultaneous submissions; accepts dot-matrix printing; does not publish research notes; publishes review articles; accepts advertising. Especially looking for articles written by specialists but in everyday language. Selection process--Editorial Board. Requires 2 copies of manuscript. Length requirements--maximum, 20 pages; minimum, 8 pages. Indexed: Cath.Ind., New Test.Abstr.

56. LUTHERAN THEOLOGICAL JOURNAL
    John Strelan, Ed.
    Lutheran Seminary
    Ward and Jeffcott Streets, North Adelaide, 5006
    South Australia

    Subscription--3/yr.--$10 Australian. Subject matter of journal-- Scripture, Ethics, Church History, Theology, Evangelism, and Religious Education. For: professors, students, and laypersons. Submissions must be in English. Accepts advertising. Parent Organization--Lutheran Church of Australia. Indexed: Old Test.Abstr., New Test.Abstr., Rel.Ind.One.

57. MELANGES DE SCIENCE RELIGIEUSE
    Jacques Liebaert, Ed.
    Institut Catholique de Lille
    60 bd. Vauban
    59046 Lille, France

    Subscription--4/yr.--$17. Subject matter of journal--Scripture,

Ethics, Church History, Theology, Religion and Culture. For:
professors, students, and laypersons. Submissions must be in
French. Accepts unsolicited articles and unsolicited reviews. Indexed: Bull.Signal, Int.Z.Bibelwiss., New Test.Abstr., Old Test.
Abstr., Rel.Per., Rel.&Theol.Abstr., Rel.Ind.One.

58. MELITA THEOLOGICA
    Hector M. Scerri, Secretary
    Theology Students' Association
    Faculty of Theology
    Tal-Virtu, Rabat, Malta

Subscription--2/yr.--LM 1.00,0 (LM = Maltese Lira). Description of subject matter of journal--Matters of special interest for
philosophy and theology circles. Publishes articles in Scripture,
Ethics, Church History, Theology, Evangelism, Church Administration, Pastoral Counseling, Missions, Psychology of Religion, Sociology
of Religion, World Religions, Philosophy of Religion, Dogma, Moral
Theology, Canon Law, Ascetical Theology, Liturgy, Philosophy and
Sociology. For: professors, students, and laypersons. Submissions must be in French, English or Italian. We accept articles in
Spanish and German, occasionally. Seeks academic, methodologically
sound articles. Accepts unsolicited articles; sometimes accepts unsolicited reviews; does not accept simultaneous submissions; does not
publish research notes or review-articles; accepts advertising--within
limits. Requires one copy of manuscript. Length requirements--
maximum, about 25 pages; minimum, 2/3 page. Selection process--
Editorial Board. Responds to a submission in 2-6 months. Approximate proportion of submissions accepted for publication--4-6 articles
per issue.

59. MERLEG
    Janos Boor, Ed.
    Ladislaus Balint, Ed.
    Verlag Herder
    Wollzeile 33
    A-1010 Vienna, Austria

Subscription--4/yr.--S.252. Publishes articles in Scripture,
Ethics, Church History, Theology, Evangelism, Church Administration, Pastoral Counseling, Missions, Psychology of Religion, Sociology
of Religion, World Religions, Philosophy of Religion, Judaism, Islam,
Hinduism, Buddhism, Eastern Religions, and Religious Education.
For: professors, students, laypersons, and priests. Submissions
must be in Hungarian. We translate articles which have already ap-
peared in leading foreign-language publications. Does not accept
unsolicited articles, unsolicited reviews; accepts dot-matrix printing,
simultaneous submissions; does not publish research notes; publishes
review-articles; accepts advertising--books and periodicals. Style of
journal--digests. Indexed: Old Test.Abstr.

60. MISCELANEA COMILLAS
    Revista de Teologia y Ciencias Humanas
    Universidad Pontificia Comillas
    E-28049 Madrid, Spain

Subscription--2/yr.--1,200 ptas. Subject matter of journal--
Theology, Scripture, Ethics, Church History, Psychology of Religion, Philosophy of Religion, Sociology of Religion, World Religions,
and Religious Education. For: professors, students, laypersons.
Submissions must be in Spanish. Does not accept unsolicited articles,
unsolicited reviews, dot-matrix printing, simultaneous submissions;
publishes research notes, review-articles; accepts advertising--
theological. Requires one copy of manuscript. Responds to a submission in 15 days. Approximate proportion of manuscripts accepted
for publication--80 percent. Indexed: New Test.Abstr.

61. MONTH
    John McDade, S.J., Ed.
    Society of Jesus
    English Province
    114 Mount St.
    London W1Y 6AH, England

Subscription--Monthly--$24. Subject matter of journal--Scripture,
Ethics, Church History, and Theology. For: professors, students,
and laypersons. Submissions must be in English. Selection process--
Editorial Board advises the Editor. Indexed: Br.Hum.Ind., Cath.
Ind., New Test.Abstr.

62. NEDERLANDS THEOLOGISCH TIJDSCHRIFT
    P. W. van der Horst, Ed.
    Boekencentrum B.V.
    Box 84176
    The Hague, Netherlands 2508 AD

Subscription--4/yr.--78 fl. Description of subject matter of
journal--In principle, every field of study within theology/religious
studies. Publishes articles in Scripture, Ethics, Church History,
Theology, Pastoral Counseling, Missions, Psychology of Religion,
World Religions, Philosophy of Religion, Judaism, Islam, Hinduism,
Buddhism, and Eastern Religions. For: professors, students, and
ministers. Submissions must be in German, English, or Dutch. Accepts unsolicited articles; does not accept unsolicited reviews, dot-
matrix printing, simultaneous submissions; does not publish research
notes; publishes review-articles; does not accept advertising. Seeks
articles that are not too technical but of a high level. Especially
seeking articles that describe the status of the questions (status
quaestionis) of a specific field of problem. Requires one copy of
manuscript. Length requirements--maximum, 10,000 words; minimum,

1000 words. Selection process--The editor and one other (or, in cases of doubt, two other) members of the board read the manuscript and decide. Responds in about 2 months. Approximate proportion of submissions accepted for publication--65 percent. Indexed: Old Test.Abstr., Rel.Per., New Test.Abstr., Rel.Ind.One, Rel.&Theol. Abstr.

63. NORSK TEOLOGISK TIDSSKRIFT/NORWEGIAN THEOLOGICAL
    JOURNAL
    Prof. Dr. Theol. Svein Aage Christoffersen, Ed.
    De teologiske institutter
    Postboks 1023, Blindern
    N-0315 Oslo 3, Norway

Subscription--4/yr.--$31. Publishes articles in Scripture, Ethics, Church History, Theology, and Philosophy of Religion. Submissions must be in Norwegian. Accepts unsolicited articles; sometimes accepts unsolicited reviews; publishes review-articles. Selection process--Editorial Board reaches a decision based on the recommendation of assigned readers. Indexed: Old Test.Abstr., New Test.Abstr., Rel.Per., Rel.Ind.One.

64. NOUVELLE REVUE THEOLOGIQUE
    D. Dideberg, S.J., Director
    Centre de Documentation et de Recherche Religieuses de la
      Compagnie de Jésus
    rue de Bruxelles, 61
    B-5000 Namur, Belgium

Subscription--6/yr.--$37. Publishes articles in Scripture, Ethics, Church History, Theology, Ecclesiology, and Spirituality. Submissions must be in French. Selection process--Editorial Board. Indexed: Cath.Ind., Old Test.Abstr., Canon Law Abstr., New Test.Abstr., Rel.&Theol.Abstr.

65. PERSPECTIVES IN RELIGIOUS STUDIES
    Dr. Watson E. Mills, Ed.
    Mercer University Press
    Mercer University
    Macon, GA   31207

Subscription--4/yr.--$12.00 (1987). Publishes articles in Scripture, Ethics, Church History, Theology, World Religions, Philosophy of Religion, and Religious Education. For: professors. Submissions must be in English. Sometimes accepts unsolicited articles and unsolicited reviews; accepts dot-matrix printing; does not accept simultaneous submissions; does not publish research notes; publishes review-articles; accepts advertising. Seeks articles concerning the

teaching of religion courses. Style of journal--Chicago. Two copies
of the manuscript are required. Length requirements--none. Selection process--peer review, 2 readers. Responds in 3-6 months. Approximate proportion of submissions that are accepted for publication--
30 percent. Parent Organization--National Association of Baptist
Professors of Religion. Indexed: Bk.Rev.Mo., Old Test.Abstr.,
Rel.Per., New Test.Abstr., Rel.Ind.One, Rel.&Theol.Abstr.

66. POSITIONS LUTHERIENNES
     Prof. Dr. Jacques-Noël Pérès, Editor-in-Chief
     Association "Positions Lutheriennes"
     16 rue Chauchat
     75009 Paris, France

     Subscription--4/yr.--140 francs. Description of subject matter
of journal--Lutheran thought and dialogue. Publishes articles in
Scripture, Ethics, Church History, Theology, Psychology of Religion,
and Sociology of Religion. For: professors, students, laypersons.
Submissions must be in French. Requires one copy of manuscript.
Sometimes accepts unsolicited articles; does not accept unsolicited
reviews, dot-matrix printing, simultaneous submissions; does not
publish research notes or review-articles. Length requirements--
maximum, 18 pages; minimum, 6 pages. Selection process--Readers
appointed by Editorial Board. Responds to a submission in one year.
Indexed: Bull.Signal.

67. PRESBYTERION
     Covenant Theological Seminary
     12330 Conway Rd.
     St. Louis, MO 63141

     Subscription--2/yr.--$6.00. Description of subject matter--a
theological journal representing historical Presbyterianism. Publishes
articles in Scripture, Ethics, Church History, Theology, Evangelism,
Church Administration, Pastoral Counseling, and Missions. For:
professors, students, and laypersons. Submissions must be in English. Sometimes accepts unsolicited articles and unsolicited reviews;
accepts dot-matrix printing; does not accept simultaneous submissions;
does not publish research notes; publishes review-articles; does not
accept advertising. Seeks interesting, relevant, excellently researched and written articles. Style of journal--Turabian. Requires
one copy of manuscript. Length requirements--(double space typ-
ing)--Articles--maximum, 35-40 pages, and minimum, 8-10 pages;
Book Reviews--maximum, 6-8 pages, and minimum, 1 page. Selection
process--a committee decides the nature of each issue. Responds--
average 3-4 mos. Approximately 50 percent of all submissions are
accepted for publication. Indexed: Rel.&Theol.Abstr.

68. PROTESTANTESIMO
    Vittorio Subilia, Ed.
    Vittorio Subilia, Ed. & Pub.
    Via Pietro Cossa 42
    00193 Rome, Italy

Subscription--4/yr.--Lire 22.000. Publishes articles in Scripture, Ethics, Church History, Theology. For: professors, students, laypersons. Submissions must be in Italian. Sometimes accepts unsolicited articles, unsolicited reviews; does not accept dot-matrix printing, simultaneous submissions; publishes research notes, review-articles; does not accept advertising. Requires 2 copies of manuscript. Indexed: Bull.Signal, Int.Z.Bibelwiss., Rel.Ind.One.

69. RECHERCHES DE SCIENCE RELIGIEUSE
    Joseph Moingt, Ed.
    Association Recherches de Science Religieuse
    15 rue Monsieur
    75007 Paris, France

Subscription--4/yr.--190 francs. Subject matter of journal--Scripture, Church History, Theology, Sociology of Religion, World Religions, Philosophy of Religion, Judaism, Islam, Hinduism, Buddhism, Eastern Religions. For: professors. Submissions must be in French. Indexed: Bull.Signal, Old Test.Abstr., Rel.Per., New Test.Abstr., Rel.Ind.One.

70. REFORMED REVIEW
    James I. Cook, Ed.
    Western Theological Seminary
    Holland, MI   49423

Subscription--3/yr.--$10. Publishes articles in Scripture, Ethics, Church History, Theology, Evangelism, Pastoral Counseling, Missions, Religious Education. For: professors, students, laypersons, and clergy. Does not accept unsolicited articles, unsolicited reviews; accepts advertising--book publishers. Indexed: Int.Z.Bibelwiss., Rel.Per., New Test.Abstr., Rel.Ind.One, Rel.&Theol.Abstr.

71. REFORMED THEOLOGICAL REVIEW
    The Rev. R. Swanton, Ed.
    The Rev. David Peterson, Ed.
    Box 2587W
    Elizabeth St. P.O.
    Melbourne, Victoria 3001, Australia

Subscription--3/yr.--$6.90. Description of subject matter of journal--Exposition of the Christian faith. Publishes articles in

Scripture, Church History, Theology. Submissions must be in English. Accepts unsolicited reviews and dot-matrix printing. Selection process--Editorial Board makes a decision based on recommendation of readers. Indexed: Rel.Per., New Test.Abstr., Int.Z.Bibelwiss., Rel.&Theol.Abstr., Rel.Ind.One.

72. REFORMED WORLD
    Edmond Perret, Ed.
    World Alliance of Reformed Churches
    150 Route de Ferney
    1211 Geneva 20, Switzerland

Subscription--4/yr.--$2. Description of subject matter of journal--issues of significance for Reformed Churches worldwide. Publishes articles in Scripture, Church History, Theology, Evangelism, Church Administration, Pastoral Counseling, Missions, Social Justice Issues, and Third World Theologies. For: professors, students, and pastors. Submissions must be in English. Sometimes accepts unsolicited articles and unsolicited reviews; does not accept dot-matrix printing or simultaneous submissions; does not publish research notes or review-articles; accepts advertising. Type of article journal seeks--theologies currently articulated among Reformed Churches; church and society matters; ecclesiastical concerns. Especially seeking articles concerning third world views on all of the above. Style of journal--presently shifting from British to American--Chicago manual. Requires 2 copies of manuscript. Length requirements--maximum, 5000 words; minimum, 1000 words. Selection process of articles--try to achieve a balance among academic, pastoral and social issues. Responds from 2 weeks to 2 months to a submission. Approximate proportion of submissions accepted for publication--one-third. Indexed: Rel.Per., Rel.Ind.One, Rel.&Theol. Abstr.

73. RELIGIOUS HUMANISM
    Paul H. Beattie, Ed.
    Fellowship of Religious Humanists
    Box 278
    Yellow Springs, OH 45387

Subscription--4/yr.--$15. Description of subject matter of journal--anything of interest to religious and secular humanists. Publishes articles in Ethics, Church History, Theology, Pastoral Counseling, Psychology of Religion, Sociology of Religion, World Religions, Philosophy of Religion, Judaism, Islam, Hinduism, Buddhism, Eastern Religions, and Religious Education. For: professors and laypersons. Submissions must be in English. Accepts unsolicited articles, unsolicited reviews, dot-matrix printing; does not accept simultaneous submissions; does not publish research notes; publishes review-articles; accepts advertising. Seeks articles showing

dimensions of humanism. Especially looking for articles of liberal
religion, humanism, the Humanist Movement, biographies of leaders,
history, philosophy. Style of journal--standard college paper format.
Requires 2 copies of manuscript. Length requirements--maximum,
10 double-spaced pages; minimum, --. Selection process--editor
reads and decides. Responds to a submission in 2-4 months. Indexed: Curr.Cont., Arts&Hum.Cit.Ind., Phil.Ind., G.Soc.Sci.&Rel.
Per.Lit., Phil.Ind., Rel.&Theol.Abstr., Rel.Ind.One.

74. RELIGIOUS STUDIES
    Prof. S. Sutherland, Ed.   32 E. 57th St.
    Cambridge University Press   New York, NY   10022
    Edinburgh Bldg.
    Shaftesbury Rd.
    Cambridge CB2 2RU, England

    Subscription--4/yr.--$50, individuals; $105, institutions. De-
scription of subject matter of journal-- Religious Studies, is concerned
with the main problems that present themselves in various fields of
religious study. Publishes articles in Psychology of Religion, Sociology of Religion, World Religions, Philosophy of Religion, and Historical and Comparative Study of Religion. Submissions must be in
English. Accepts unsolicited articles; does not accept simultaneous
submissions. Especially seeking articles which maintain high standards
of precision and clarity. Length requirements--maximum, 10,000
words; minimum, 5000 words. Comments: Footnotes should be used
sparingly. Indexed: Br.Hum.Ind., Curr.Cont., Hum.Ind., Rel.
Per., Arts&Hum.Cit.Ind., New Test.Abstr., Rel.Ind.One, Rel.&
Theol.Abstr.

75. RELIGIOUS STUDIES REVIEW
    Glenn Yocum, Managing Ed.
    Department of Religion
    Whittier College
    Whittier, CA   90608

    Subscription--4/yr.--$24, individuals; $20, institutions. De-
scription of subject matter of journal--Journal spanning the entire
field of religious studies; publishes 6-8 major "review essays" and
250-300 "book notes" per issue. Publishes articles in Scripture,
Ethics, Church History, Theology, Psychology of Religion, Sociology
of Religion, World Religions, Philosophy of Religion, Judaism, Islam,
Hinduism, Buddhism, and Religious Studies. For: professors, students, some clergy. Submissions must be in English. Does not accept unsolicited articles, unsolicited reviews, simultaneous submissions; accepts dot-matrix printing; does not publish research notes;
publishes review-articles; accepts advertising--ads from publishers.
Type of article that is sought--3000-6000 word review essays and
100-150 word book notes. Style of journal--"Social Science" format;

references at end of major reviews. Requires 1 copy of manuscript. Selection process--area editors identify major reviews and solicit review essays from scholars expert in field; "networks" of scholars in particular fields identify new publications and write book notes on them. Indexed: Old Test.Abstr., Rel.Per., New Test.Abstr., Rel. Ind.One.

76. REVIEW AND EXPOSITOR
R. Alan Culpepper, Ed.
Southern Baptist Theological Seminary
2825 Lexington Rd.
Louisville, KY 40280

Subscription--4/yr.--$9. Subject matter of journal--try to cover the range of topics represented in their seminary programs: Theology, Christian Education, Church Music, Church Social Work. One issue each year is devoted to a book of the Bible. For: professors, students, laypersons, and ministers. Submissions must be in English. Does not accept unsolicited articles, unsolicited reviews, simultaneous submissions; accepts dot-matrix printing; does not publish research notes; publishes review-articles; accepts advertising. One copy of the manuscript should be submitted. Length requirements -- maximum, 40 pages; minimum, 12 pages. Comments--Virtually all of the articles that are published in the R&E are commissioned. Each issue is devoted to a certain topic; the Editorial Board designs each issue and selects the writers. Instructions are then sent along with the invitation to submit an article. Indexed: Old Test.Abstr., Rel. Per., New Test.Abstr., Rel.Ind.One, Rel.&Theol.Abstr., South Bap.Per.Ind.

77. REVIEW OF RELIGIOUS RESEARCH
Edward L. Lehman, Ed.
State University of New York at Brockport
Sociology Dept.
Brockport, NY 14420

Subscription--4/yr.--$22, individuals; $30, institutions. Review of Religious Research is the official journal of the Religious Research Association. Publishes articles in Ethics, Church History, Theology, Psychology of Religion, and Sociology of Religion. Seeks articles that further the role of religion in contemporary life. Requires 4 copies of manuscript. Accepts unsolicited articles (but there is a charge of $15 for reviewing manuscripts of individuals who do not subscribe to the Review); sometimes accepts unsolicited reviews; accepts advertising. For: professors, students, laypersons, social scientists, church researchers to planners, theologians, teachers, administrators, clergy, editors, religious educators. Indexed: Curr. Cont., Rel.Per., SSCI, Sociol.Abstr., Arts&Hum.Cit.Ind., G.Soc. Sci.&Rel.Per.Lit., Rel.Ind.One, Rel.&Theol.Abstr.

78. REVISTA ECLESIASTICA BRASILEIRA
    Elói Dionísio Piva, O.F.M., Redator
    Editora Vozes Ltda.
    Caixa Postal 23
    25600 Petrópolis
    Rio de Janeiro, Brazil

Subscription--4/yr.--$60. Subject matter of journal--Scripture,
Ethics, Church History, Theology, Evangelism, Missions, Sociology
of Religion, Religious Education, Liberation Themes. Submissions
must be in English. Selection process--Editorial Board decides.
Comments: Issues are usually organized around a theme. Indexed:
Cath.Ind., Old Test.Abstr., New Test.Abstr.

79. REVUE AFRICAINE DE THEOLOGIE
    Prof. A. Vanneste, Secrétaire
    Faculte de Theologie Catholique de Kinshasa
    B.P. 1534
    Kinshasa/Limete, Zaïre

Subscription--2/yr.--$20. Subject matter of journal--Scripture,
Ethics, Church History, Theology, Evangelism, Missions, Psychology
of Religion, Sociology of Religion, Philosophy of Religion, Christianity
and African Culture. For: professors, students, and laypersons.
Submissions must be in French. Selection process--the Editorial
Board upon advice of appointed readers. Indexed: New Test.Abstr.

80. REVUE D'HISTOIRE ET DE PHILOSOPHIE RELIGIEUSES
    M. Philonenko, Ed.
    Presses Universitaires de France
    108 bd. Saint Germain
    75279 Paris Cedex 6, France

Subscription--4/yr.--140 francs. Description of subject matter
of journal--The Revue is open to all theological disciplines and all
theological currents of thought. It is non-sectarian and is an
academic journal. Publishes articles in Scripture, Ethics, Church
History, Theology, Philosophy of Religion, and Judaism. For: professors, students, and ministers. Submissions must be in French.
Accepts unsolicited articles; sometimes accepts unsolicited reviews;
does not accept dot-matrix printing or simultaneous submissions; does
not publish research notes; publishes review-articles; does not accept advertising. Requires one copy of manuscript. Length requirements for a submission--maximum, 20 pages; minimum, 10 pages.
Selection process--Articles are submitted to an Editorial Committee.
Responds to a submission in 2 months. Parent Organization--Uni-
versité de Strasbourg II. Indexed: Curr.Cont., Rel.Per., Arts&
Hum.Cit.Ind., New Test.Abstr., Rel.Ind.One, Rel.&Theol.Abstr.

81. REVUE DE THEOLOGIE ET DE PHILOSOPHIE
    Revue de Theologie et de Philosophie
    7 Chemin des Cedres
    Lausanne, Switzerland

Subscription--4/yr.--56 francs. Publishes articles in Scripture, Ethics, Church History, Theology, World Religions, Philosophy of Religion, and Philosophy. For: professors, students, and layper-sons. Submissions must be in French, German, English, or Italian. Accepts unsolicited articles; sometimes accepts unsolicited reviews; does not accept dot-matrix printing; accepts simultaneous submissions; does not publish research notes or review-articles; does not accept advertising. Style of journal--academic. Requires three copies of manuscript. Length requirements--maximum, 50,000 words. Selec-tion process--articles read by each member of the Editorial Board and then discussed. Responds in three months. Approximate pro-portion of submissions that are accepted for publication--60 percent. Indexed: Bull.Signal, Old Test.Abstr., New Test.Abstr., Phil. Ind., Rel.Ind.One.

82. REVUE DES SCIENCES RELIGIEUSES
    René Epp, Dir.
    Bureau De La Revue Des Sciences Religieuses
    Palais Universitaire
    67084 Strasbourg Cedex, France

Subscription--4/yr.--140 francs. Subject matter of journal--Scripture, Church History, and Theology. Accepts unsolicited ar-ticles and unsolicited reviews. For: professors, students, and laypersons. Submissions must be in French. Selection process--Editorial Board. Indexed: Old Test.Abstr., Rel.Per., New Test. Abstr., Rel.Ind.One.

83. REVUE THEOLOGIQUE DE LOUVAIN
    J. Ponthot, Ed.
    Université Catholique de Louvain
    Facultés de Theologie et de Droit Canonique
    Grand-Place 45
    1348 Louvain-la-Neuve, Belgium

Subscription--4/yr.--1000 francs. Description of subject mat-ter of journal--reflection, research and critical information of aca-demic standards--especially concerning doctrinal and pastoral aspects of the Christian tradition, past and present. Publishes articles in Scripture, Ethics, Church History, Theology, Evangelism, Church Administration, Pastoral Counseling, Missions, Psychology of Re-ligion, Sociology of Religion, World Religions, Philosophy of Religion, Judaism, Islam, Hinduism, Buddhism, Eastern Religions, Religious Education. For: professors, students, laypersons, clergy.

Submissions must be in French. Sometimes accepts unsolicited articles; does not accept unsolicited reviews, simultaneous submissions; accepts dot-matrix printing; publishes research notes, review-articles; does not accept advertising. Style of journal--publications of an academic standard but not written in technical jargon. Requires one copy of manuscript. Length requirements--maximum, 30 pages; minimum, 5 pages. Selection process--once a year, the Editorial Committee suggests topics and authors. Unsolicited manuscripts are refereed by two members of the Board of Directors or of the Redaction Committee. Responds to a submission in about a month. Acceptance depends on the quality of the paper submitted. Indexed: Cath.Ind., Arts&Hum.Cit.Ind., New Test.Abstr.

84. REVUE ZAIROISE DE THEOLOGIE PROTESTANTE
    Munduku Ngamayamu Dagoga, Red.
    Faculte de Theologie Protestant au Zaïre
    Croisement des Avenues du 24 Novembre et de la Victoire
    B.P. 4745 Kinshasa II, Zaïre

Subscription--1/yr. Subject matter of journal--Scripture, Ethics, Church History, Theology, Sociology of Religion, Religion and Culture. Submissions must be in French.

85. ST. LUKE'S JOURNAL OF THEOLOGY
    John M. Gessell, Ed.
    University of the South
    School of Theology
    Sewanee, TN 37375

Subscription--4/yr.--$10. Description of subject matter of journal--Articles that seek to relate Christian faith and witness to contemporary issues. Publishes articles in Scripture, Ethics, Church History, Theology, Evangelism, Church Administration, Pastoral Counseling, Missions, Psychology of Religion, Sociology of Religion, World Religions, Philosophy of Religion, Judaism, Islam, Hinduism, Buddhism, Eastern Religions, Religious Education. For: professors, students, laypersons. Submissions must be in English. Accepts unsolicited articles, simultaneous submissions; sometimes accepts unsolicited reviews; does not accept dot-matrix printing; does not publish research notes; publishes review-articles; accepts advertising --books, scholarly events. Seeks articles written for clergy and laity engaged in practice of ministry. Style of journal--MLA. Requires 2 copies of manuscript. Length requirements--maximum, about 20 pages; minimum--none. Selection process--on reader's recommendations. Responds in 3-6 months. Approximate proportion of submissions accepted for publication--50 percent. Indexed: Old Test. Abstr., Rel.Per., Rel.Ind.One.

86. ST. VLADIMIR'S THEOLOGICAL QUARTERLY
Very Rev. John Breck, Ed.
St. Vladimir's Orthodox Theological Seminary
575 Scarsdale Rd., Crestwood
Tuckahoe, NY 10707

Subscription--4/yr.--$18. Description of subject matter--Orthodox theology--scholarly articles on Scripture, Patristics, and Ethics. For: professors, students, and laypersons. Submissions must be in English. Accepts unsolicited articles, unsolicited reviews, dot-matrix printing; does not accept simultaneous submissions; publishes research notes and review-articles; does not accept advertising. Seeks scholarly articles dealing with an Orthodox perspective on the above topics. Style of journal--10-20 page articles, properly footnoted; book reviews. Requires 1, preferably 2, copies of manuscript. Length requirements--maximum, 25 pages; minimum, 10 pages. Selection process--Academic/scholarly competence in an area of interest to our readers--quality of writing, grammar, etc. are important considerations. Responds in 2-3 months, after review by the Editorial Board. About 2/3 of the submissions in the past 3 years have been published, including reviews. Indexed: Old Test.Abstr., Rel.Per., New Test.Abstr., Rel.&Theol.Abstr., Rel.Ind.One, Theol.&Rel.Ind.

87. SALESIANUM
Università Pontificia Salesiana
Piazza Alteneo Salesiano 1
00139 Rome, Italy

Subscription--4/yr.--L. 45.000. Publishes articles in Scripture, Ethics, Church History, Theology, and Philosophy of Religion. For: professors. Submissions must be in French, German, Spanish, English, or Italian. Does not accept unsolicited articles, unsolicited reviews, dot-matrix printing, simultaneous submissions; publishes research notes and review-articles; does not accept advertising. Seeks scholarly or academic articles only of the professors of the Pontifical Salesian University. Indexed: Canon Law Abstr., New Test.Abstr., Rel.&Theol.Abstr.

88. SCRIPTA THEOLOGICA
Pedro Rodríguez, Ed.
Universidad de Navarra
Apdo. 170
31080 Pamplona, Spain

Subscription--3/yr.--$33. Description of subject matter of journal--research articles and notes: commentary on scripture, theology, history of the church, patristic studies, etc. For: professors, students, laypersons, priests. Submissions must be in French, German, Spanish, English, Italian, or Portuguese. Sometimes accepts unsolicited articles, unsolicited reviews; does not accept dot-matrix printing, simultaneous submissions; publishes research notes, review-articles; does not accept advertising. Seeks articles that are documented and written for an academic audience. Especially looking for articles concerned with Catholic Doctrine. Style of journal-- a style proper to research and scientific commentary. Requires 2 copies of manuscript. Length requirements--maximum, 9000 words; minimum, 1200 words. Selection process--Favorable report of two members of the Editing Board and approval of the Direction Committee. Responds in 60 days. Approximate proportion of submissions accepted for publication--30 percent. Indexed: Old Test.Abstr., New Test.Abstr.

89. SCUOLA CATTOLICA
    A. Rimoldi, Ed.
    Seminario Arcivescovile di Milano
    21060 Venegono Inferiore
    Varese, Italy

Subscription--6/yr.--$32. Publishes articles in Scripture, Ethics, Church History, Theology, and Evangelism. Sometimes accepts unsolicited articles; does not accept unsolicited reviews, dot-matrix printing, simultaneous submissions; publishes research notes and review-articles; does not accept advertising. Requires one copy of manuscript. Indexed: New Test.Abstr., Rel.&Theol.Abstr.

90. STUDIA PATAVINA, RIVISTA DI SCIENZE RELIGIOSE
    Seminario Vescovile
    Via del Seminario 29
    35122 Padua, Italy

Subscription--3/yr.--$22. Publishes articles in Scripture, Ethics, Church History, Theology, Evangelism, Church Administration, Pastoral Counseling, Missions, Psychology of Religion, Sociology of Religion, World Religions, Philosophy of Religion, Judaism, Islam, Hinduism, Buddhism, Eastern Religions, Religious Education. For: professors, students, laypersons. Submissions must be in Italian. Sometimes accepts unsolicited articles, unsolicited reviews; does not publish review-articles; does not accept advertising. Style of journal--academic. Requires 1 copy of manuscript. Length requirements--maximum, 30 pages; minimum, 5 pages. Selection process-- recommendation by three members of the Editorial Staff and the approval of all the Editorial Staff. Responds in 3 months. Approximate proportion of submissions accepted for publication--70 percent. Indexed: Old Test.Abstr., New Test.Abstr.

91. STUDIA THEOLOGICA
    Prof. Arvid S. Kapelrud, Ed.
    Prof. Jacob Jervell, Ed.

P.O. Box 1023 Blindern
Oslo 3, Norway

Subscription--2/yr.--$27. Subject matter of journal--Scripture,
Theology, Hermeneutics, Biblical Criticism, Religion and Literature.
Submissions must be in French, German, or English. Accepts un-
solicited articles. Selection process--Editorial Board reviews and se-
lects articles to be included in journal. Indexed: Curr.Cont., Rel.
Per., Arts&Hum.Cit.Ind., New Test.Abstr., Rel.Ind.One, Rel.&
Theol.Abstr.

92. STUDIES IN RELIGION/SCIENCES RELIGIEUSES
     Tom Sinclair-Faulkner, Ed.
     Dalhousie University
     Halifax, Nova Scotia B3H 3J5, Canada

Subscription--4/yr.--$30 Canadian. Publishes articles and re-
views in the areas of scholarship represented by the Canadian Society of Biblical Studies, the Canadian Society of Church History, the
Canadian Society of Patristic Studies, the Canadian Society for the
Study of Religion, and the Canadian Theological Society. Accepts
unsolicited articles and unsolicited reviews. Selection process--mem-
bers of the Editorial Board read the articles and advise the Editor
who then decides which articles to accept. Indexed: Old Test.
Abstr., Rel.Per., New Test.Abstr., Arts&Hum.Cit.Ind., Rel.Ind.
One, Rel.&Theol.Abstr.

93. SVENSK TEOLOGISK KVARTALSKRIFT
     Bengt Hagglund, Ed.
     P. E. Persson, Ed.
     Liber Forlag
     S-205 10
     Malmoe, Sweden

Subscription--4/yr.--Kr 95. Description of subject matter of
journal--Theology in all its facets. Publishes articles in Scripture,
Ethics, Church History, Theology, Psychology of Religion, Sociology
of Religion, Missions, World Religions, Philosophy of Religion, Judaism,
Islam, Hinduism, Buddhism, Eastern Religions, and Religious Education. Sometimes accepts unsolicited articles and unsolicited reviews;
does not accept dot-matrix printing; does not publish research notes;
publishes review-articles; accepts advertising. For: professors,
students, and laypersons. Submissions must be in Swedish. Seeks
articles that are not too long, on an academic level. Requires 2
copies of manuscript. Length requirements--maximum, 15 A-4 pages.
Responds to a submission in 4 weeks. Indexed: Old Test.Abstr.,
Rel.Per., New Test.Abstr., Rel.Ind.One.

94. TEOLOGIA Y VIDA
    Marciano Barrios, Ed.
    Facultad de Teologia de la Universidad Católica
    Diagonal Oriente 3300
    Casilla 114-D
    Santiago, Chile

Subscription--4/yr.--$25. Subject matter of journal--Scripture,
Ethics, Church History, Theology, Evangelism, Sociology of Religion, and Philosophy of Religion. Accepts unsolicited articles and
unsolicited reviews. For: professors, students, and laypersons.
Submissions must be in Spanish. Selection process--the Editor acts
upon the advice of Advisory Board. Indexed: Bull.Signal, Cath.
Ind., Old Test.Abstr., Canon Law Abstr., New Test.Abstr.

95. TERESIANUM--EPHEMERIDES CARMELITICAE
    P. Virgilio Pasquetto, Director
    Edizioni del Teresianum
    Piazza S. Pancrazio 5-A
    00152 Rome, Italy

Subscription--2/yr.--$30. Publishes articles in Theology, Scrip-
ture, Ethics, Church History, Evangelism, Psycholgy of Religion.
For: professors, students. Submissions must be in Italian, French,
German, Spanish, or English. Accepts unsolicited articles; publishes research notes. Style of journal--academic. Requires 2 copies
of manuscript. Length requirements--maximum, 30 pages; minimum,
20 pages. Selection process--Editorial Board. Responds in 30 days.
Parent Organization--Pontificia Facolta Teresianum. Indexed: Old
Test.Abstr., New Test.Abstr.

96. THEMELIOS
    David Wenham, Ed.
    Universities & Colleges Christian Fellowship
    38 De Montfort St.
    Leicester LE1 7GP, England

Subscription--3/yr.--$25. Description of subject matter of
journal--Issues relevant to theological students, especially under-
graduates. Publishes articles in Scripture, Ethics, Church History,
Theology, Evangelism, Pastoral Counseling, Missions, World Religions,
and Philosophy of Religion. For: students. Submissions must be
in English. Sometimes accepts unsolicited articles, unsolicited reviews; accepts dot-matrix printing; does not accept simultaneous
submissions; does not publish research notes; publishes review-
articles; does not accept advertising. Seeks nontechnical, but
scholarly, surveys of and introductions to issues of current importance to students. Requires one copy of manuscript. Length
requirements for submissions--maximum, 6000 words; minimum, 2000

words (normally). Selection process--general editor's decision in consultation with readers. Responds to a submission in 1-3 months (normally). Approximate proportion of submissions that are accepted for publication--maybe a third or half of the unsolicited articles. Comments: authors to be in agreement with the theological position of TSF and IFES. Co-sponsor--International Fellowship of Evangelical Students. Indexed: Old Test.Abstr.

97. THEOLOGISCHE LITERATURZEITUNG
     Prof. Dr. Ernst-Heinz Amberg, Ed.
     Redaktion
     Scherlstrasse 2 - PSF 448
     7010 Leipzig, East Germany (D.D.R.)

Subscription--12/yr.--DM 60.--. Publishes articles in Theology, Scripture, Ethics, Church History, Pastoral Counseling, Missions, Psychology of Religion, World Religions, Philosophy of Religion, Judaism, and Religious Education. For: professors, students, and libraries. Submissions must be in French, German, or English. Sometimes accepts unsolicited articles, unsolicited reviews; does not accept dot-matrix printing, simultaneous submissions; publishes research notes and review-articles; does not accept advertising. Seeks reviews. Requires two copies of manuscript. Indexed: Old Test. Abstr., Rel.Per., New Test.Abstr., Rel.&Theol.Abstr., Rel.Ind.One.

98. THEOLOGISCHE RUNDSCHAU
     J. Baur, Ed.
     L. Perlitt, Ed.
     Verlag J.C.B. Mohr (Paul Siebeck)
     Wilhelmstrasse 18
     Postfach 2040
     7400 Tuebingen, West Germany (B.R.D.)

Subscription--4/yr.--DM 98, individuals; DM 58, students. Description of subject matter of journal--review-articles. Publishes articles in Scripture, Ethics, Church History, Theology, Evangelism, Church Administration, Pastoral Counseling, Missions, Psychology of Religion, Sociology of Religion, World Religions, Philosophy of Religion, Judaism, Islam, Hinduism, Buddhism, Eastern Religions, Religious Education. For: professors, students, pastors. Submissions must be in German. Does not accept unsolicited articles, unsolicited reviews, dot-matrix printing, simultaneous submissions; does not publish research notes; publishes review-articles; does not accept advertising. Requires one copy of manuscript. Length requirements-- maximum, 60 pages; minimum, 7 pages. Responds to a submission in 2 weeks. Indexed: Old Test.Abstr., Rel.Per., New Test.Abstr., Rel.Ind.One, Rel.&Theol.Abstr.

99. TRIERER THEOLOGISCHE ZEITSCHRIFT
     Paulinus-Verlag
     Fleischstrasse 61-65
     5500 Trier, West Germany (B.R.D.)

     Subscription--4/yr.--DM 64.80. Publishes articles in Scripture,
Ethics, Church History, Theology, Evangelism, Church Administra-
tion, Pastoral Counseling, Missions, and Religious Education. For:
professors, students, and laypersons. Submissions must be in Dutch.
Does not accept unsolicited articles; publishes research notes. Parent
Organization--Theologische Fakultaet Trier. Indexed: Old Test.
Abstr., Canon Law Abstr., New Test.Abstr.

100. TRINITY JOURNAL
      D. A. Carson, Ed.
      Douglas J. Moo, Ed.
      Trinity Evangelical Divinity School
      2065 Half Day Road
      Deerfield, IL   60015

     Subscription--2/yr.--$7.50, nonstudents; $6.50, students. De-
scription of subject matter--those studies which are a normal aspect
of Divinity School curriculum. Publishes articles in Scripture, Ethics, Church History, Theology, Evangelism, Church Administration,
Pastoral Counseling, Missions, Religious Education. For: professors,
students, pastors. Submissions must be in English. Seeks articles
which are in the forefront of academic research, contribute new
knowledge, and have relevance to Christian understanding. Especially looking for well thought out articles which are relevant to life
situations. Style of journal--classical academic writing with footnotes or endnotes. Requires one copy of manuscript. Length re-
quirements--maximum, 100 pages; minimum, 10 pages. Selection pro-
cess--Articles are reviewed blind by the Editorial Board. Decisions
are yes, no, yes with revision. Basis of evaluation is the quality
of research, writing style, and relevance to life. Responds in 2-3
months. Approximate proportion of submissions accepted for publi-
cation--50 percent. Indexed: Bull.Signal, Old Test.Abstr., New
Test.Abstr., Bk.Rev.Ind., Bk.Rev.Mo., Chr.Per.Ind., Curr.Bk.
Rev.Cit., G.Soc.Sci.&Rel.Per.Lit., Int.Z.Bibelwiss., Rel.&Theol.
Abstr., Rel.Ind.One.

101. UNION SEMINARY QUARTERLY REVIEW
      Alexandra Coe, Co-editor
      Earl Kooperkamp, Co-editor
      Union Theological Seminary
      3041 Broadway
      New York, NY   10027

     Subscription--4/yr.--$10, individuals; $14, institutions.

Publishes articles in Scripture, Ethics, Church History, Theology, Sociology of Religion, Psychology of Religion, World Religions, Philosophy of Religion, Judaism, Biblical Studies, and Hermeneutics. For: professors, students, clergy, laypersons. Submissions must be in English. Accepts unsolicited articles, unsolicited reviews, dot-matrix printing, simultaneous submissions; does not publish research notes; publishes review-articles; accepts advertising--mostly from publishing houses, but other appropriate ads may be accepted. Seeks articles which make a positive contribution to contemporary theology, ethics, or Biblical studies, which provoke thought and contribute to the knowledge in the field. Style of journal--MLA. Requires one copy of manuscript. Length requirements--maximum, 40 pages double-spaced; minimum, 15 pages double-spaced. Selection process--articles are read by the editors and members of the Advisory Board of Union Seminary faculty. Responds in 2-3 weeks. Approximate proportion of submissions accepted for publication--50 percent. Indexed: Old Test.Abstr., Rel.Per., New Test.Abstr., Rel.Ind.One, Rel.&Theol.Abstr.

102. UNITED EVANGELICAL ACTION
Donald R. Brown, Ed.
National Association of Evangelicals
Box 28
Wheaton, IL 60189

Subscription--6/yr.--$10. Description of subject matter--important Biblical, moral, and ethical questions. Publishes articles in Scripture, Ethics, Theology, Evangelism, Church Administration, Missions, and World Religions. For: professors, students, laypersons, and pastors. Submissions must be in English. Does not accept unsolicited articles, unsolicited reviews; accepts dot-matrix printing, simultaneous submissions; publishes research notes and review-articles; accepts advertising. Seeks articles that are well-researched pertaining to the magazine's theme. Especially looking for well-written pieces by well-known evangelicals. Style of Journal--AP. Requires 1 copy of manuscript. Length requirements--maximum, 1200 words; minimum, 800 words. Selection process: Editor solicits the articles published. In editorial planning sessions the articles are determined and then writers are hired accordingly. Responds in 2 weeks. Approximate proportion of submissions that are accepted for publication--unsolicited manuscripts--0 percent; solicited--100 percent. Comments--open to query letters. On several occasions, suggested topics were developed into issues themselves. Indexed: Chr.Per.Ind., G.Soc.Sci.&Rel.Per.Lit.

103. VERKUENDIGUNG UND FORSCHUNG
Christian Kaiser Verlag
Isabellastrasse 20
8000 Munich 40, West Germany (B.R.D.)

Subscription--2/yr.--DM 28. Publishes articles in Theology, Scripture, Ethics, Missions. For: professors, students, laypersons. Submissions must be in German. Does not accept unsolicited articles, unsolicited reviews, dot-matrix printing, simultaneous submissions; publishes review-articles; accepts advertising. Length requirements-- maximum, 100 pages; minimum, 70 pages. Selection process--Editorial Board. Indexed: New Test.Abstr.

104. VIDYAJYOTI
S.Arokiasamy, Ed.
23 Raj Nivas Marg
Delhi 110054, India

Subscription--11/yr.--$12. Subject matter of journal--Scripture, Ethics, Church History, Theology, Psychology of Religion, Sociology of Religion, Philosophy of Religion, Islam, Christianity and Culture. For: professors, students, laypersons. Submissions must be in English. Accepts unsolicited articles and unsolicited reviews. Selection process--Editorial Board acting on behalf of the Vidyajyoti Educational and Welfare Society selects materials to be included in issues. Indexed: Old Test.Abstr., Canon Law Abstr., New Test. Abstr.

105. WESLEYAN THEOLOGICAL JOURNAL
Dr. A. R. G. Deasley, Ed.
Nazarene Theological Seminary
1700 East Meyer Boulevard
Kansas City, MO 64131

Subscription--2/yr. Individuals and libraries, $6; students, $2. Description of subject matter of journal--journal seeks to en- courage the exchange of ideas among Wesleyan-Arminian theologians. Publishes articles in Scripture, Ethics, Church History, Theology, Evangelism, Church Administration, Pastoral Counseling, Missions, Religious Education, and Wesleyan Theology. Submissions must be in English. For: professors and students. Sometimes accepts un- solicited articles and unsolicited reviews. Preference is given to papers assigned for and presented at the annual meetings of the Wesleyan Theological Society and the WTS seminar at the annual con- vention of the Christian Holiness Association. Style of journal-- University of Chicago Style as set forth in Kate Turabian, A Manual .... Selection process--Members of Editorial Committee read and communicate reactions to the Editor. Majority approval. Indexed: Chr.Per.Ind., Rel.Ind.One.

106. WESTMINSTER THEOLOGICAL JOURNAL
Moises Silva, Ed.
Westminster Theological Seminary

Chestnut Hill
Philadelphia, PA   19118

Subscription--2/yr.--$15, individuals; $20, institutions. Description of subject matter--broad theological disciplines. Subject
matter of journal--(primary)--Scripture, Church History, and Theology; (secondary)--Ethics, Evangelism, Pastoral Counseling, and
Missions. For: professors, students, and pastors. Submissions
must be in English. Accepts unsolicited articles and dot-matrix
printing, if near-letter quality; does not accept unsolicited reviews
or simultaneous submissions; publishes research notes and review-
articles; and accepts advertising--only academic and scholarly. Seeks
scholarly articles. Style of Journal--JBL. Submit one copy of manuscript. Length requirements--no set requirements, preferably 25-
35 pages. Selection process--evaluation by someone with expertise
in topic. Responds in 6-8 weeks. Approximately 40 percent of all
submissions are accepted for publication. Indexed: Rel.Per., Chr.
Per.Ind., Int.Z.Bibelwiss., New Test.Abstr., Old Test.Abstr., Rel.
Ind.One, Rel.&Theol.Abstr.

107. ZEITSCHRIFT FUER RELIGIONS UND GEISTESGESCHICHTE
      E. J. Brill GmbH   Editorial address:
      Antwerpener Str 6   Dr. Regina Johann
      5000 Cologne 1, West   Universität-Gh-Duisburg
          Germany (B.R.D.)   Bürgerstrasse 15, Postfach
                                        10 16 29
                                    4100 Duisburg 1, West
                                        Germany (B.R.D.)

Subscription--4/yr.--DM 96. Subject matter of journal--Scrip-
ture, Ethics, Church History, Theology, Psychology of Religion,
Sociology of Religion, World Religions, Philosophy of Religion, Judaism, Islam, Hinduism, Buddhism, Religious Education, Intellectual
History of Mankind. For: professors and students. Submissions
must be in English or German. Sometimes accepts unsolicited articles, unsolicited reviews; accepts dot-matrix printing; does not accept simultaneous submissions; publishes research notes, review-
articles; accepts advertising--academic, publishers. Style of jour-
nal--objective, academic. Requires one copy of manuscript. Length
requirements--maximum, 30 pages; minimum, --. Articles that are
selected must enhance the knowledge in religious sciences. Responds
in about 2 weeks. Approximate proportion of submissions accepted
for publication--20 percent. Indexed: Rel.Per., Rel.&Theol.Abstr.,
Arts&Hum.Cit.Ind., New Test.Abstr., Rel.Ind.One.

108. ZEITSCHRIFT FUER THEOLOGIE UND KIRCHE
      Prof. Dr. Wilfrid Werbeck
      Stoecklestr. 22
      7400 Tuebingen, West Germany (B.R.D.)

Subscription--4/yr.--66 DM. Subject matter of journal--
Scripture, Ethics, Church History, and Theology. For: professors,
students, and laypersons. Submissions must be in German. Accepts
unsolicited articles; accepts advertising. Selection process--Editorial
Board in consultation with assigned readers. Indexed: Curr.Cont.,
Old Test.Abstr., Rel.Per., Arts&Hum.Cit.Ind., Rel.Ind.One, Rel.&
Theol.Abstr.

2. CHURCH HISTORY

109. AMERICAN CATHOLIC HISTORICAL SOCIETY OF PHILADELPHIA
RECORDS
Thomas R. Greene, Ed.
American Catholic Historical Society of Philadelphia
Box 84
Philadelphia, PA   19105

Subscription--4/yr.--$15. Description of subject matter of
journal--Journal is devoted exclusively to the study of the history
of the Catholic Church in America. Publishes articles in Church
History, and History of the Catholic Church in America. For: professors, students, laypersons, and Catholic clergy. Sometimes accepts unsolicited articles; does not accept unsolicited reviews. Seeks
articles on the documentary sources of Catholic history of America.
Indexed: Cath.Ind.

110. AMERICAN PRESBYTERIANS: JOURNAL OF PRESBYTERIAN
HISTORY
James H. Smylie, Ed.
Presbyterian Historical Society and Historical Foundation
Presbyterian Church USA
425 Lombard St.
Philadelphia, PA   19147

Subscription--4/yr.--$15. Description of subject matter of
journal--We focus on the history of Presbyterians and others in the
"Reformed" family in the USA. For: professors and laypersons.
Submissions must be in English. Accepts unsolicited articles, unsolicited reviews; does not accept simultaneous submissions; publishes
review-articles; does not accept advertising. Type of article that is
sought--we consider any well-researched, well-documented, and well-
written essay on Presbyterian and Reformed subjects. We also like
illustrations. We would like to increase our coverage of areas, e.g.,
the Mid West, the North West, the South West, California--especially
in regard to history, women's history, and the histories of other
minorities. Requires 1 copy of manuscript. Length requirements--
maximum, 25 pages, including notes, double-spaced. Selection pro-
cess--articles go to the Editorial Committee and to readers with special expertise; editor has final say. Responds to a submission in

2-4 months. Comments: when we receive an essay which has prom-
ise we attempt to work with the author to produce a publishable
article. We wish to encourage writing in our special area of interest.
Parent Organization--United Presbyterian Church in the USA, Presbyterian Historical Society and Historical Foundation. Indexed: Curr.
Cont., Hist.Abstr., Rel.Per., Amer.Hist.&Life, Arts&Hum.Cit.Ind.,
Rel.Ind.One, Rel.&Theol.Abstr.

111.   BAPTIST HISTORY AND HERITAGE
        Lynn E. May, Jr., Ed.
        Southern Baptist Convention
        Historical Commission
        901 Commerce St.
        Ste. 400
        Nashville, TN   37203-3620

   Subscription--4/yr.--$8.50, ($11.00--outside of U.S.A.); 2/yr.
subscription for $15.50 ($20.50 outside of U.S.A.); 3/yr. subscription for $22.95 ($30.50 outside of U.S.A.). Description of subject
matter--focuses on Baptist history throughout the world. For: professors, students, and laypersons. Submissions must be in English.
Accepts unsolicited articles, unsolicited reviews, dot-matrix printing;
does not publish research notes or review-articles; does not accept
advertising. Seeks articles that are well documented, that take a
fresh approach, and that reflect historical objectivity. Especially interested in an article that relates to Southern Baptist heritage.
Style of journal--style sheet may be obtained by writing journal.
Two copies of manuscript are required. Length requirements--
maximum, 20 pages--double-spaced; minimum, 10 pages--double-
spaced. Selection process--Evaluation is done both by staff and by
outside readers. Responds in 6 weeks. Approximately 60 percent
of all submissions are accepted for publication. Indexed: Amer.
Hist.&Life, Rel.Ind.One, South.Bap.Per.Ind.

112.   BAPTIST QUARTERLY N.S.
        John Briggs, Ed.
        Department of History
        University of Keele
        Staffordshire ST5 5BG, England

   Subscription--4/yr.--13 pounds, nonmembers; 16 pounds, libraries. Description of subject matter of journal--Whilst, as the
periodical of the Baptist Historical Society, the main concern of the
journal is Baptist history, with a focus (but not an exclusive focus)
on the British story. It also seeks to lay a record for the future by
allowing space to Baptist authors engaged in serious theological study.
It is also keen to record Baptist attitudes to the major theological
developments of the day. It is now clear that developments in the
western world need to be placed in the context of worldwide Christian

concerns and developments. Baptist History also needs to be seen as belonging to the nonestablished reformed tradition and, accordingly, articles in this area are also welcome. For: professors, students, laypersons, historians, ministers--pastorate. Submissions must be in English. Accepts unsolicited articles, dot-matrix printing (if clear), simultaneous submissions; (rarely) accepts unsolicited reviews; publishes research notes and review-articles; accepts advertising. Requires 2 copies of manuscript. Style of journal--academic, request journal style sheet. Length requirements--maximum, 15,000 words; minimum, 1500 words. Selection process--in keeping with the editorial guidelines and by reference to panel of referees. Responds to a submission--acknowledgment in about a week; and then dependent upon readers' responses. Approximate proportion of submissions accepted for publication--60 percent. Indexed: Br.Hum.Ind., Hist. Abstr., Rel.Per., Rel.Ind.One, Rel.&Theol.Abstr.

113. CATHOLIC HISTORICAL REVIEW
     Rev. Robert Trisco, Ed.
     Catholic University of America Press
     620 Michigan Ave., N.E.
     Washington, DC   20064

Subscription--4/yr.--$20. Description of subject matter for journal--for articles: history of the Catholic Church broadly conceived (all times and places); for book reviews: history of Christianity (all branches or denominations). For: professors, laypersons, clergy. Submissions must be in English. Accepts unsolicited articles; does not accept unsolicited reviews, dot-matrix printing, simultaneous submissions; publishes research notes, review articles; accepts advertising--advertisements of books, microform publications, etc. Seeks scholarly, original, significant articles. At present, for the sake of proper distribution over various fields, they are seeking articles in ancient, medieval, and Latin American church history. Style of journal--University of Chicago Manual of Style (modified). Length requirements--maximum, 30 pages; minimum, 15 pages. Selection process--The articles are judged by the editor, by one or more of the associate and advisory editors, and by one or more experts serving as referees. Responds in less than 3 months (normally). Approximate proportion of submissions that are accepted for publication--25-33 percent. Parent Organization--American Catholic Historical Association. Indexed: Cath.Ind., Curr.Cont., Hum.Ind., Old Test.Abstr., Arts&Hum.Cit.Ind., Rel.&Theol.Abstr.

114. CEHILA
     Dirección y Redacción
     Apartado 52790
     Bogotá, Colombia

Subscriptions--4/yr.--$8.00. Subject matter of journal--

Church History, Theology, Sociology of Religion. Submissions must be in Spanish.

115. CHURCH HISTORY
     American Society of Church History
     University of Chicago
     Swift Hall
     1025 E. 58th St.
     Chicago, IL 60637

Subscription--4/yr.--$25. Description of subject matter of journal--The scholarly study of the history of Christianity from the first century to the present. Publishes articles in Church History. For: Professors and graduate students. Submissons must be in English. Accepts unsolicited articles, dot-matrix printing, simultaneous submissions; does not accept unsolicited reviews; does not publish research notes; publishes review-articles; accepts advertising. Style of journal--Chicago Manual of Style. Requires 2 copies of manuscript. Length requirements--25 pages double-spaced; minimum --. Selection process--Manuscript is sent to two outside readers who are experts in the subject area. The editors then decide whether or not to publish the article based on the evaluations and recommendations of the outside readers. Responds in 4-6 months. Approximate proportion of submissions accepted for publication--1 in 6 accepted. Indexed: Curr.Cont., Hum.Ind., Old Test.Abstr., Rel.Per., Arts& Hum.Cit.Ind., Chr.Per.Ind., Rel.&Theol.Abstr., Rel.Ind.One, RILA.

116. CONCORDIA HISTORICAL INSTITUTE QUARTERLY
     Hilton C. Oswald, Ed.
     Concordia Historical Institute
     801 DeMun Ave.
     St. Louis, MO 63105

Subscription--4 issues/yr.--$15.00. Description of subject matter of journal--broadly speaking, all aspects of the history of Lutheranism in America; also sometimes accepts articles on European antecedents and contemporary overseas developments. Accepts unsolicited articles, unsolicited reviews, dot-matrix printing; does not accept simultaneous submissions; accepts research notes; publishes review-articles; accepts advertising--camera-ready, one color. For: professors, students, and laypersons. Submissions must be in English. Seeks both popular and scholarly articles depicting all aspects of Lutheranism in America: research, memoirs, translations of significant documents, oral histories, etc. Especially seeking articles by new authors or in new areas of research in American Lutheran history. Style of journal--Chicago Manual of Style; articles typed double-spaced, notes at end. Requires two copies of manuscript. Length requirements--maximum, 25-30 pages. Selection process-- circulates copies past 3 Associate Editors and Editor-in-Chief.

Responds to a submission in 6 months. Approximate proportion of submissions accepted for publication--25-50 percent.

117. CHRISTIANESIMO NELLA STORIA
Prof. Giuseppe Alberigo, Ed.
Istituto per le Scienze Religiose
Centro Editoriale Dehoniano
Via San Vitale 114
40125 Bologna, Italy

Subscription--3/yr.--Lit.--50.000. Description of subject matter of journal--history of Christianity from its origins to the present. Publishes articles in Scripture, Church History, Theology and Judaism. For: professors, students, and laypersons. Submissions must be in French, German, Spanish, English, or Italian. Sometimes accepts unsolicited articles, unsolicited reviews; accepts dot-matrix printing; does not accept simultaneous submissions; publishes research notes and review-articles; accepts advertising--short notices about books or other religious reviews. Seeks original research essays. Style of journal--academic and scientific. Requires one copy of manuscript. Length requirements--maximum, 50 pages; minimum, 15 pages. Selection process--Submission to the scientific board of the review. Responds in one month. Approximate proportion of submissions accepted for publication--70 percent. Text in English, French, German, Italian and Spanish; summaries in English. Parent Organization--Istituto per le Scienze Religiose. Indexed: Old Test. Abstr., Canon Law Abstr., Rel.&Theol.Abstr.

118. INDIAN CHURCH HISTORY REVIEW
Dr. S. Immanuel David, Executive Editor
United Theological College
17 Miler's Road
Bangalore 560 046, India

Subscription--2/yr.--$12. Description of subject matter of journal--History of Christianity in India. For: professors, students, laypersons. Submissions must be in English. Publishes articles in Church History, Evangelism, Missions, Sociology of Religion, World Religions, Philosophy of Religion, Islam, Hinduism. Accepts unsolicited articles and unsolicited reviews. Selection process--Editorial Board. Indexed: Rol.Per., Rel.Ind.One.

119. JOURNAL OF ECCLESIASTICAL HISTORY
Brendan Bradshaw, Ed.
Peter Linehan, Ed.
St. John's College
Cambridge CB2 1TP, England

Subscription--2/yr.--$57, individuals; $110, institutions. Seeks significant contributions to a variety of subjects in Church History. Submissions must be in English. Style of journal--style sheet available upon request. Accepts unsolicited articles, unsolicited reviews; publishes review-articles; does not accept advertising. Indexed: Br.Hum.Ind., Curr.Cont., Hist.Abstr., Rel.Per.Lit., New Test. Abstr., Rel.&Theol.Abstr., Rel.Ind.One.

120. JOURNAL OF RELIGIOUS HISTORY
     B. E. Mansfield, Ed.
     A. E. Cahill, Ed.
     Department of History
     University of Sydney
     N.S.W., Australia

Subscription--2/yr.--$A16.00 Australian (US$18.50), individuals; $A29.00 (US$33.40), institutions. Description of subject matter of journal--Religious history and the bearing of religion on human history in general. Publishes articles in Church History. For: professors and students. Submissions must be in English. Accepts unsolicited articles, dot-matrix printing; sometimes accepts unsolicited reviews; does not accept simultaneous submissions; does not publish research notes; publishes review-articles; accepts advertising--other journals, mainly by exchange--possibly books. Seeks scholarly historical articles. Style of journal--Sydney University Press (adaptation of Oxford University Press). Requires one copy of manuscript. Length requirements--maximum, 9000 words; minimum, 4000 words. Selection process--reading by editors and specialist readers. Immediate acknowledgment of a submission; decision within 2-3 months. Approximate proportion of submissions accepted for publication--70 percent, including specified revisions. Parent Organization--Association for the Journal of Religious History. Indexed: Curr. Cont., Rel.Per., Aus.P.A.I.S., Arts&Hum.Cit.Ind., Rel.Ind.One, Rel.&Theol.Abstr.

121. METHODIST HISTORY
     Charles Yrigoyen Jr., Ed.
     United Methodist Church
     Commission on Archives and History
     Box 127
     Madison, NJ   07940

Subscription--4/yr.--$10. Description of subject matter--Methodist History. For: professors, students, laypersons, and clergy. Submissions must be in English. Accepts unsolicited articles; does not accept unsolicited reviews, dot-matrix printing, simultaneous submissions; publishes research notes and review-articles; accepts advertising--books and materials related to Methodist History. Seeks--any quality material on Methodist history, preferably based on primary research/documented mss. One copy of mss. required. Length requirements--maximum, 6500 words; minimum--none. Selection process--Editorial Committee and editor review submissions. Responds in 2-3 months. Approximately 50 percent of all submissions are accepted for publication. Indexed: Hist.Abstr., Meth.Per.Ind., Rel.Per., Rel.Ind.One, Rel.&Theol.Abstr.

122. MOREANA
Germain Marc'hadour, Ed.
Moreana Publications
B.P. 808
49005 Angers, France

Subscription--4/yr.--$34, individuals; $50, institutions. (Appears 3 times a year--Autumn issue is double.) Description of subject matter of journal--Anything that bears on the "world" of Thomas More--his era (Early Tudor England), his main pursuits: classical humanism, Catholic faith, the best government. Publishes articles in Scripture, Church History, Philosophy of Religion, Martyrdom, Natural Religion (in More's Utopia), and Reformation Controversy. For: professors, students, lawyers, and priests. Submissions: French and English are the editorial languages; we have also published articles in German, Spanish, Italian, Dutch, and Portuguese. Accepts unsolicited articles, unsolicited reviews; does not accept simultaneous submissions; publishes research notes and review-articles; accepts advertising--a maximum of 3 pages about books in our field. Seeks articles that add to our knowledge of More's life, works: sources, documents, translations or other forms of influence--textual or historical or philological information (also on Erasmus, Tyndale, Fisher). Especially seeking notes tracing More's life (e.g., a deed bearing his signature), or his impact, especially on STC books and outside of England. Style of journal--all styles are welcome, depending on authors' cultural traditions. Requires 3 copies of manuscript. Length requirements of submission--maximum, 30 pages; minimum, no minimum. Selection process--Each submission goes to 3 assessors. A high percentage return to authors for revision. Assessors usually make suggestions. Editor writes on the ms. Responds to a submission--acknowledgment is immediate; assessment takes up to 7-8 months. Approximate proportion of submissions accepted for publication--about 40 percent for English, 60 percent in French. Comments: We tend to be less demanding for French material because it is less abundant and also to be partial to Amici Thomae Mori, since Moreana is their bulletin. Indexed: Abstr.Engl. Stud., Curr.Cont., Hist.Abstr., M.L.A., Arts&Hum.Cit.Ind., Amer. Hist.&Life.

123. NEDERLANDS ARCHIEF VOOR KERKGESCHIEDENIS--DUTCH REVIEW OF CHURCH HISTORY
Editorial Board (Cornelis Augustijn, Amsterdam; Sip de Boer, Amsterdam; Olivier Fatio, Geneva; Otto J. de Jong, Utrecht;

Johannes C. P. A. van Laarhoven, Nijmegen; Marc Lienhard, Strasbourg; Steven E. Ozment, Cambridge [Mass.]; Guillaume H. M. Posthumus Meyjes, Leiden; Johannes Roldanus, Groningen)
E. J. Brill
Oude Rijn 33a-35
2312 HB Leiden, Netherlands

Subscription--2/yr.--72 fl. Subject matter of journal--Church History, Theology, Sociology of Religion and Philosophy of Religion. For: professors, students. Submissions must be in French, German, English, or Dutch. Seeks articles which are scholarly, new material (not previously published). Accepts unsolicited articles, unsolicited reviews, dot-matrix printing; does not accept simultaneous submissions; sometimes publishes research notes; publishes review-articles; does not accept advertising. Requires 2 copies of manuscript. Length requirements--maximum, 25-30 pages. Selection process--joint editorial decision. Responds in 6 weeks. Approximate proportion of submissions accepted for publication--30 percent. Indexed: Rel.Ind.One.

124. RECHERCHES DE THEOLOGIE ANCIENNE ET MEDIEVALE
D. H. Bascour, Ed.
Abbaye du Mont Cesar
202 Mechelse Straat
B-3000 Louvain, Belgium

Subscription--1/yr.--750 francs. Publishes articles in History of Theology, Ancient and Medieval. Submissions must be in French, German, Spanish, English, or Italian. Accepts unsolicited articles; sometimes accepts unsolicited reviews; publishes research notes, review-articles; accepts advertising. Seeks scholarly articles. Requires one copy of manuscript. Length requirements--maximum, 50 pages. Approximate proportion of submissions accepted for publication--90 percent. Indexed: New Test.Abstr., Rel.&Theol.Abstr.

125. RECUSANT HISTORY
The Editor
44 Pearson Park
Hull, HU5 2TG, England

Subscription--2/yr.--12-13 pounds. Description of subject matter of journal--Research in Post-Reformation Roman Catholic History in the British Isles, 16th to early 20th century. Publishes articles in Church History, History of Church Administration, History of Religious Education, Biography and Bibliography. For: professors, students, laypersons, and clergy. Seeks research articles on all aspects of the Post-Reformation Roman Catholic community in England, particularly on topics as yet little explored. Accepts

unsolicited articles; does not accept unsolicited reviews; accepts
simultaneous submissions; publishes research notes; does not publish
review-articles; accepts advertising--booksellers specializing in Roman
Catholicism. Requires one copy of manuscript. Selection process--
selection is by members of the Editorial Committee assisted by expert
advisers. Responds to a submission in 1-6 weeks. Submissions must
be in English. Style of journal--directions for contributors are provided within the cover of the journal. Indexed: Br.Hum.Ind.,
CERDIC.

126. RESTORATION QUARTERLY
Everett Ferguson, Ed.
Restoration Quarterly Corporation
Box 8227
Abilene, TX 79699

Subscription--4/yr.--$11. Description of subject matter of
journal--Biblical and Restoration history. Publishes articles in
Scripture, Ethics, Church History, Theology, Evangelism, Pastoral
Counseling, Missions, Philosophy of Religion, and Religious Education. For: professors, students, laypersons, and clergymen. Submissions must be in English. Accepts unsolicited articles, unsolicited
reviews, dot-matrix printing; does not accept simultaneous submissions; does not publish research notes; publishes review-articles;
accepts advertising--book. Style of journal--quasi scholarly. Requires 2 copies of manuscript. Length requirements--maximum, 30
typed pages; minimum, 5 typed pages. Selection process--at least
one reader with expertise in subject. Responds in 2 months--1 year
to publish after acceptance. Approximate proportion of submissions
accepted for publication--1/3. Indexed: Old Test.Abstr., New Test.
Abstr., Rel.&Theol.Abstr., Rel.Ind.One.

127. REVUE BENEDICTINE
Dir. Pierre Patrick Verbraken
Abbaye de Maredsous
B-5198 Denée, Belgium

Subscription--2/yr. (two double issues)--$40. Description of
articles--Ecclesiastical erudition. Publishes articles in Church History, Patristic Texts, and Monastic History. For: professors, students, laypersons, universities and monasteries. Submissions must
be in French, German, English, or Italian. Sometimes accepts unsolicited articles, unsolicited reviews; sometimes publishes research
notes, review-articles; does not accept advertising. Seeks articles
of textual editions and historical studies. Especially seeking articles
on monastic history. Style of journal--highly scientifical. Requires
one copy of manuscript. Length requirements--maximum, 50 pages;
minimum, 10 pages. Selection process--Advisory Board--Directory
Committee--Director. Responds in one month. Approximate proportion

of submissions that are accepted for publication--varies every year.
Text in English, French, German, and Italian. Comments--We are
at present in 41 countries. All past volumes are available in an ex-
ceptional offer: A complete collection from 1884-1983 for 50.000
Belgian francs or 1,000 U.S. dollars. Indexed: Bull.Signal, Old
Test.Abstr., New Test.Abstr.

128. REVUE D'HISTOIRE ECCLESIASTIQUE
Roger Aubert, Ed.
Collège Erasme, Place Blaise Pascal
1348 Louvain-La-Neuve, Belgium

Subscription--4/yr.--$45. Subject matter of journal--Church
History. Accepts unsolicited articles. For: professors and students.
Submissions must be in French. Selection process--Editorial Board.
Indexed: Rel.Per., Arts&Hum.Cit.Ind., New Test.Abstr., Rel.Ind.
One, Rel.&Theol.Abstr.

129. REVUE DES ETUDES AUGUSTINIENNES
Claude Lepelley, Dir.
Institut des Etudes Augustiniennes
3 rue de l'Abbaye
75006 Paris, France

Subscription--4/yr.--$44. Description of subject matter of
journal--Articles which give special insight into the life and thought
of St. Augustine. Submissions must be in French, German, or English. Publishes articles in Scripture, Ethics, Church History, Theology, and Patristics. Accepts unsolicited articles; sometimes accepts
unsolicited reviews. Selection process--Editorial Board reviews and
selects appropriate articles. Indexed: Bull.Signal, New Test.Abstr.

130. RIVISTA DI STORIA E LETTERATURA RELIGIOSA
Franco Bolgiani, Ed.
Casa Editrice Leo S. Olschki
Casella Postale 66
50100 Florence, Italy

Subscription--3/yr.--45.000 lire. Description of subject matter
of journal--religious history which either directly or indirectly concerns Christianity. Publishes articles in Scripture, Church History,
Evangelism, and Judaism. For: professors and students. Submissions must be in French, German, English, or Italian. Accepts unsolicited articles; sometimes accepts unsolicited reviews; publishes
research notes and review-articles. Requires one copy of manuscript.
Length requirements for submissions--maximum, 30-35 pages. Selection process--Articles are discussed at an Editorial Board meeting
once a week. Responds to a submission in 2 months. Indexed: New
Test.Abstr.

131. ROEMISCHE QUARTALSCHRIFT FUER CHRISTLICHE ALTER-
     TUMSKUNDE UND KIRCHENGESCHICHTE
     Redaktion der Roemischen Quartalschrift
     Via della Sagrestia, 17
     I-00120, Vatican City

Subscription--2/yr.--142 DM. Subject matter of journal--
Church History, Theology, and Patristics. Submissions must be in
German. Accepts unsolicited articles; sometimes accepts unsolicited
reviews. Indexed: RILA.

132. SECOND CENTURY
     Everett Ferguson, Ed.
     ACU Station
     Box 8227
     Abilene, TX 79699

Subscription--4/yr.--$10. Description of subject matter--
primarily second-century Christianity. Publishes articles in Scripture,
Church History, and Judaism. For: professors and students. Submissions must be in French, German, Spanish, English, Italian or
Dutch. However, after the article is translated, it is only published
in English. Accepts unsolicited articles, reviews; does not accept dot-
matrix printing, simultaneous submissions; publishes research notes
and review articles; accepts advertising--mostly book publishers.
Seeks scholarly, original research, relating second-century to scripture
or to the Greco-Roman or Jewish background. Style of journal--
Univ. of Chicago Manual of Style. Requires one copy of manuscript.
Length requirements--none. Selection process--sent to readers for
advice. Responds in 2 months. Approximate proportion of submissions accepted for publication--50 percent. Indexed: Rel.&Theol.
Abstr., Rel.Ind.One.

133. STUDIA MONASTICA
     Rev. Josep Massot Muntaner, Ed.
     Publicacions de l'Abadia de Montserrat
     Ausias March 92-98
     Ap. 244
     Barcelona 13, Spain

Subscription--2/yr.--$50. Description of subject matter of
journal--monastic history and spirituality. Publishes articles in
Church History. Accepts unsolicited articles; sometimes accepts unsolicited reviews; does not accept dot-matrix printing, simultaneous
submissions; publishes research notes and review-articles; does not
accept advertising. For: professors and students. Submissions must
be in French, German, Spanish, English, Italian, Latin, Catalan, or
Portuguese. Seeks scientific articles. Requires one copy of manuscript. Responds to a submission in 4 days. Approximate proportion

of submissions accepted for publication--90 percent. Indexed:
Arts&Hum.Cit.Ind.

134. UNITED REFORMED CHURCH HISTORY SOCIETY JOURNAL
     Clyde Binfield, Ed.
     United Reformed Church History Society
     Church House
     86 Tavistock Pl
     London WC1H 9RT, England

Subscription--2/yr.--3.26 pounds. Description of subject matter of journal--material relevant to an understanding of the development of the British congregational Presbyterian and Churches of
Christ tradition--social, cultural, theological mission etc. from 16th
to 20th century. Publishes articles in Church History. For: professors, students, and laypersons. Submissions must be in English.
Accepts unsolicited articles and dot-matrix printing; sometimes accepts
unsolicited reviews; does not accept simultaneous submissions (there
are very occasional exceptions); publishes research notes and review-
articles; does not accept advertising. Seeks articles--that are sufficiently authoritative to appeal to the scholarly and sufficiently literary to appeal to the generalist. Style of journal--scholarly and
literary. Requires one copy of manuscript. Length requirements--
maximum, 10,000 words; minimum, --. Selection process--consulta-
tion with colleagues and members of council--final decision resting
with editor: Criteria are the appropriate mix of original work; literary merit; representativeness; and the balance of the moment with
regard to period, tradition, region, and theme. Responds to a sub-
mission--Prompt acknowledgment; decision is made in 2 weeks to 2
months. Approximate proportion of submissions that are accepted
for publication--70 percent at the moment. Comments--We try to be
as flexible as possible given the inevitable constraints of space.
Indexed: Br.Hum.Ind.

135. VIGILIAE CHRISTIANAE
     Prof. J. H. Waszink, Secretary of Editorial Board
     "Park Overbosch," Sportlaan 3, Flat 311
     2215 NB Voorhout, The Netherlands

Subscription--4/yr.--$53. Description of subject matter of
journal--Articles on an historical and cultural, linguistic or philological nature on Early Christian Literature posterior to the New Testament as well as on Christian epigraphy and archaeology. Interested in the Social History of the Early Christian period. Submissions must be in French, German, or English. Accepts unsolicited
articles, unsolicited reviews; does not accept simultaneous submissions;
publishes research notes. Style of journal--Instructions are supplied
on the back cover of the journal. Selection process--Editors are ad-
vised by readers who review and evaluate the submissions. Indexed:

Curr.Cont., Rel.Per., Arts&Hum.Cit.Ind., New Test.Abstr., Rel.
Ind.One, Rel.&Theol.Abstr.

136. WESLEY HISTORICAL SOCIETY. PROCEEDINGS.
E. A. Rose, Ed.
Wesley Historical Society
c/o Mrs. V. Vickers
87 Marshall Avenue
Bognor Regis
West Sussex, P021 2TW,
England

Subscription--3/yr.--$10. Description of subject matter--History of Wesleys and Methodism, chiefly in Britain. For: professors, students, and laypersons. Submissions must be in English. Accepts unsolicited articles, dot-matrix printing; does not accept unsolicited reviews, simultaneous submissions; publishes research notes and review-articles; accepts advertising--display and "small ads." Requires one copy of manuscript. Length requirements--maximum, 10,000 words; minimum, 1000 words. Responds in one month. Approximate proportion of submissions that are accepted for publication--75 percent. Indexed: Br.Hum.Ind.

137. ZEITSCHRIFT FUER KIRCHENGESCHICHTE
Erich Meuthen u.a.
W. Kohlhammer GmbH (Stuttgart),
Hessbruehlstrasse 69
Postfach 800430
7000 Stuttgart 80, West Germany (B.R.D.)

Subscription--3/yr.--78.- DM. Subject matter of journal--Church History. For: professors, students. Submissions must be in German, (sometimes) English. Sometimes accepts unsolicited articles; does not accept unsolicited reviews, dot-matrix printing, simultaneous submissions; publishes research notes and review-articles; accepts advertising. Style of journal--Science. Requires 2 copies of manuscript. Length requirements--maximum, ca. 70 pages; minimum, ca. 30 pages. Selection process--chief editor and 6 coeditors, each specialized for every period of Church History. Responds in 2-4 weeks. Approximate proportion of submissions accepted for publication--50 percent. Indexed: Rel.Per., Rel.Ind.One, Rel.&Theol.Abstr.

OTHER JOURNALS THAT PUBLISH ARTICLES
IN CHURCH HISTORY

AFER 501   Africa Theological Journal 502

3. PHILOSOPHY OF RELIGION

138. DIWA
Fr. Constante C. Floresca, Managing Editor
Divine Word Seminary
Tagaytay City, 2721, Philippines

Subscription--2/yr.--P. 30.00; $7.50, overseas. Subject matter of journal--Theology and Philosophy of Religion. Accepts unsolicited articles. Submissions must be in English.

139. FAITH AND PHILOSOPHY
William P. Alston, Ed.
Syracuse University
Department of Philosophy
Syracuse, NY 13244-1170

Subscription--4/yr.--$18, individuals; $30, institutions. Publishes articles in Philosophy of Religion and Philosophy. Accepts unsolicited articles, unsolicited reviews, dot-matrix printing. Seeks articles which address philosophical issues from a Christian perspective, for discussions of philosophical issues which arise within the Christian Faith, and for articles from any perspective which deal critically with the philosophical credentials of the Christian faith. Style of journal--MLA. Requires 2 copies of manuscript. Two copies of a 100-word abstract must accompany manuscript. Indexed: Phil.Ind., Rel.Ind.One.

140. FREIBURGER ZEITSCHRIFT FUER PHILOSOPHIE UND THE-OLOGIE
Prof. J.-B. Brantschen, R. Imbach, G. Vergauwen, Dr. M. Brun
Editions Saint Paul
Perolles 42
CH-1700 Fribourg, Switzerland

Subscription--2/yr.--50 francs + postal charge. Publishes articles in Theology and Philosophy. Sometimes accepts unsolicited articles, unsolicited reviews; accepts dot-matrix printing; does not accept simultaneous submissions; publishes research notes and review-articles; does not accept advertising. For: professors and students. Submissions must be in French, German, Spanish, English, or Italian. Requires one copy of manuscript. Length requirements--maximum, 25 pages. Selection process--Editorial Board. Responds to a submission in 3-6 months. Approximate proportion of submissions accepted for publication--2/3.

141. INTERNATIONAL JOURNAL FOR PHILOSOPHY OF RELIGION
Bowman L. Clarke, Ed.
The University of Georgia
Department of Philosophy and Religion
Athens, GA 30602

Subscription--4/yr.--$35.50, individuals; $22.00, institutions. Subject of journal--Philosophy of Religion. For: professors, students, and laypersons. Submissions must be in English. Accepts unsolicited articles, unsolicited reviews, advertising. Style of journal--MLA. Selection process--Editorial Board reaches a decision on advice of readers. Indexed: Curr.Cont., Hum.Ind., Arts&Hum. Cit.Ind., Rel.Ind.One, Rel.&Theol.Abstr.

142. THE JOURNAL OF RELIGIOUS STUDIES
Wazir Singh, Ed.
Punjabi University
Department of Religious Studies
Patiala 147002
Punjab, India

Subscription--2/yr.--$7, one issue by airmail; $13, two issues by airmail; $10, surface mail. Description of subject matter of journal--Religious Studies/Philosophy of Religion. Publishes articles in Scripture, Ethics, Theology, Psychology of Religion, Sociology of Religion, World Religions, Philosophy of Religion, Judaism, Islam, Hinduism, Buddhism, Sikhism. For: professors, students, laypersons, others interested in Religious Studies. Submissions must be in English. Accepts unsolicited articles, dot-matrix printing; sometimes accepts unsolicited reviews; does not accept simultaneous submissions; publishes research notes (in special cases); publishes review-articles; does not accept advertising. Seeks articles bearing on religion, religious life and thought, textual studies, philosophy, ethics, sociology of religion. Especially seeks articles that are philosophical/scholarly studies of world faiths; theological issues, dialogue of religions. Style of journal--scholarly/documented presentation of materials. Requires two copies of manuscript. Length requirements--maximum, 20 pages; minimum, 5-6 pages, in print. Selection process--determined by Editorial Board in line with the policy outlined above. Responds to a submission in 3-6 months. Approximate proportion of submissions accepted for publication--60 percent. Comments: Articles are welcome on prayer; understanding of religious faiths; and Bible studies. Indexed: Rel.Ind.One.

143. LAVAL THEOLOGIQUE ET PHILOSOPHIQUE
Pierre Gaudette, Ed.
L. Ponton, Ed.
Presses de L'Université Laval
C.P. 2447
Quebec G1K 7R4, Canada

Subscription--3/yr.--$20 Canadian. Subject matter of journal--
Scripture, Ethics, Theology, Philosophy of Religion, Psychology of
Religion, and Philosophy. For: professors and students. Submissions must be in English or French. Accepts unsolicited articles;
sometimes accepts unsolicited reviews; does not accept simultaneous
submissions; publishes research notes. Seeks articles on Greek,
French, and German Philosophy. Especially seeking in-depth studies.
Requires 3 copies of manuscript. Length requirements--maximum,
45 pages; minimum, 12 pages. Selection process--A reading committee chooses the texts to be published. Responds to a submission
in 2 years. Approximate proportion of submissions accepted for pub-
lication--15 percent. Indexed: Cath.Ind., Curr.Cont., Old Test.
Abstr., Arts&Hum.Cit.Ind., New Test.Abstr., Ptde Rep.

144. THE NIGERIAN JOURNAL OF PHILOSOPHY
Dr. J. I. Omoregbe, Ed.
University of Lagos
Department of Philosophy
Faculty of Arts
Lagos, Nigeria

Subscription--$20, individuals; $40, institutions. Subject matter of journal--Theology and Philosophy of Religion. Accepts unsolicited articles, unsolicited reviews, and advertising. Submissions
must be in English. Requires 2 copies of manuscript. Length re-
quirements--maximum, 25 pages; minimum, 15 pages.

145. PROCESS STUDIES
Lewis S. Ford, Ed.
School of Theology at Claremont
Center for Process Studies
1325 N. College Ave.
Claremont, CA 91711

Subscription--4/yr.--$15, individuals; $20, institutions. De-
scription of subject matter of journal--essays of most fields, but par-
ticularly philosophy and religious studies, devoted to the thought of
A. N. Whitehead and his intellectual associates, most notably,
Charles Hartshorne. Publishes articles in Theology, Philosophy of
Religion and Process Philosophy. For: professors and students.
Submissions must be in English. Accepts unsolicited articles, dot-
matrix printing; sometimes accepts unsolicited reviews, does not

accept simultaneous submissions; publishes research notes and review-articles; accepts advertising--mostly journal exchanges but open to book advertising. Seeks articles which will make a scholarly contribution to the field. Style of journal--style of its own; listed on the back cover. Requires one copy of manuscript. Selection process-- The editor judges most of the manuscripts but defers them to outside readers if he feels they are beyond his competence. Responds in 3 months. Approximate proportion of submissions accepted for publication--30 percent. Indexed: Curr.Cont., Old Test.Abstr., Rel.Per., Arts&Hum.Cit.Ind., Phil.Ind., Rel.Ind.One, Rel.&Theol. Abstr.

146. ULTIMATE REALITY AND MEANING
    Tibor Horvath, Ed.
    University of Toronto Press
    Front Campus
    Toronto, Ont. M5S 1A6, Canada

    Subscription--10/yr.--$25 Canadian, individuals; $43, Canadian, institutions. Subject matter of journal--Scripture, Ethics, Church History, Theology, Psychology of Religion, Sociology of Religion, World Religions, Philosophy of Religion, Judaism, Islam, Hinduism, Buddhism, Eastern Religions, and Religious Education. For: professors. Submissions must be in English. Style sheet for contributors may be obtained. Accepts unsolicited articles, dot-matrix printing; does not accept unsolicited reviews, simultaneous submissions; does not publish research notes; does not accept advertising. Requires 3 copies of manuscript. Length requirements--maximum, 40 double-spaced pages; minimum, 10 pages. Selection process-- referee system, experts in the field, Editorial Board. Responds to a submission in 1-2 months. Approximate proportion of submissions accepted for publication--unsolicited: accepted without revision--3-4 percent; with revision--60-70 percent. Indexed: Arts&Hum.Cit.Ind., Amer.Bibl.Slavic&E.Eur.Stud., G.Soc.Sci.&Rel.Per.Lit., Lang.&Lang. Behav.Abstr., Phil.Ind., Rel.Ind.One, Rel.&Theol.Abstr.

OTHER JOURNALS THAT PUBLISH ARTICLES IN
PHILOSOPHY OF RELIGION

4. PSYCHOLOGY OF RELIGION

147. JOURNAL OF PSYCHOLOGY AND CHRISTIANITY
Harold Ellens, Ed.
Christian Association for Psychological Studies International
26705 Farmington Rd.
Farmington Hills, MI   48018

Subscription--4/yr.--$50. Description of subject matter of
journal--concerns in the Social Sciences, Humanities, and exact sciences related to Psychology and Christianity. For: professors,
students, and clinicians. Submissions must be in English. Accepts
unsolicited articles, unsolicited reviews, dot-matrix printing, simultaneous submissions; publishes research notes and review-articles;
accepts advertising--any kind $600.--per page, or fractions thereof.
Seeks articles in the above areas, new work, in APA manual style.
Requires 3 copies of manuscript. Length requirements--maximum,
20 pages; minimum, none. Selection process--Referee board selec-
tion--2/3 majority. Responds in 4 months. Approximate proportion
of submissions accepted for publication--10 percent. Indexed:
A.S.&T.Ind., Psychol.Abstr., Educ.Ind., R.G., Soc.Sci.Ind., Rel.
Ind.One.

148. JOURNAL OF PSYCHOLOGY AND JUDAISM
Dr. Reuven P. Bulka, Ed.
Human Sciences Press, Inc.
72 Fifth Ave.
New York, NY   10011

Subscription--4/yr.--$24, individuals; $49, institutions. Description of subject matter of journal--Anything dealing with the
Psychology-Judaism connection on a clinical, theoretical, or practical
level. Publishes articles in Ethics, Theology, Pastoral Counseling,
Psychology of Religion, Sociology of Religion, Philosophy of Religion, Judaism, and Religious Education. For: professors, students,
laypersons, clinicians, counselors, social workers. Submissions must
be in English. Accepts unsolicited articles, unsolicited reviews,
dot-matrix printing; does not (except under rare circumstances) accept simultaneous submissions; publishes review-articles; does not
publish research notes; accepts advertising--only for other journals
or books. Journal seeks case histories, original research, and

insights relating to psychological matters unique to Jews and Judaism. Especially seeking articles that make significant contributions to the literature. Style of journal--APA. Requires 3 copies of manuscript. Length requirements--maximum, 25 pages; minimum, 8 pages. Selection process--after initial screening, blind review by 2 members of the Editorial Board. Responds to a submission in 3 months (average). Approximate proportion of submissions accepted for publication--25 percent. Indexed: Curr.Cont., Excerp.Med., M.L.A., Psychol.Abstr., SSCI, G.Soc.Sci.&Rel.Per.Lit., Ind.Jew.Per., Past. Care&Couns.Abstr., Rel.&Theol.Abstr., Rel.Ind.One.

149. JOURNAL OF PSYCHOLOGY AND THEOLOGY
     William F. Hunter, Ed.
     Biola University
     Rosemead School of Psychology
     13800 Biola Ave.
     La Mirada, CA   90639

Subscription--4/yr.--$20. Description of subject matter of journal--The purpose of the Journal of Psychology and Theology is to communicate recent scholarly thinking on the interrelationships of psychological and theological concepts and to consider the application of these concepts to a variety of professional settings. For: professors, students, clergy, and psychologists. Submissions must be in English. Accepts unsolicited articles. Articles should be consistent with evangelical theological position. Style of journal--APA--include an abstract--150 words. Requires 4 copies of manuscript. Length requirements--maximum, 20 pages. Selection process--blind review. Responds to a submission in 3-5 months. Approximate proportion of submissions accepted for publication--50 percent (JPT rarely accepts an article outright--most frequently requires revision). Indexed: Curr.Cont., Old Test.Abstr., Psychol.Abstr., SSCI, Arts&Hum. Cit.Ind., Chr.Per.Ind., G.Soc.Sci.&Rel.Per.Lit., R.G., Rel.&Theol. Abstr., Rel.Ind.One.

150. PASTORAL PSYCHOLOGY
     Professor Lewis Rambo, Ed.   Ralph Underwood, Ph.D., Book
     San Francisco Theological   Review Ed.
       Seminary   Austin Presbyterian Theological
     San Anselmo, CA   94960   Seminary
                                        Austin, TX   78705

Subscription--4/yr.--$32, individuals; $82, institutions. Description of subject matter of journal--provides a forum for discussion of the work of ministry as this work is illuminated by comments from other professions and professionals, by behavioral science research and theory, and by theological awareness and critique. Publishes articles in Ethics, Theology, Pastoral Counseling, Pastoral Psychology, and Psychology of Religion. For: professors, students, and

laypersons. Submissions must be in English. Accepts unsolicited
articles; sometimes accepts unsolicited reviews; accepts advertising--
inquiries to Business Office--Human Sciences Press; 72 5th Avenue;
New York, NY 10011-8004. Requires 3 copies of manuscript. Length
requirements--maximum, 15 double-spaced pages; minimum, further
information may be obtained from Editor. Indexed: Curr.Cont.,
Psychol.Abstr., SSCI, G.Soc.Sci.&Rel.Per.Lit., Rel.Per., Past.Care
&Couns.Abstr., Rel.&Theol.Abstr., Rel.Ind.One.

OTHER JOURNALS THAT PUBLISH ARTICLES IN
PSYCHOLOGY OF RELIGION

AJS Review   479
America   448
American Jewish Archives   480
American Scientific Affiliation
   Journal   249
Anglican Theological Review   4
Anima   423
Antonianum   271
Asbury Theological Journal   5
Banner   6
Benedictines   316
Berliner Theologische Zeit-
   schrift   7
Biblical Theology Bulletin   174
Bijdragen   9
Buddhist-Christian Studies   411
Burgense   10
Caribbean Journal of Religious
   Studies   525
Centre for the Study of Islam
   and Christian Muslim Rela-
   tions Newsletter   472
Cercle Ernest Renan. Cahiers
   13
Christian Century   224
Christian Jewish Relations   424
Christian Medical Society Journal
   226
Christian Ministry   318
Christianity & Crisis   227
Christianity Today   228
Christus   252
Church History   115
Churchman (London)   15
Churchman (St. Petersburg,
   FL)   16

Civiltà Cattolica   19
Communio Viatorum   426
Conservative Judaism   483
Cristianismo y Sociedad   526
Cross Currents   255
Crux   230
Diaconate Magazine   323
Diakonia   324
Dialogue and Alliance   427
The Drew Gateway   27
Duke Divinity School Review   28
East Asian Pastoral Review   328
Expository Times   181
Heythrop Journal   285
Human Development   379
Iliff Review   43
International Kirchliche Zeit-
   schrift   433
Japanese Journal of Religious
   Studies   522
Journal for the Scientific Study
   of Religion   46
The Journal of Pastoral Care
   151
Journal of Religion   47
Journal of Religion and Aging
   152
Journal of Religion and Health
   234
Journal of Religious Studies
   142
Journal of Religious Thought
   49
Journal of the American Academy
   of Religion   50
The Journal of the Interdenom-

5. PASTORAL COUNSELING; PASTORAL CARE;
AND PASTORAL THEOLOGY

151. THE JOURNAL OF PASTORAL CARE
Orlo Strunk, Ed.
Journal of Pastoral Care Publications, Inc.
901 N. Kings Highway
Myrtle Beach, SC   29577

Subscription--4/yr.--$15.   Subject matter of journal--Pastoral
Care, Pastoral Counseling, Mental Health, Psychology of Religion.
For: professors, students, laypersons, chaplains.   Submissions
must be in English.   Accepts unsolicited articles, unsolicited reviews, dot-matrix printing, simultaneous submissions; does not publish research notes; publishes review-articles; accepts advertising--
book publishers, training centers.   Seeks articles that are concerned
with the theory and practice of pastoral care and counseling.   Especially looking for articles concerned with the integration of theory
(theology) and clinical.   Style of journal--own style manual.   Requires three copies of manuscript.   Length requirements--maximum,
20 typewritten pages; minimum, none.   Selection process--Recom-
mendations from two editorial advisors to editor who then makes decision.   Responds in 8 weeks.   Approximate proportion of submissions accepted for publication--20 percent.   Indexed: Psychol.
Abstr., Rel.Per., Rel.&Theol.Abstr., Rel.Ind.One.

152. JOURNAL OF RELIGION AND AGING
William M. Clements, Ph.D., Ed.
The Haworth Press, Inc.
12 West 32nd Street
New York, NY   10001

Subscription--4/yr.--$28, individuals; $36, institutions; $48,
libraries.   Publishes articles in Theology, Pastoral Counseling, Psychology of Religion, Sociology of Religion, Philosophy of Religion,
and Religious Gerontology.   For: professors and professionals.
Submissions must be in English.   Sometimes accepts unsolicited articles, unsolicited reviews; accepts dot-matrix printing, does not
accept simultaneous submissions; publishes research notes and
review-articles; accepts advertising--paid and exchange.   Style of

journal--University of Chicago Manual of Style; "Instructions for Authors" sheet may be obtained from the journal. Requires 3 copies of manuscript. Length requirements--maximum, 20 pages; minimum, 10 pages. Selection process--Editorial Board selection. The Journal of Religion and Aging has 3 broad goals--1) to inform religious professionals about developments in the new field of religious gerontology; 2) to inform "secular" professionals who work with elderly people and their families within the context of religious institutions; 3) to focus the attention of the traditional academic disciplines within religion on human aging. Sample topics the editors would like to see in the journal--ethical issues in nursing home care; adult day-activities programs in the local church; the right to die; pastoral care of the adult whose parent is dying; remarriage in old age within the religious community; theological themes in the decision for nursing home care; theological education and human aging, retirement planning as a religious activity; pastoral care of the child whose grandparent has died, mandatory retirement and religious belief; white male suicide in old age as a religious statement; etc. Indexed: CLOA.

153. LOUVAIN STUDIES
   Raymond F. Collins, Ed.
   Katholieke Universiteit Leuven
   Faculty of Theology
   St. Michielsstraat, 2
   3000 Leuven, Belgium

   Subscription--4/yr.--$18. Description of subject matter of journal--theology with pastoral orientation. Publishes articles in Scripture, Ethics, Church History, Theology, and Religious Education. For: professors, students, and clergy. Submissions must be in English. Sometimes accepts unsolicited articles and unsolicited reviews; does not accept dot-matrix printing, simultaneous submissions; does not publish research notes; publishes review-articles; does not accept advertising. Seeks articles of scientific theology for those involved in pastoral ministry. Style of journal--MLA style sheet. Requires one copy of manuscript. Length requirements--maximum, 20 printed pages; minimum, 10 printed pages. Selection process--Reports are solicited from two members of the Editorial Board assigned as readers by the Editor-in-Chief. Full board makes the final selection from among solicited and/or approved articles. Responds in 4-6 weeks. Approximate proportion of submissions accepted for publication--35 percent. Indexed: Cath.Ind., Old Test. Abstr., Canon Law Abstr., New Test.Abstr., Rel.&Theol.Abstr.

154. MARRIAGE AND FAMILY LIVING
   Keith McClellan, Ed.
   Abbey Press
   Hill Dr.
   St. Meinrad, IN 47577

Subscription--monthly--$11.95. Description of subject matter
of journal--marriage and family-oriented articles. For: laypersons.
Submissions must be in English. Accepts unsolicited articles, dot-
matrix printing, simultaneous submissions; sometimes accepts unsolicited reviews; does not publish research notes; publishes review-
articles; accepts advertising--consumer, book. Seeks practical, ex-
periential, value-based articles. Style of journal--popular. Requires
one copy of manuscript. Length requirements--maximum, 2500 words;
minimum, none. Selection process--Editorial Committee evaluates.
Responds in 6 weeks. Approximate proportion of submissions accepted for publication--10 percent. Indexed: Cath.Ind., CERDIC.

155. SAL TERRAE
     José Antonio García, S.J., Dir.
     San Leopoldo, 8, 3°A
     28029 Madrid, Spain

Subscription--Monthly--$23. Description of subject matter of
journal--Subjects of Pastoral Theology. Submissions must be in Spanish. Publishes articles in Scripture, Ethics, Church History, Theology, Evangelism, Missions, Psychology of Religion, Sociology of Religion, Philosophy of Religion, and Religious Education. Sometimes
accepts unsolicited articles. The journal is often organized around
a particular theme. Indexed: Canon Law Abstr.

156. TELEMA
     Boka di Mpasi Londi
     B.P. 3277
     Avenue P Boka 7
     Kinshasha-Gombe, Zaïre

Subscription--4/yr.--$30. Description of subject matter of
journal--Pastoral Theology, Evangelism, Pastoral Counseling, Missions,
World Religions. For: everyone. Submissions must be in French.
Accepts unsolicited articles; sometimes accepts unsolicited reviews;
does not accept dot-matrix printing, simultaneous submissions; does
not publish research notes; sometimes publishes review-articles; accepts advertising--in good taste and appropriate to the audience of
the journal. Seeks articles on spirituality and Christian experiences.
Not interested in abstract theory. Especially seeking articles concerning witnessing and pastoral activity. Style of journal--straight
forward, strong thought. Length requirements--maximum, 15 pages;
minimum, 8 pages. Selection process--Editorial Board. Responds in
2 months. Indexed: Old Test.Abstr.

157. WESLEYAN ADVOCATE
     Wayne Caldwell, Th.D., Ed.
     Wesley Press

Box 2000
Marion, IN 46952

Subscription--22/yr.--$10. Description of subject matter--
practical. Publishes articles in Scripture, Ethics, Theology, Evangelism, and Missions. For: professors, students, laypersons, and
ministers. Submissions must be in English. Sometimes accepts unsolicited articles, unsolicited reviews; accepts dot-matrix printing,
simultaneous submissions; does not publish research notes; sometimes
publishes review-articles; accepts advertising--display only. Seeks
articles--about a unique subject or at least written in a unique style.
Themes of projected issues are given to those who write and request
them. Style of journal--practical, pragmatic, nonacademic or classroom. Requires 2 copies of manuscript. Length requirements--maxi-
mum, 1200 words; minimum, 250 words. Chooses articles that contribute to seasonal and thematic scheme. Responds almost immediately,
1 week maximum. Approximately 50 percent of all submissions are accepted for publication. Indexed: G.Soc.Sci.&Rel.Per.Lit.

OTHER JOURNALS THAT PUBLISH ARTICLES IN
PASTORAL COUNSELING; PASTORAL CARE; PASTORAL THEOLOGY

AFER 501
America 448
American Baptist Quarterly 1
Antonianum 271
Asbury Theological Journal 5
Banner 6
Baptist Program 442
Bibliotheca Sacra 8
Calvin Theological Journal 11
Caribbean Journal of Religious
 Studies 525
Catalyst: Social Pastoral Maga-
 zine for Melanesia 223
Centre for the Study of Islam
 and Christian Muslim Rela-
 tions Newsletter 472
Christian Century 224
Christian Medical Society Jour-
 nal 226
Christian Ministry 318
Christianity Today 228
Churchman (London) 15
Concordia Journal 23
Currents in Theology and Mis-
 sion 320
Diaconate Magazine 323

Diakonia 324
The Drew Gateway 27
East Asian Pastoral Review 328
Expository Times 181
Faith and Mission 35
The Furrow 37
Gregorios Ho Palamas 41
His Dominion 330
Homiletic and Pastoral Review
 400
Human Development 379
Japan Christian Quarterly 521
Journal of Christian Nursing
 233
Journal of Psychology and Chris-
 tianity 147
Journal of Psychology and Juda-
 ism 148
Journal of Psychology and The-
 ology 149
Journal of Religion and Health
 234
Journal of Religious Thought 49
The Journal of the Interdenomina-
 tional Theological Center 51
Journal of Theology for

6. ETHICS AND RELIGION

158. JOURNAL OF RELIGIOUS ETHICS
James Johnson, Ed.
Religious Ethics, Inc.
University of Notre Dame Press
Notre Dame, IN 46556

Subscription--2/yr.--$12, individuals; $15, institutions. Description of subject matter of journal--Systematic historical or comparative perspectives on religious ethics. Publishes articles in Ethics, Church History, Theology, World Religions, Philosophy of Religion, Judaism, Islam, Hinduism, Buddhism, and Eastern Religions. Accepts unsolicited articles; sometimes accepts unsolicited reviews; does not accept simultaneous submissions; does not publish research notes; sometimes publishes review-articles; accepts advertising-- books and journals related to Religious Ethics--systematic, historical, or comparative. For: professors. Submissions must be in English. Seeks scholarly, analytical articles. Style of journal--modified social science style. Requires 2 copies of manuscript. Length requirements-- maximum, 40 pages; minimum, 20 pages. Selection process--Each submission is read by the general editor and 2 "blind" readers. Critiques are provided to authors. Responds to a submission--total review, 3-6 months. Approximate proportion of submissions accepted for publication--20 percent. Indexed: Curr.Cont., Hum.Ind., Old Test.Abstr., Rel.Per., Arts&Hum.Cit.Ind., Phil.Ind., Rel.Ind.One, Rel.&Theol.Abstr.

159. "LE SUPPLEMENT," REVUE D'ETHIQUE ET DE THEOLOGIE MORALE
Editions du Cerf
29 bd. Latour Mauborg
75007 Paris, France

Subscription--4/yr.--207 francs. Description of subject matter of journal--Ethics and Moral Theology. Publishes articles in Ethics, Church History, Theology, Church Administration, Pastoral Counseling, Psychology of Religion, Sociology of Religion, World Religions, Philosophy of Religion, Religious Education, and Canon Law. For: professors, students, people interested in medical ethics. Accepts unsolicited articles, unsolicited reviews, simultaneous submissions;

does not accept dot-matrix printing; publishes research notes, review-
articles; accepts advertising--of other reviews. Seeking issues that
are oriented to specific themes in Ethics and Moral Theology. Especially looking for articles pertaining to bio-ethic problems. Style
of journal--University of Chicago Style. Requires 2 copies of manuscript. Length requirements--maximum, 16 pages; minimum, 8 pages.
Selection process--Board of Review, committee decision. Responds
in 6 months. Indexed: Cath.Ind.

160. ZEITSCHRIFT FUER EVANGELISCHE ETHIK
      Chr. Frey, Ed.
      Guetersloher Verlagshaus Gerd Mohn
      Koenigstrasse 23-25
      Postfach 1343
      4830 Guetersloh, West Germany (B.R.D.)

      Subscription--4/yr.--64 DM. Description of subject matter of
journal--Ethical research, public discussions of problems on an
academic level. Publishes articles in Scripture, Ethics, Theology,
Sociology of Religion. For: professors, students, laypersons. Articles appear in German, translations from French, English, Dutch
possible. Sometimes accepts unsolicited articles, unsolicited reviews;
publishes research notes and review articles; accepts advertising--
literature (theology, ethics). Seeks articles which are academic
studies and reviews. Especially seeking discussions of actual social
and political problems. Length requirements--maximum, 20 pages.
Selection process--One person from the Board of Editors and the
chief editor have to agree to the printing of the article (sometimes
they discuss the article with the author and demand alterations).
Responds in 3 months. Requires one copy of manuscript. Approximately 50 percent of the submissions are accepted for publication.
Indexed: Curr.Cont., Rel.Per., Rel.&Theol.Abstr., Arts&Hum.Cit.
Ind., Rel.Ind.One.

OTHER JOURNALS THAT PUBLISH ARTICLES IN
ETHICS AND RELIGION

7. SCRIPTURE; BIBLICAL ARCHAEOLOGY

161. ANNUAL OF THE JAPANESE BIBLICAL INSTITUTE
c/o Japan Bible Society
5-1, 4-Chome, Ginza
Tokyo, Japan

Subscription--1/yr. Subject matter of journal--Scripture.
Submissions must be in German or English.

162. ARCHAEOLOGY AND BIBLICAL RESEARCH
David Livingston, Ed.
Associates for Biblical Research
15 Broadwing Drive
Denver, PA 17517

Subscription--4/yr.--$12. Publishes articles in Archaeology
related to the Bible. For: professors, students, laypersons. Submissions must be in English. Seeks articles that help to confirm and
illuminate the Scriptures. Reports well-known archaeological finds
which substantiate the Bible; reports excavations in progress; suggests solutions to difficult Bible passages; reviews articles and other
biblical archaeology magazines. Especially interested in articles on
creationist subjects which touch on archaeology. Accepts unsolicited
articles, unsolicited reviews, dot-matrix printing, simultaneous submissions; publishes research notes and review-articles; does not accept advertising. Requires one copy of manuscript. Length re-
quirements--maximum, 2500 words; minimum, --. Style of journal--
will provide information upon request. Indexed: Chr.Per.Ind.

163. BIBBIA E ORIENTE
Fausto Sardini, Ed.
Centro Studi Arti Grafiche
25040 Bornato (Brescia), Italy

Subscription--4/yr.--$68. Subject matter of journal--Scripture,
Ethics, Church History, Theology, Evangelism, Judaism, Eastern Religions, Archaeology, and Anthropology. For: professors, students,
laypersons. Submissions must be in French, German, Spanish,
English, or Italian. Accepts unsolicited articles, unsolicited reviews,

dot-matrix printing, simultaneous submissions; publishes research notes; review-articles; accepts advertising--books on Bible. Especially seeks articles of biblical archaeology. Style of journal-- academic. Requires one copy of manuscript. Length requirements-- maximum, 10 pages; minimum, 2-3 pages. Responds to a submission in 1 month. Indexed: Old Test.Abstr., Rel.&Theol.Abstr., New Test.Abstr.

164. BIBEL UND KIRCHE
    P. G. Mueller, Ed.
    Katholisches Bibelwerk E.V.
    Silberburgstrasse 121
    7000 Stuttgart 1, West Germany (B.R.D.)

Subscription--4/yr.--22 DM. Description of subject matter of journal--biblical studies. Publishes articles in Scripture, Evangelism, Judaism, Islam. For: professors, students, laypersons. Submissions must be in German. Does not accept unsolicited articles, unsolicited reviews, dot-matrix printing, simultaneous submissions; publishes research notes, review-articles; does not accept advertising. Seeks articles that are exegetical--thematical. Requires 2 copies of manuscript. Length requirements--maximum, 15 pages; minimum, 10 pages. Selection process--Editorial Board. Responds in 1 month. Indexed: Old Test.Abstr., New Test.Abstr.

165. BIBEL UND LITURGIE
    Norbert W. Hoeslinger, Ed.
    Pius-Parsch Institut
    Stiftsplatz 8
    A-3400 Klosterneuburg, Austria

Subscription--4/yr.--248 S. Publishes articles in Scripture and Liturgy. For: professors, students, laypersons, and clergy. Submissions must be in German. Accepts unsolicited articles and unsolicited reviews. Seeks studies in biblical criticism, biblical theology, and worship. Especially seeking articles that bridge the gap between scientific study and pastoral activity. Indexed: Old Test. Abstr., New Test.Abstr.

166. BIBLE TODAY
    Sr. Dianne Bergant, C.S.A.
    Liturgical Press
    St. John's Abbey
    Collegeville, MN 56321

Subscription--6/yr.--$14 U.S.; $16 (foreign). Description of subject matter of journal--biblical, with a pastoral focus. Publishes articles in Scripture. For: professors, students, laypersons.

Submissions must be in English. Sometimes accepts unsolicited articles; does not accept unsolicited reviews, simultaneous submissions; does not publish research notes or review-articles; accepts advertising--camera-ready, and will set type at no additional charge. Seeks articles that bring the findings of contemporary scholarship to the broader church. Requires one copy of manuscript. Length requirements--maximum, 8-9 pages. Selection process--articles must be biblical and rather popular (level). Responds to a submission--immediate acknowledgment; decision in a few weeks. Approximate proportion of submissions accepted for publication--since we accept only a few unsolicited articles, this number is slight. Indexed: Cath.Ind., Old Test.Abstr., New Test.Abstr.

167. BIBLEBHASHYAM
Matthew Vellanickal, Ed.
St. Thomas Apostolic Seminary
Post Box No. 1
Vadavathoor
Kottayam 686010, India

Subscription--4/yr.--$7. Subject matter of journal--Scriptural - Biblical. For: professors, students, laypersons, priests, and sisters. Submissions must be in English. Accepts unsolicited articles, unsolicited reviews, simultaneous submissions; does not accept dot-matrix printing; publishes research notes, review-articles; does not accept advertising. Seeks articles that are scientific but with pastoral and spiritual orientations. Length requirements--maximum, 15 pages; minimum, 12 pages. Requires 2 copies of the manuscript. Responds in one month. Approximate proportion of submissions that are accepted for publication--75 percent. Indexed: Old Test. Abstr., New Test.Abstr.

168. BIBLIA REVUO
Dir. Angelo Duranti
Internacia Asocio de Bibliistoj Kaj Orientalistoj
Piazza Duomo 4
48100 Ravenna, Italy

Subscription--4/yr.--$6. Description of subject matter of journal--Biblical themes. Publishes articles in Scripture, Church History, Sociology of Religion, Exegesis, Archaeology, Literary Criticism. For: professors, students, laypersons, clergy. Submissions must be in Italian. Accepts unsolicited articles; sometimes accepts unsolicited reviews. Selection process--reviewed by Board members. Indexed: Old Test.Abstr., New Test.Abstr.

169. BIBLIA Y FE
Escuela Bíblica

Fermín Caballero, 53
28034 Madrid, Spain

Subscription--1.500 ptas; $15.00, overseas. Subject matter of journal--Scripture, Theology, and Sociology of Religion. Sometimes accepts unsolicited articles and unsolicited reviews; accepts advertising. Submissions must be in Spanish.

170. BIBLICA
     Prof. H. Simian-Yofre
     Biblical Institute Press
     Piazza della Pilotta 35
     00187 Rome, Italy

Subscription--4/yr.--$35. Subject matter of journal--Scripture--Exegesis OT/NT, Biblical Theology, Semitics, Biblical Linguistic. Accepts unsolicited articles, dot-matrix printing; sometimes accepts unsolicited reviews; does not accept simultaneous submissions; publishes research notes and review-articles; does not accept advertising. For: professors and students. Submissions must be in French, German, Spanish, English or Italian. Seeks research articles. Requires one copy of manuscript. Length requirements--maximum, 35 pages; minimum, --. Selection process--Editorial Board. Responds in one to two months. Approximate proportion of submissions accepted for publication--40 percent. Text in English, French, German, Italian, Latin and Spanish. Parent Organization--Pontificio Istituto Biblico. Indexed: Curr.Cont., Old Test.Abstr., Rel.Per., Arts&Hum.Cit.Ind., New Test.Abstr., Rel.Ind.One, Rel.&Theol.Abstr.

171. BIBLICAL ARCHAEOLOGIST
     Eric M. Meyers, Ed.
     ASOR Publications Office
     Box H.M.
     Duke Sta.
     Durham, NC 27706

Subscription--4/yr.--$18, individuals; $25, institutions. Description of subject matter of journal--archaeological discoveries as they are related to the Bible. Publishes articles in Scripture, Theology, Sociology of Religion, Judaism, and Biblical Archaeology. For: professors, students, laypersons, and clergy. Submissions must be in English. Accepts unsolicited articles; sometimes accepts unsolicited reviews; publishes review-articles; accepts advertising. Seeks readable, non-technical, yet thoroughly reliable accounts of archaeological discoveries. Parent Organization--American Schools of Oriental Research. Indexed: Cath.Ind., Hum.Ind., M.L.A., Old Test.Abstr., Rel.Per., Art Ind., Abstr.Anthropol., Chr.Per.Ind., New Test.Abstr., Numis.Lit., Rel.Ind.One, Rel.&Theol.Abstr.

172. BIBLICAL ARCHAEOLOGY REVIEW
     Hershel Shanks, Ed.
     Biblical Archaeology Society
     1317 F. St., N.W.
     Washington, DC 20004

Subscription--12/yr.--$24. Description of subject matter of
journal--articles concerning archaeological discoveries in the Biblical
world. For: professors, students, laypersons. Submissions must
be in English. Accepts unsolicited articles; does not accept unsolicited
reviews; accepts advertising. Seeks summaries of archaeological
finds, well illustrated with photographs, written in a popular style.
Length requirements for submission--maximum, 6 pages. Parent Or-
ganization--Biblical Archaeology Society. Indexed: Old Test.Abstr.,
G.Soc.Sci.&Rel.Per.Lit., New Test.Abstr., Rel.&Theol.Abstr., Rel.
Ind.One.

173. BIBLICAL ILLUSTRATOR
     Michael J. Mitchell
     Baptist Sunday School Board
     127 Ninth Ave., North
     Nashville, TN 37234

Subscription--4/yr.--$11. Description of subject matter--
factual biblical background articles illustrated with photographs,
maps, charts, and sketches. Subject matter of journal--Theology,
Archaeology, Biblical Background. For: professors, students, laypersons, and Bible teachers. Submissions must be in English.
Sometimes accepts unsolicited articles; does not accept unsolicited
reviews and simultaneous submissions; accepts dot-matrix printing;
publishes research notes; does not publish review-articles; does not
accept advertising. Style of journal--easy-to-read, nontechnical.
Selection process--articles are assigned based on subjects contained
in focal passages of three adult Sunday School curricula produced
by BSSB. Indexed: South.Bap.Per.Ind.

174. BIBLICAL THEOLOGY BULLETIN
     David M. Bossman, Ed.
     Leland J. White, Ed.
     St. John's University
     Jamaica, NY 11439

Subscription--4/yr.--$12. Description of subject matter of
journal--Biblical theology--scientific but not technical presentations.
Publishes articles in: (principally)--Scripture and Theology; (sec-
ondarily)--Psychology of Religion, Sociology of Religion, Philosophy
of Religion, Judaism, and Religious Education. For: professors,
students, laypersons. Submissions must be in English. Accepts unsolicited articles, unsolicited reviews, dot-matrix printing; does not

accept simultaneous submissions; does not publish research notes; publishes review-articles; accepts advertising--publishers. Style of journal--Social Science method of citation--no footnotes. Requires 3 copies of manuscript. Length requirements--maximum, 25 pages; minimum, 10 pages. Selection process--Peer review--Associate editors (3) review and advise editors. Responds to a submission-- promptly. Approximate proportion of submissions that are accepted for publication--usually 50 percent. Parent Organization--St. Bonaventure University. Indexed: Old Test.Abstr., Rel.Per., New Test.Abstr., Rel.Ind.One, Rel.&Theol.Abstr.

175. BIBLICAL VIEWPOINT
Stewart Custer, Ed.
Bob Jones University
Greenville, SC 29614

Subscription--2/yr.--$3.50. A journal in the exposition of Scripture, usually a different Biblical book each issue. Publishes articles in Scripture and Theology. For: students, pastors, and Bible teachers. Articles appear in English. Sometimes accepts unsolicited articles; accepts dot-matrix printing; does not accept unsolicited reviews, simultaneous submissions. Does not publish research notes; publishes review-articles. Does not accept advertising. Seeks messages on specific texts that Bible teachers would enjoy. Submissions should be scholarly exegesis of Scripture. Length requirements--maximum of 10 typed pages, minimum of 5 typed pages. Selection process/how article is chosen for publication--is the article true to Scripture? Is it conservative, orthodox, warm-hearted? Responds in 2 mos. Indexed: Chr.Per.Ind., Rel.&Theol.Abstr.

176. BIBLISCHE ZEITSCHRIFT
J. Schreiner, Ed.
R. Schnackenburg, Ed.
Ferdinand Schoeningh
Juehenplatz 1
Postfach 2540
4790 Paderborn, West Germany (B.R.D.)

Subscription--2/yr.--$55 DM. Description of subject matter of journal--the whole area of biblical studies (O.T. & N.T.). Publishes articles in Scripture. For: professors, students, etc. Submissions must be in French, German or English. Accepts unsolicited articles; does not accept unsolicited reviews, dot-matrix printing, simultaneous submissions; publishes research notes and review-articles; does not accept advertising. Seeks research articles, exegesis, minor contributions. Especially seeking new material and new insights for biblical questions. Style of journal--objective, academic. Requires one copy of manuscript. Length requirements-- maximum, about 25 typewritten pages (sometimes longer); minimum,

5 pages. Selection process--on the editors' judgment. Responds in
1-3 weeks. Approximate proportion of submissions that are accepted
for publication--for each issue: 2 longer articles for O.T. and 2
for N.T. and some minor contributions, reviews, and reports. Indexed: Curr.Cont., Old Test.Abstr., Rel.Per., Arts&Hum.Cit.Ind.,
New Test.Abstr., Rel.Ind.One, Rel.&Theol.Abstr.

177. BURIED HISTORY
     P. T. Crocker, Ed.
     Australian Institute of Archaeology
     174 Collins St.
     Melbourne 3000
     Victoria, Australia

Subscription--4/yr.--$10 Australian ($11). Publishes articles
in--Biblical and Ancient Near Eastern (Egypt/Mesopotamia) Archaeology and History, Scripture. For: professors (a small percentage),
laypersons, and ministers of religion. Submissions must be in English. Sometimes accepts unsolicited articles, unsolicited reviews; does
not accept dot-matrix printing, simultaneous submissions; does not
publish research notes; publishes review-articles; does not accept
advertising. Seeks a semi-popular conservative evangelical viewpoint
on above subject matter; recent discoveries relating to above subject
matter. Style of journal--semi-popular, semi-academic. Requires two
copies of manuscript. Length requirements--maximum, 3000 words;
minimum, none. Selection process--balance of subject matter in the
magazine as a whole; available space; probable interest to general
readership. Responds in one month, usually less. Comments:
Legible manuscripts can be considered. Publication is only 16-20
pages, circulation--500. Indexed: Old Test.Abstr., Chr.Per.Ind.

178. CAHIERS EVANGILE
     F. Tricard, Dir.
     Service Biblique Evangile et Vie
     6, Avenue Vavin
     75006 Paris, France

Subscription--4/yr.--197 francs. Description of subject matter of journal--booklets are devoted to a topic which is of concern
to Protestant Biblical scholarship. The purpose of the writings is
to inform the non-specialist of developments in biblical interpretation.
For: students and laypersons. Submissions must be in French. Indexed: Old Test.Abstr., Pt.de Rep.

179. CATHOLIC BIBLICAL QUARTERLY
     John P. Meier, Ed.
     Catholic Biblical Assoc. of America
     Catholic University of America
     Washington, DC 20064

Subscription--4/yr.--$15. Description of subject matter of journal--Textual studies, redaction, literary, source, and historical criticism of the Bible. Publishes articles in Scripture. For: professors and students. Submissions must be in English. Accepts unsolicited articles, unsolicited reviews; does not accept simultaneous submissions; publishes research notes; accepts advertising. Style of journal--Chicago Manual of Style. Selection process--Editor makes a decision based on the positive recommendation of assigned readers. Responds to a submission in 3 months. Indexed: Cath.Ind., Curr. Cont., Hum.Ind., Rel.Per., Arts&Hum.Cit.Ind., New Test.Abstr., Old Test.Abstr., Rel.Ind.One, Rel.&Theol.Abstr.

180. ENCOUNTER
Dr. J. William Thompson
Southern Baptist Convention
Sunday School Board
127 Ninth Ave., North
Nashville, TN   37234

Subscription--4/yr.--$3.75. Description of subject matter of journal--Devotional thoughts on Scripture passages, poetry, prayer suggestions. This is a Youth Worship Guide. Publishes articles in Scripture. For: youth (ages 12-17). Submissions must be in English. Does not accept unsolicited articles, unsolicited reviews, simultaneous submissions; accepts dot-matrix printing; does not publish research notes, review-articles; does not accept advertising. Articles are assigned. Requires one copy of manuscript. Length requirements--maximum/minimum--30 lines/50 characters. Responds in 3 days. Approximate proportion of submissions that are accepted for publication--99 percent. Comments--no freelance. No unsolicited. No queries. Indexed: Arts&Hum.Cit.Ind., G.Soc.Sci.&Rel.Per.Lit., Rel.&Theol.Abstr., Rel.Ind.One.

257. EXPOSITORY TIMES
Rev. Dr. C. S. Rodd, Ed.
43 Higher Dr.
Banstead
Surrey SM7 1PL, England

Subscription--12/yr.: UK--12.95 pounds; USA--$24; Canada--$27.50; Elsewhere--14.50 pounds. Publishes articles in Scripture, Ethics, Church History, Theology, Pastoral Counseling, Psychology of Religion, Sociology of Religion, World Religions, Philosophy of Religion, and Religious Education. Also, publishes sermons and book reviews. For: professors, students, laypersons, ministers, and clergy. Submissions must be in English. Accepts unsolicited articles, dot-matrix printing; does not accept unsolicited reviews, simultaneous submissions; does not publish research notes; publishes review-articles; accepts advertising. Especially seeking biblical exposition and

critical scholarship, pastoralia. Style of journal--academic. Requires one copy of manuscript. Length requirements--maximum, 3500
words; minimum, 500 words. Selection process--Editor assesses the
article for academic value and readers' interests. Responds in approximately 2 weeks. Approximate proportion of submissions accepted for publication--50 percent. All literary correspondence
should be addressed to the Editor. Subscription and advertising
inquiries should be addressed to T&T Clark Ltd., 36 George St.,
Edinburgh EH2 2LQ, Scotland. Indexed: Br.Hum.Ind., Curr.Cont.,
Old Test.Abstr., Arts&Hum.Cit.Ind., New Test.Abstr., Rel.&Theol.
Abstr., Rel.Ind.One.

182. HOKHMA
     1, rue Beauregard
     CH-1204 Geneva, Switzerland

Subscription--3/yr.--23 FS, students; 28 FS, institutions.
Subject matter of journal--Scripture and Theology. Accepts advertising.

183. HORIZONS IN BIBLICAL THEOLOGY
     Ulrich Mauser, Ed.
     Pittsburgh Theological Seminary
     Pittsburgh, PA 15206

Subscription--2/yr.--$10.00; $7.00--students; $14.00--institu-
tions. Accepts unsolicited articles, unsolicited reviews. Subject
matter of journal--Scripture and Theology. Submissions must be in
English.

184. INTERPRETATION
     Paul J. Achtemeier, Ed.
     Union Theological Seminary in Virginia
     3401 Brook Rd.
     Richmond, VA 23227

Subscription--Quarterly--$13.50, domestic; $15.00, foreign,
$20.00, library. Description of subject matter--Exegetical-biblical
theology. Publishes articles in Scripture, Ethics, and Theology.
Seeking well-written, original work. For: professors, students, and
laypersons. Submissions must be in English. Accepts unsolicited
articles, dot-matrix printing; sometimes accepts unsolicited reviews;
does not accept simultaneous submissions; does not publish research
notes; publishes review-articles; accepts advertising. One copy of
manuscript is required. Selection process--all articles read by editor and passed on to member(s) of Editorial Board for their opinion.
Approximately 5 percent of volunteered material is accepted for publication. Indexed: Biol.Abstr., Bk.Rev.Ind., Int.Z.Bibelwiss.,

New Test.Abstr., Hum.Ind., Chr.Per.Ind., Old Test.Abstr., Soc.
Sci.Ind., G.Soc.Sci.&Rel.Per.Lit., Rel.Per., Rel.Ind.One, Rel.&
Theol.Abstr.

185. **JOURNAL OF BIBLICAL LITERATURE**
Victor Paul Furnish, Ed.
Perkins School of Theology
Southern Methodist University
Dallas, TX 75275

Subscription--4/yr.--$50, nonmembers (annually). Description
of subject matter of journal--Biblical and related literature of the
ANE and the Greco-Roman world. Publishes articles in Scripture.
For: professors and students. Submissions must be in English,
French, or German. Accepts unsolicited articles; does not accept
unsolicited reviews, dot-matrix printing, simultaneous submissions;
publishes research notes; does not publish review-articles; accepts
advertising--books and related matters. Seeks articles that make
original contributions to scholarship in the above areas. Style of
journal--own stylebook. Requires one copy of manuscript. Length
requirements--negotiable. Selection process--Review by Editorial
Board; final decision by Editor. Responds in 4-24 weeks (normally).
Approximate proportion of submissions accepted for publication--
25 percent. Parent Organization--Society of Biblical Literature. Indexed: Curr.Cont., Hum.Ind., Old Test.Abstr., Rel.Per., Arts&
Hum.Cit.Ind., Bk.Rev.Ind., G.Soc.Sci.&Rel.Per.Lit., Ind.Jew.Per.,
New Test.Abstr., Rel.&Theol.Abstr., Rel.Ind.One.

186. **LINGUISTICA BIBLICA**
Erhardt Guettgemanns, Ed.
Postfach 13 0154
D-5300 Bonn, West Germany (B.R.D.)

Subscription--2/yr.--DM.35. Subject matter of journal--Scrip-
ture and Language Studies. For: professors and students. Submissions must be in German. Accepts unsolicited articles. Indexed:
Curr.Cont., M.L.A., Old Test.Abstr., Arts&Hum.Cit.Ind., CERDIC,
Lang.&Lang.Behav.Abstr., Rel.&Theol.Abstr., New Test.Abstr.

187. **PRACTICAL PAPERS FOR THE BIBLE TRANSLATOR**
E. McG. Fry, Ed.
United Bible Societies
c/o University of Aberdeen
Dept. of Religious Studies
Aberdeen AB9 2UB, Scotland

Subscription--2/yr.--$6. Description of subject matter of jour-
nal--Bible translation and related subjects. Publishes articles in

Scripture and Bible Translation. For: professors, students, lay-persons, and Bible translators. Submissions must be in English. Contributions in French are referred to Cahier de Theologie Biblique. Accepts unsolicited articles, dot-matrix printing; does not accept un-solicited reviews, simultaneous submissions; does not publish research notes; publishes review-articles; accepts advertising--camera-ready copy. Seeks articles which will help translators to improve their un-derstanding of the biblical text and/or their translation of it. Es-pecially seeking exegetical and linguistic contributions not limited in application to a single language or area. Style of journal--style sheet available. Requires one copy of manuscript. Length require-ments--maximum, 7500 words; minimum--short, more acceptable. Se-lection process--Editor consults other members of an Editorial Com-mittee and decides whether to publish, revise with author's agree-ment, ask author to revise, or reject. Responds to a submission--immediate acknowledgment; decision, 2-3 months. Approximate pro-portion of submissions accepted for publication--70 percent; 20 per-cent without substantial revision. Indexed: Old Test.Abstr., Chr. Per.Ind., New Test.Abstr., Rel.Ind.One, Rel.&Theol.Abstr.

188. REVISTA BIBLICA
Armando Levoratti, Ed.
Sociedad Argentina de Profesores de Sagrada Escritura
Casilla Postal 33
1425 Buenos Aires, Argentina

Subscription--4/yr.--$16. Description of subject matter of journal--Biblical exegesis, theology and hermeneutic studies in an ecumenical fashion by Catholic and Protestant scholars. Publishes articles in Scripture. For: professors and students. Submissions must be in Spanish. Sometimes accepts unsolicited articles, unsolic-ited reviews; accepts simultaneous submissions; publishes research notes, review-articles; accepts advertising--only about Biblical books. Seeks articles--high level diffusion. Especially seeking research articles avoiding technical terminology. Requires one copy of manu-script. Length requirements--maximum, 20 pages; minimum, --. Responds in 3 months to a submission. Indexed: New Test.Abstr.

189. REVUE BIBLIQUE
R. P. Tournay, Ed.
Ecole Biblique et Archéologique Française
P.O.Box 19053-91000 Jerusalem, Israël

Subscription--4/yr.--668 francs. Subject matter of journal--Exegetical Research on a critical level; History of Bible Land and Palestine; Epigraphy; Archaeology; Old Semitic Languages; Scripture. For: professors and students. Articles are in French or English. Sometimes accepts submissions in German and Spanish. Seeks aca-demic, critical articles. Accepts unsolicited articles, simultaneous submissions; does not accept unsolicited reviews, dot-matrix printing; publishes research notes and review-articles; does not accept advertising. Especially seeking: first publication of newly discovered texts (Epigraphy related to the Old or New Testament) and Methodology in Exegeses. Style of journal--classical, fully academic. Requires one copy of manuscript. Length requirements--maximum, 40 printed pages; minimum, 4 printed pages. Selection process--All the professors of the Ecole Biblique are from the Board of the Revue. They may have an opinion when the article is in their field; the Director of the Revue makes the first choice. Tries to respond to submissions in three months. Approximate proportion of submissions accepted for publication--50 percent. Comments: The Revue Biblique is nearly one century old; it has classical traditions.... Parent Organization--Ecole Biblique et Archeologique de Jerusalem. Indexed: Curr.Cont., Old Test.Abstr., Rel.Per., Arts&Hum.Cit.Ind., New Test.Abstr., Rel.Ind.One, Rel.&Theol.Abstr.

190. SCRIPTURE BULLETIN
     The Editor
     St. Mary's College
     Strawberry Hill, Twickenham
     Middlesex TW1 4SX, England

Subscription--2/yr.--$10. Description of subject matter of journal--The journal seeks to keep the members of the Catholic Biblical Association informed of current Biblical events and new publications. Publishes articles in Scripture. For: professors, students, and laypersons. Submissions must be in English. Indexed: Cath. Ind., Old Test.Abstr.

191. SEARCHING TOGETHER
     John Zens, Ed.
     Word of Life Church
     Box 548
     St. Croix Falls, WI 54024

Subscription--4/yr.--$6. Description of subject matter--deal with crucial issues facing the church in light of the Bible. Publishes articles in Scripture, Ethics, Church History, Theology, Evangelism, Church Administration, Pastoral Counseling, Missions, Sociology of Religion, and Church Renewal. For: any serious Bible student. Submissions must be in English. Accepts unsolicited articles, unsolicited reviews, dot-matrix printing, simultaneous submissions; publishes research notes and review-articles; accepts advertising--select books or events. Seeks articles that are provocative, often those which question or challenge traditions of the past. Especially looking for articles with a cutting edge, a "prophetic" thrust. Usually tackle one topic in each issue and give several angles of the topic. Requires one manuscript to be submitted. Length requirements--

maximum, 2000-3000 words; minimum, 500 words. Selection process--
if focusing on one issue, then articles are selected which are related to this issue. Sometimes the articles that are received determine the issue that will be dealt with. Responds in 10 days. Approximately 70 percent of submissions are accepted for publication.
Indexed: Rel.Per., Rel.Ind.One, Rel.&Theol.Abstr.

192. SEMEIA
Robert C. Culley, General Ed.
Scholars Press
819 Houston Mill Road
Atlanta, GA   30329

   Subscription--Semeia was published irregularly in issues numbered consecutively from 1974 to 1979. Since 1980-81 it is published
quarterly in August, November, February, and May, but still in issues numbered consecutively. Subscription units consist of four
numbers and cost $18. Single issues are $5; ten or more copies to
the same address--$4 each. Publishes articles in Scripture. For:
professors and students. Submissions must be in English. Sometimes accepts unsolicited articles; does not accept unsolicited reviews.
Semeia is an experimental journal devoted to the exploration of new
and emergent areas and methods of biblical criticism. Studies employ-
ing the methods, models, and findings of linguistics, folklore studies,
contemporary literary criticism, structuralism, social anthropology,
and other such disciplines and approaches are invited. Although experimental in both form and content, Semeia proposes to publish work
that reflects a well-defined methodology that is appropriate to the material being interpreted. Issues of Semeia are unified around a central theme and edited by an individual member of the Editorial Board.
Future themes and editors are given at the back of each issue of
Semeia. Inquiries or manuscripts should be sent directly to the individual editor of the appropriate thematic volume. Semeia and
Semeia Studies are sponsored by the Society of Biblical Literature as
part of its research and publications program. Indexed: Old Test.
Abstr., Arts&Hum.Cit.Ind., New Test.Abstr., Rel.&Theol.Abstr.,
Rel.Ind.One.

193. SOUTHWESTERN JOURNAL OF THEOLOGY
Dan Kent, Ed.
Southwestern Baptist Theological Seminary
Box 22000 2E
Fort Worth, TX   76122

   Subscription--3/yr.--$13. Description of subject matter--study,
analysis, and application of Scripture. Publishes articles in Scripture, Ethics, Church History, Theology, Evangelism, Church Administration, Pastoral Counseling, Missions, Psychology of Religion,
Philosophy of Religion, and Homiletics. For: professors, students,

and pastors. Submit article in French, German, Spanish or English. Sometimes accepts unsolicited articles and unsolicited reviews; does not accept simultaneous submissions; does not publish research notes; publishes review-articles; accepts advertising--publishers, conferences, full page, half page, multiple pages. Seek scholarly articles related to the theme of the particular issue. Style of manual--Turabian. Requires 2 copies of manuscript. Length requirements--maximum, 50 pages double spaced; minimum, 12-15 pages double spaced. Selection process--articles are usually solicited by the board of the journal. Unsolicited articles are selected on their relevance, thoroughness, documentation, and clarity. Responds in 2-4 weeks. Approximately 1 percent of all submissions are accepted. Indexed: Old Test.Abstr., Rel.Per., Chr.Per.Ind., New Test.Abstr., Rel. Ind.One, Rel.&Theol.Abstr., South.Bap.Per.Ind.

194. TECHNICAL PAPERS FOR THE BIBLE TRANSLATOR
Paul Ellingworth, Ed.
United Bible Societies
c/o University of Aberdeen
Dept. of Religious Studies
Aberdeen AB9 2UB, Scotland

Subscription--2/yr.--$6. Description of subject matter of journal--Bible translation and related subjects. Publishes articles in Scripture and Bible Translation. For: professors, students, laypersons, and Bible translators. Submissions must be in English. Contributions in French are referred to Cahier de Theologie Biblique. Accepts unsolicited articles, dot-matrix printing; does not accept unsolicited reviews, simultaneous submissions; does not publish research notes; publishes review-articles; accepts advertising--camera-ready copy. Seeks articles which will help translators to improve their understanding of the Biblical text and/or their translation of it. Especially seeking exegetical and linguistic contributions not limited in application to a single language or area. Style of journal--style sheet available. Requires one copy of manuscript. Length requirements--maximum, 7500 words; minimum--short, more acceptable. Selection process--Editor consults other members of an Editorial Committee and decides whether to publish, revise with author's agreement, ask author to revise, or reject. Responds to a submission--immediate acknowledgment; decision, 2-3 months. Approximate proportion of submissions accepted for publication--70 percent; 20 percent without substantial revision. Indexed: Old Test.Abstr., Chr. Per.Ind., New Test.Abstr., Rel.Ind.One, Rel.&Theol.Abstr.

195. THEOLOGISCHE BEITRAEGE
R. Brockhaus Verlag
Champagne 7
Postfach 110152
5600 Wuppertal 11, West Germany (B.R.D.)

Subscription--6/yr.--DM 44; students, DM 2. Description of subject matter of journal--The renewal of "Biblical Hermeneutics" and "Biblical Theology" and the unity of faith and thinking. Publishes articles in Scripture, Ethics, Biblical Hermeneutics, Church History, Theology, Evangelism, Pastoral Counseling, Missions, Philosophy of Religion, Judaism, and Religious Education. For: professors, students, pastors. Submissions must be in German. Articles must be easily understood by students and pastors. Sometimes accepts unsolicited articles, unsolicited reviews; accepts dot-matrix printing; does not accept simultaneous submissions; does not publish research notes; publishes review-articles; accepts advertising--Theological Publishing Houses. Length requirements--maximum, 20 typed pages. Selection process--Editors decide. Responds in 1-6 months. Approximate proportion of submissions accepted for publication--50 percent. Indexed: Old Test.Abstr., New Test.Abstr.

7A. THE OLD TESTAMENT; HEBREW SCRIPTURE

196. BETH MIKRA
Ben-Zion Luria, Ed.
World Jewish Bible Center
Box 7024
Jerusalem, Israel

Subscription--4/yr.--$12. Description of subject matter--Bible research. Publishes articles in Scripture and Judaism. For: professors, students, and laypersons. Submissions must be in Hebrew. Accepts unsolicited articles, unsolicited reviews; does not accept simultaneous submissions; publishes research notes, review-articles; does not accept advertising. Seeks articles of academic reviews on biblical subjects. Type of article especially searching for--history of the land of Israel during biblical times. Manuscripts should be correct and clear. Requires one copy of manuscript. Selection process--Editor's decision. Responds in 2 weeks. Approximate proportion of submissions accepted for publication--70 percent. Indexed: Ind.Heb.Per., Rel.&Theol.Abstr.

197. BULLETIN OF THE INTERNATIONAL ORGANIZATION FOR SEPTUAGINT AND COGNATE STUDIES
Prof. Eugene Ulrich, Ed.
University of Notre Dame
Department of Theology
Notre Dame, IN   46556

Subscription--1/yr.--$5.00. Subject matter of journal--Scripture, Church History, Judaism. Submissions must be in English, French, or German. Invites the following contributions: 1) Record of work published or in progress. 2) Record of Septuagint and cognate theses and dissertations completed or in progress. 3) Reports significant for Septuagint and cognate studies. Items of newly discovered manuscripts or of original groundbreaking research will be given primary consideration. Reports should be brief and informative and may be written in English, French, or German. Greek and Hebrew need not be transliterated. 4) Abstracts of Septuagint papers read before international, national, and regional academic meetings. Abstracts should be previously unpublished, not more than one page, double spaced, including the time, place and occasion of presentation.

198. JOURNAL FOR THE STUDY OF THE OLD TESTAMENT
      JSOT Press
      343 Fulwood Road
      Sheffield S10 3BP, England

Subscription--3/yr.--$19.50, individuals; $50, institutions. Description of subject matter of journal--Exegesis of the Old Testament. For: professors, students, clergy. Submissions must be in English. Seeks original research in Old Testament studies. Accepts unsolicited articles, dot-matrix printing; does not accept unsolicited reviews, simultaneous submissions; does not publish research notes; publishes review-articles; accepts advertising--relevant publications, announcements of conferences, etc. Style of journal--JSOT has its own style (style guide available on request); similar to that of JBL. Requires 1 copy of manuscript. Selection process--Editors select according to 1) inherent value as a contribution to research; 2) academic competence; 3) level of general interest to scholars; 4) readability. Responds in 2-3 months. Approximate proportion of submissions accepted for publication--35 percent. Indexed: Bull.Signal, Old Test. Abstr., Rel.Per., Int.Z.Bibelwiss., New Test.Abstr., Rel.Ind.One, Rel.&Theol.Abstr.

199. REVUE DE QUMRAN
      Florentino García Martínez, Secretaire de la Revue
      Qumrân Instituut, Nieuwe Kijk in 't Jatstraat 104
      9712 SL Groningen, The Netherlands

Subscription--Sept.-April--352 francs. Description of subject matter of journal--all aspects of Qumrân research. Submissions must be in French, German, Spanish, or English. Publishes articles in Scripture and Judaism. Publishes research notes and accepts advertising. Selection process--Editorial Board on the advice of readers. Indexed: Old Test.Abstr., Rel.Per., New Test.Abstr., Rel. Ind.One, Rel.&Theol.Abstr.

200. VETUS TESTAMENTUM

Prof. W. L. Holladay, Ed.
210 Herrick Road
Newton Centre, MA   02159

Subscription--4/yr.   Description of subject matter of journal--
studies which shed new light on the Old Testament.   Publishes articles in Scripture, Hermeneutics, Biblical Criticism, and Textual
Studies.   Submissions must be in French, German, or English.   Accepts unsolicited articles, unsolicited reviews; does not accept simultaneous submissions; publishes research notes.   Style of journal--
style directions are provided on the inside cover of the journal.
Priority is given to Short Notes and to articles of less than 5000
words.   Parent Organization: International Organization for the
Study of the Old Testament.   Indexed: Curr.Cont., Old Test.Abstr.,
Rel.Per., Arts&Hum.Cit.Ind., New Test.Abstr., Rel.Ind.One, Rel.&
Theol.Abstr.

201.   ZEITSCHRIFT FUER DIE ALTTESTAMENTLICHE WISSENSCHAFT
       Prof. Dr. Otto Kaiser, Ed.
       Am Krappen 29
       D 3550 Marburg/Lahn, West Germany (B.R.D.)

Subscription--3/yr.- $61.85.   Description of subject matter of
journal--Subjects which shed light on the formation, history, and
meaning of the Old Testament.   Publishes articles in Scripture, Iler-
meneutics, Biblical Criticism, and Textual Studies.   Submissions
must be in French, German, or English.   Selection process--Editorial
Board acts on the recommendation of readers.   Indexed: Curr.Cont.,
Old Test.Abstr., Rel.Per., Rel.&Theol.Abstr., Arts&Hum.Cit.Ind.,
New Test.Abstr., Rel.Ind.One.

7B.   THE NEW TESTAMENT

202.   JOURNAL FOR THE STUDY OF THE NEW TESTAMENT
       JSOT Press
       343 Fulwood Road
       Sheffield S10 3BP, England

Subscription--3/yr.--$19.50, individuals; $50, institutions.
Description of subject matter of journal--Exegesis of the New Testament.   For: professors, students, clergy.   Submissions must be in
English.   Seeks original research in New Testament study.   Accepts
unsolicited articles, dot-matrix printing; does not accept unsolicited
reviews, simultaneous submissions; does not publish research notes;
publishes review-articles; accepts advertising--relevant publications
of books, software; conference announcements, etc.   Style of journal--
JSOT style (guide available upon request), similar to JBL style.

Requires one copy of manuscript. Length requirements--maximum, 15,000 words; minimum, 1000 words. Selection process--Editors select according to 1) inherent value as original research; 2) academic competence; 3) level of general interest to scholars; 4) readability. Responds in 2 months. Approximate proportion of submissions accepted for publication--50 percent. Indexed: New Test.Abstr., Rel. Ind.One, Rel.&Theol.Abstr.

203. NEOTESTAMENTICA
      Dr. P. G. R. de Villiers, Ed.
      New Testament Society of South Africa
      C. B. Powell Bible Centre
      UNISA
      P.O. Box 392
      Pretoria 0001, South Africa

Subscription--2/yr.--$15. Publishes articles in Scripture, New Testament Studies and related fields. Accepts unsolicited articles; sometimes accepts unsolicited reviews; does not accept dot-matrix printing, simultaneous submissions; publishes research notes, review-articles; accepts advertising--advertisements with an academic nature (e.g.--publishers, indexing institutions). For: professors, students, scholars. Submissions must be in English--other languages accepted only after consultation with editor. Seeks academic articles on the various subdisciplines in New Testament studies. Style of journal--advanced academic style (for highly qualified scholars). Requires 3 copies of manuscript. Length requirements--maximum, 6000 words; minimum, --. Selection process--articles submitted for evaluation to three independent specialists on the topic of the article. If articles reflect original input, expertise and an acceptable scientific level, they are accepted. Responds in 3-6 months. Approximate proportion of submissions accepted for publication--60 percent. Comments: Articles must be submitted in guideline form (available from the editor). Indexed: New Test.Abstr., Int.Z.Bibelwiss.

204. NEW TESTAMENT ABSTRACTS
      D. J. Harrington, Ed.
      Weston School of Theology
      3 Phillips Place
      Cambridge, MA   02138

Subscription--3/yr.--$24. Description of subject matter--summaries of books and articles in the New Testament field. Subject matter of journal--Scripture. For: professors and students. Submissions must be in English. Does not accept unsolicited articles, unsolicited reviews, dot-matrix printing, simultaneous submissions; does not publish research notes or review-articles; accepts advertising--books in the New Testament field. Copies of manuscript--N/A. Length requirements--maximum, 200 words; minimum, 15 words.

Selection process--All abstracts are assigned. Comments--This abstraction journal does not fit the general pattern of other journals. Indexed: Int.Z.Bibelwiss.

205. NEW TESTAMENT STUDIES
Prof. G. N. Stanton, Ed.
King's College, Strand
London, WC2R 2LS, England

Subscription--4/yr.--$48, individuals; $69, institutions. Description of subject matter of journal--New Testament and early Christianity. Publishes articles in Scripture. For: professors and graduate students. Submissions must be in French, German, or English. New Testament Studies publishes original research from scholars of all denominations from all parts of the world. Articles cover all aspects of the text and theology of the New Testament. Reports of SNTS seminars are also included. Accepts unsolicited articles, dot-matrix printing; does not accept unsolicited reviews, simultaneous submissions; publishes research notes (as short articles); (rarely) publishes review-articles; accepts advertising--scholarly books. Seeks substantial, creative contributions to New Testament scholarship. Requires 2 copies of manuscript. Length requirements--maximum, 20 printed pages; minimum, - . Selection process--Editor and members of Editorial Board. Style of journal--detailed instructions for contributors are printed in NTS regularly. Responds in 3 weeks (average). Approximate proportion of submissions accepted for publication--less than half. Comments: The scholarship is careful, balanced, well written, and documented. The audience is the general reader to specialist. This is a journal that no theological seminary can afford to be without and should be in any research library that supports biblical studies. Indexed: Curr.Cont., Hum. Ind., Rel.Per., Arts&Hum.Cit.Ind., New Test.Abstr., Rel.Ind.Onc, Rel.&Theol.Abstr.

206. NOVUM TESTAMENTUM
E. J. Brill,
Plantoin Straat 2
POB 9000, 2300 PA, Netherlands

Subscription--4/yr.--115 fl. Description of subject matter of journal--the New Testament and the history of its study. Publishes articles in Scripture and Theology. For: professors. Submissions must be in French, German, or English. Accepts unsolicited articles; sometimes accepts unsolicited reviews; accepts dot-matrix printing; does not accept simultaneous submissions; does not publish research notes; publishes review-articles; accepts advertising--for scholarly books. Seeks articles of new scholarly research on all aspects of the above. Style of journal--Chicago Manual. Requires one copy of manuscript. Length requirements--maximum, 30 pages; minimum, 5 pages. Selection process--articles are read by one reviewer and a member of the Editorial Board. The decision is by the whole Editorial Board which receives recommendations and abstracts. Approximate proportion of submissions accepted for publication--25 percent. Text in English, French, and German. Indexed: Curr.Cont., Rel.Per., Arts&Hum.Cit.Ind., New Test.Abstr., Rel.&Theol.Abstr.

207. ZEITSCHRIFT FUER DIE NEUTESTAMENTLICHE WISSENSCHAFT
UND DIE KUNDE DER AELTEREN KIRCHE
Erich Graesser, Ed.
Walter de Gruyter und Co.
Genthiner Str. 13
1000 Berlin 30, West Germany (B.R.D.)

Subscription--2/yr.--$43.20. Description of subject matter of journal--New Testament Exegesis and matters pertaining to the early church. Publishes articles in Scripture and Theology. For: professors, students, and laypersons. Submissions must be in French, German, or English. Does not accept unsolicited articles, unsolicited reviews, dot-matrix printing, simultaneous submissions; does not publish research notes, review-articles; does not accept advertising. Requires one copy of manuscript. Length requirements for submissions--maximum, 30 pages; minimum, 1 page. Selection process-- Editorial Board. Responds to a submission in one year. Indexed: Rel.Per., New Test.Abstr., Rel.Ind.One, Rel.&Theol.Abstr.

OTHER JOURNALS THAT PUBLISH
ARTICLES IN SCRIPTURE

8. LITERATURE AND RELIGION; LINGUISTICS

208. AFROASIATIC LINGUISTICS
c/o Russell G. Schuh
UCLA
Department of Linguistics
Los Angeles, CA 90024

Subscription--1/yr.--$24.00. Subject matter of journal--Scripture, Judaism, and Islam. Accepts unsolicited articles. Submissions must be in English. Style of journal--style sheet is provided on the back cover of the journal.

209. BULLETIN DE LITTERATURE ECCLESIASTIQUE
Henri Crouzel, Ed.
Institut Catholique de Toulouse
31 rue de la Fonderie
31068 Toulouse Cedex, France

Subscription--4/yr.--$21. Description of subject matter of journal--All matters concerning the religious literature. Publishes articles in Scripture, Church History and Theology. For: professors, students, and laypersons. Submissions must be in French. Accepts unsolicited articles, unsolicited reviews, and simultaneous submissions; publishes research notes and review-articles; does not accept advertising. Style of journal--scientific. Requires one copy of manuscript. Length requirements--maximum, 30 pages; minimum, 10 pages. Selection process for choosing an article for publication-- If articles are of true scientific quality, to the judgment of the editor and to the judgment of other scholars he consults. Responds in one month (usually). Approximate proportion of submissions accepted for publication--70 percent. Indexed: Bull.Signal, Old Test. Abstr., New Test.Abstr.

210. CHRISTIANITY AND LITERATURE
James Barcus, Ed.
Conference on Christianity and Literature
Baylor University
Waco, TX 76798

Subscription--4/yr.--$10, individuals; $15, institutions. Description of subject matter of journal--scholarly essays, book reviews, occasional short poems, general forums, and new items that explore the relationships between Christianity and literature. For: professors, students, laypersons. Submissions must be in English. Accepts unsolicited articles, unsolicited reviews, dot-matrix printing, does not accept simultaneous submissions; does not publish research notes; publishes review-articles; accepts advertising--appropriate to audience and scope of journal. Seeks interdisciplinary, scholarly but not pedantic writing. Requires 2 copies of manuscript. Style of journal--MLA. Selection process--reviewed by two or more experts. Responds to a submission in 6-8 months. Approximate proportion of submissions accepted for publication--1 in 15. Comments: We also accept poetry of a religious nature or theme. Indexed: Abstr.Engl. Stud., Curr.Cont., Chr.Per.Ind., M.L.A., Arts&Hum.Cit.Ind., Amer.Bibl.Slavic&E.Eur.Stud., CERDIC, LCR, Rel.Ind.One.

211. JOURNAL OF NORTHWEST SEMITIC LANGUAGES
Prof. F. C. Fensham, Ed.
University of Stellenbosch
Department of Semitic Languages
Stellenbosch 7600, South Africa

Subject matter of journal--Scripture, Judaism, and Semitic Languages. Accepts unsolicited articles; sometimes accepts unsolicited reviews; does not accept advertising. Submissions must be in French, German, English, or Afrikaans.

212. ORIENTALIA CHRISTIANA PERIODICA
Richard Caplice, Editor
Pontifical Biblical Institute
Via della Pilotta 25
I-00187 Rome, Italy

Subscription--4/yr.--$60. Publishes articles in Scripture, Sociology of Religion, Archaeology, Literary Studies, Textual Studies, Linguistics, and Semitic Documents. Submissions must be in French, German, English, or Italian. Accepts unsolicited articles; sometimes accepts unsolicited reviews. Selection process--Editor reaches a decision on recommendation of readers. Indexed: Bull.Signal, Rel.& Theol.Abstr., New Test.Abstr., Rel.Ind.One.

213. PARABOLA
Lorraine Kisly, Ed.
656 Broadway
New York, NY 10012-2317

Subscription--4/yr.--$18.00. Subject matter of journal--Sociology

of Religion, Myth, Tradition, and Art. Accepts unsolicited articles
and accepts advertising. Submissions must be in English. Indexed:
Rel.Ind.One, Abstr.Engl.Stud., Bk.Rev.Ind.

214. RELIGION AND LITERATURE
Thomas Werge, Ed.
James Dougherty, Ed.
University of Notre Dame
Department of English
Notre Dame, IN 46556

Subscription--3/yr.--$12, individuals; $15, libraries. Description of subject matter of journal--the religious interpretation of literature and the use of imaginative techniques in religious writing.
For: professors. Submissions must be in English. Accepts unsolicited articles; sometimes accepts unsolicited reviews; does not accept dot-matrix printing, simultaneous submissions; does not publish
research notes; publishes review-articles; accepts advertising--book
publishers from their field, also exchanges journal ads. Seeks scholarly articles addressed to a general academic audience. Also seeks
reviews of books in their field. Especially seeking articles that are
informed by theories of interpretation but not preoccupied with theory.
Style of journal--MLA plus Chicago. Requires three copies of manuscript. Length requirements--maximum, 7000 words; minimum, 4000
words (reviews are shorter). Selection process--in-house review,
editors' review, experts' opinions, editors' decision. Responds in 3-5
months. Approximate proportion of submissions accepted for publica-
tion--1/10. Indexed: Abstr.Engl.Stud., Cath.Ind., Curr.Cont.,
M.L.A., Amer.Hum.Ind., Arts&Hum.Cit.Ind., CERDIC, Rel.&Theol.
Abstr., Rel.Ind.One.

215. SEMIOTIQUE ET BIBLE
Jean Delorme, Ed.
Centre pour l'Analyse du Discours Religieux
25 rue du Plat
69002 Lyon Cedex, France

Subscription--4/yr.--France, 110 francs; other countries 150
francs. Description of subject matter of journal--Linguistic studies
of biblical texts and religious texts. Publishes articles in Scripture,
Linguistics, and Semiotics. For: professors, students, laypersons.
Submissions must be in French. Sometimes translates articles into
French. Accepts unsolicited articles; sometimes accepts unsolicited
reviews; does not accept dot-matrix printing; accepts simultaneous
submissions; publishes research notes and review-articles; accepts
advertising. Seeks Semiotic studies on biblical or religious texts;
theoretical and methodological reflections. Style of journal academic,
well-referenced. Requires 2 copies of manuscript. Selection process--
Editoral Board, blind review. Responds to a submission in 3 months.
Indexed: New Test.Abstr.

OTHER JOURNALS THAT PUBLISH ARTICLES IN
LITERATURE AND RELIGION; LINGUISTICS

9. SOCIOLOGY OF RELIGION; CHURCH AND STATE

216. CHURCH AND SOCIETY
Gaspar Langella, Ed.
Frederick Nesetril, Production Mgr.
The United Presbyterian Church (U.S.A.)
Room 1244K
475 Riverside Dr.
New York, NY 10115

Subscription--6 issues/yr.--$7.50; 3 yr.--$20. Description of subject matter of journal--subjects of social concern for Christians. Publishes articles in Scripture, Ethics, Church History, Theology, Evangelism, Sociology of Religion, World Religions, Philosophy of Religion, Religious Education, Economic and Social Justice. For: professors, students, laypersons and clergy. Submissions must be in English. Sometimes accepts unsolicited articles, simultaneous submissions; does not accept unsolicited reviews; accepts dot-matrix printing; does not publish research notes, review-articles; does not accept advertising. Description of article that journal seeks--thematic, according to issue, models and resources for individual and group study or action; articles to encourage dialogue among persons with religious commitment. Articles journal is especially seeking--thematic essays covering church history, theology, social and economic justice. Style of journal--Introduction, 3-5 essays, one theological reflection; resources including bibliographies, charts, network lists. Requires one copy of manuscript. Length requirements--maximum--475, 72-character lines; minimum--175, 72-character lines. Selection process-- Content Editor gathers, edits and combines articles into one theme issue. Content editors are chosen by Content Committee and Editor. Responds in 4-6 weeks. Indexed: Rel.Per., Rel.Ind.One.

217. JOURNAL OF CHURCH AND STATE
James E. Wood, Jr., Ed.
Baylor University
J. M. Dawson Studies in Church and State
Box 380
Waco, TX 76798

Subscription--3/yr.--$15. Description of subject matter of journal--Sociological, philosophical, constitutional, historical,

theological studies on religion and the body politic. Subject matter--
World Religions, articles must emphasize some aspect of church-state
relations. For: professors, students, laypersons. Submissions must
be in English. Accepts unsolicited articles and dot-matrix printing;
does not accept unsolicited reviews or simultaneous submissions; does
not publish research notes; publishes review-articles; and accepts
advertising--usually from publishers or universities. Seeks scholarly
and well-researched articles related to church and state. Style of
journal--Chicago Manual of Style, 13th rev. ed. Requires 3 copies
of manuscript. Length requirements--maximum, 30 pages (includ.
notes); minimum, around 20 pages. Selection process--manuscripts
are sent to members of an editorial council who evaluate and critique
the manuscripts. They must be timely, original, scholarly (not editorials), and well written. The Editor makes the final decision on
whether or not to publish an article. Responds--rarely less than 2
months, usually about 4 months--varies greatly. Approximately 15
percent of the submissions are accepted for publication. Comments--
Although articles should be scholarly, they are meant to be read by
both professionals and laypersons, so they should be clear and without
excessive jargon. Indexed: Amer.Hist.&Life, Curr.Cont., Chr.Per.
Ind., Educ.Admin.Abstr., Hist.Abstr., P.A.I.S., Rel.Per., Arts&
Hum.Cit.Ind., C.L.I., L.R.I., Rel.&Theol.Abstr., Rel.Ind.One.

218. REFORMATIO EVANGELISCHE ZEITSCHRIFT FUER KULTUR,
      POLITIK, KIRCHE
      Hans-Rudolf Schaer, Ed.
      Benteli-Verlag
      3018 Berne, Switzerland

      Subscription--6/yr.--50 francs. Evangelical journal which pub-
lishes articles in Ethics, Religion and Politics, Church History, Theology, Sociology of Religion, and Philosophy of Religion. For: professors, students, laypersons. Sometimes accepts unsolicited articles,
unsolicited reviews; does not accept dot-matrix printing, simultaneous
submissions; does not publish research notes; publishes review-
articles; accepts advertising--publishing houses or job advertisements.
Submissions must be in German, occasionally French. Requires one
copy of manuscript. Length requirements--maximum, 15 pages; minimum, 1 page. Selection process--opinions of various members of the
Editorial Committee. Responds in about 1 month. Approximate proportion of submissions accepted for publication--50 percent. Most of
the contributions are solicited. Indexed: Rel.Per., Rel.Ind.One.

219. RELIGION AND SOCIETY
      Christian Institute for the Study of Religion and Society
      Box 4600
      17 Miller's Rd.
      Bangalore 560046, India

Subscription--4/yr.--$15. Description of subject matter of jour-
nal--studies of socio-religious-political issues from a Christian point
of view. Publishes articles in Theology, Sociology of Religion, World
Religions, Social Problems, and Political Issues. For: professors,
students, laypersons. Submissions must be in English. Sometimes
accepts unsolicited articles; does not accept unsolicited reviews, dot-
matrix printing, simultaneous submissions; does not publish research
notes; publishes review-articles; does not accept advertising. Style
of journal--rather scholarly. Requires one copy of manuscript.
Length requirements--around 6000 words (but no limit). Selection
process--Editorial Board. Responds in one month. Approximate
proportion of submissions that are accepted for publication--Generally
articles arise from our own studies and conferences. We do not
often publish an unsolicited article. Indexed: Rel.Per., G.Indian
Per.Lit., Rel.Ind.One.

220. REPORT FROM THE CAPITAL
     Victor Tupitza, Ed.
     Baptist Joint Committee on Public Affairs
     200 Maryland Ave., N.E.
     Washington, DC 20002

     Subscription--10/yr.--$6. Description of subject matter of
journal--Religious Liberty; Church-State Relations; Public Policy Issues. Publishes articles in Ethics, Church History, and Theology,
especially as they pertain to the Baptist tradition. For: professors,
students, laypersons. Submissions must be in English. Accepts unsolicited articles, unsolicited reviews, simultaneous submissions, dot-
matrix printing; does not publish research notes; publishes review-
articles; does not accept advertising. Requires one copy of manuscript. Length requirements--maximum, 2000 words; minimum, 500
words. Selection process--try to maintain a balance of Baptist history and tradition, contemporary implications and public policy
(legislation, court decisions, etc.). Responds within 2 weeks as a
rule. Approximate proportion of submissions that are accepted for
publication--60 percent. Indexed: South.Bap.Per.Ind.

221. TIERRA NUEVA
     Maria B. Cabezas de Gonzalez, Ed.
     Centro de Estudios para el Desarrollo e Integracion de America
        Latina
     Carrera 90
     No. 47-54
     Apdo. Aereo 100572
     Bogota, D.E. 10, Colombia

     Subscription--4/yr.--$27. Description of subject matter of
journal--socio-Theology in Latin America. For: clergy. Submissions
must be in French, German, Spanish, English, Italian, or Dutch.

Sometimes accepts unsolicited articles; does not accept unsolicited reviews, dot-matrix printing; accepts simultaneous submissions; does not publish research notes; publishes review-articles; does not accept advertising. Seeks articles pertaining primarily to Liberation Theology and Social Doctrine of the Church. Style of journal-- academic. Requires one copy of manuscript. Length requirements-- maximum, 20 pages; minimum, 5 pages. Approximate proportion of submissions accepted for publication--10 percent. Indexed: CERDIC.

OTHER JOURNALS THAT PUBLISH ARTICLES IN SOCIOLOGY OF RELIGION

Africa Theological Journal 502
America 448
American Jewish Archives 480
American Scientific Affiliation Journal 249
Anglican Theological Review 4
Anima 423
Antonianum 271
Asbury Theological Journal 5
Asian Issues 512
Banner 6
Benedictines 316
Berliner Theologische Zeitschrift 7
Bibbia e Oriente 163
Bible Bhashyam 167
Biblia Revuo 168
Biblia y Fe 169
Biblical Archaeologist 171
Biblical Theology Bulletin 174
Bijdragen 9
Boletín Teológico 524
Buddhist-Christian Studies 411
The Bulletin of the Henry Martyn Institute of Islamic Studies 471
Burgense 10
Caribbean Journal of Religious Studies 525
Catalyst: Social Pastoral Magazine for Melanesia 223
CEHILA 114
Centre for the Study of Islam and Christian Muslim Relations Newsletter 472
Cercle Ernest Renan. Cahiers 13

Chicago Studies 277
China Study Project Journal 514
The Chinese Theological Review 515
Christian Century 224
Christian Jewish Relations 424
Christian Ministry 318
Christian Orient 425
Christianity and Crisis 227
Christianity Today 228
Church and Society 216
Church History 115
Churchman (London) 15
Churchman (St. Petersburg, FL) 16
Cithara 17
La Ciudad de Dios 18
Civiltà Cattolica 19
Commonweal 449
Communio Viatorum 426
Conservative Judaism 483
Cristianismo y Sociedad 526
The Critic 254
Cross Currents 255
Crux 230
Cuadernos de Derechos Humanos 256
Cultura Popular 527
Dansalan Quarterly 516
Diaconate Magazine 323
Diakonia 324
Dialog 25
Dialogue 505
Dialogue and Alliance 427
The Drew Gateway 27
Duke Divinity School Review 28

East Africa Journal of Evangel-
ical Theology 506
East Asian Pastoral Review 328
Ecumenical Review 428
Ecumenist 430
Etudes 231
Evangelische Theologie 34
Expository Times 181
Focus 517
Franciscanum 36
Freiburger Rundbrief 432
Harvard Theological Review 42
Herder-Korrespondenz 232
Heythrop Journal 285
ICUIS Justice Ministries 258
Iliff Review 43
Indian Church History Review
118
Indian Theological Studies 519
Inter-Religio 520
International Review of Mission
363
Internationale Kirchliche Zeit-
schrift 433
Irish Theological Quarterly 45
Islam and the Modern Age 474
Japan Christian Quarterly 521
Japanese Journal of Religious
Studies 522
Jewish Social Studies 488
Journal for the Scientific Study
of Religion 46
Journal of Church and State
217
Journal of Psychology and Chris-
tianity 147
Journal of Psychology and Juda-
ism 148
Journal of Religion 47
Journal of Religion and Aging
152
Journal of Religion and Health
234
Journal of Religion in Africa/
Religion en Afrique 507
Journal of Religious Studies
142
Journal of Religious Thought
49
The Journal of the Interdenom-
inational Theological

Center 51
Journal of Theology for Southern
Africa 508
Kairos 416
Keyhole 528
Laurentianum 54
Lucha/Struggle 259
Lumen Vitae 385
Lumière et Vie 55
Melita Theologica 58
Mérleg 59
Minaret Monthly International
476
Miscelanea Comillas 60
Missiology 365
Modern Judaism 494
Le Monde Copte 237
Nederlands Archief Voor Kerk-
geschiendenis--Dutch Review
of Church History 123
Neotestamentica 203
New Blackfriars 238
Northeast Asia Journal of The-
ology 436
Nova et Vetera 437
Oekumenische Rundschau 438
One in Christ 439
Orientalia Christiana Periodica
212
Orita 510
Orthodox Word 348
Parabola 213
Philippiniana Sacra 262
Positions Lutheriennes 66
Priests and People 337
Process Studies 145
Proyeccion 243
Puebla 264
Quaker History 463
Recherches de Science Religieuse
69
Reconciliation International 265
Reformatio Evangelische Zeitschrift
fuer Kultur, Politik, Kirche
218
Religion 418
Religion in Communist Lands
245
Religion in Southern Africa 511
Religious Education 392
Religious Humanism 73

10. CULTURE AND RELIGION

222. ANNALS MAGAZINE
Paul Stenhouse, M.S.C., Ph.D., Ed.
Chevalier Press
Box 13
Kensington, NSW 2033, Australia

Subscription--10/yr.--Australian $15. Publishes articles in
Scripture, Church History, Missions, Judaism, Islam, Religious Education. For: professors, students, laypersons, families. Submissions must be in English. Accepts unsolicited articles, unsolicited
reviews, dot-matrix printing; publishes review-articles; accepts ad-
vertising--except cigarette and alcohol. Description of article that
is sought--aspects of Catholic culture, at all levels. Pastoral material is welcome. Suitable for parish councils. Especially looking
for articles concerning a topical treatment of all dimensions of Catholic life and culture. Style of journal--not heavy, but not "Timesque"
either; sound journalism. Requires one copy of manuscript. Length
requirements--maximum, 1200 words; minimum, --. Selection process
of article chosen to be published--objectivity, raciness, clarity,
brevity. Indexed: Gdlns.

223. CATALYST: SOCIAL PASTORAL MAGAZINE FOR MELANESIA
P.O. Box 571
Goroka, E.H.P.
Papua, New Guinea

Subscription--4/yr.--K. 4.00; A $5.00, Australia; U.S. $7.50,
elsewhere. Subject matter of journal--Scripture, Ethics, Church
History, Evangelism, Psychology of Religion, Sociology of Religion,
World Religions, and Religious Education. Accepts unsolicited articles. Submissions must be in English.

223a. CATHOLIC LAWYER
Edward Fagan, Ed.
St. John's University
School of Law
Grand Central and Utopia Parkways
Jamaica, NY 11439

Subscription--4/yr.--$5. Description of subject matter of
journal--legal matters having ethical, canonical or theological implications. Publishes articles in Ethics, Theology, Religious Education, and Canon Law. For: professors, students, laypersons, and
attorneys. Submissions must be in English. Seeks scholarly articles.
Requires one copy of manuscript. No length requirements. Selection process of articles--timeliness and scholarship. Responds in
2 weeks. Approximate proportion of submissions accepted for pub-
lication--1/10. Comments--Our readers are also abroad (subscription).
This is a non-profit organization. Indexed: Cath.Ind., Leg.Per.,
C.L.I., CERDIC, Canon Law Abstr., L.R.I.

224. CHRISTIAN CENTURY
James M. Wall, Ed.
Christian Century Foundation
407 S. Dearborn St.
Chicago, IL 60605

Subscription--40/yr.--$28. A journal in religion and culture.
Publishes articles in Ethics, Church History, Theology, Church Administration, Pastoral Counseling, Psychology of Religion, Sociology
of Religion, World Religions, Philosophy of Religion, Judaism, Islam,
Hinduism, and Religious Education. For: clergy, laypersons. Articles appear in English. Sometimes accepts unsolicited articles. Does
not accept unsolicited reviews, simultaneous submissions. Does not
publish research notes; publishes review-articles. Accepts advertising. Submit one copy of manuscript. Length requirements--
maximum, 2800 words; minimum, 850 words. Responds in 4 weeks.
Accepts 20 percent of submissions. Indexed: R.G., Rel.Per., Bk.
Rev.Dig., Abstrax, G.Soc.Sci.&Rel.Per.Lit., Mag.Ind., PMR, Rel.
Ind.One, Rel.&Theol.Abstr.

225. CHRISTIAN LEGAL SOCIETY QUARTERLY
Samuel E. Ericsson
P.O. Box 1492
Merrifield, VA 22116-1492

Subscription--4/yr.--$15. Subject matter of journal--All as-
pects of law and religion. Publishes articles in Ethics. Accepts
unsolicited articles and advertising. For: lawyers, judges, law
students. Submissions must be in English.

226. CHRISTIAN MEDICAL SOCIETY JOURNAL
Edwin A. Blum, D. Theol., Th.D., Ed.
Christian Medical Society
Box 689
1616 Gateway Blvd.
Richardson, TX 75083-0689

Subscription--4/yr.--$16. Publishes articles in Scripture, Ethics, Church History, Theology, Evangelism, Church Administration, Pastoral Counseling, Missions, and Psychology of Religion. Welcomes any articles on an inspirational nature aimed at strengthening the Christian beliefs and experiences of their members and any dealings with the interface between Christianity and medicine. For: professors, students, laypersons, medical/dental professionals. Submissions must be in English. Accepts unsolicited articles, unsolicited reviews, dot-matrix printing, simultaneous submissions; does not publish research notes; publishes review-articles; does not accept advertising. Requires one copy of manuscript. Length requirements--maximum, 2500 words; minimum, none. Selection process-- at the discretion of the editor with some input from the consulting editors. Responds in 3-6 weeks, normally. Approximate proportion of submissions accepted for publication--50 percent. Indexed: Chr. Per.Ind.

227. CHRISTIANITY AND CRISIS
     Leon Howell, Ed.
     Christianity and Crisis, Inc.
     537 W. 121st St.
     New York, NY 10027

Subscription--fortnight--$21, individuals; $24, institutions. Description of subject matter of journal--The matters that compose daily life--political, cultural, social, religious--as viewed through filters refined by the Judaeo-Christian tradition. Publishes articles in Ethics, Theology, Evangelism, Missions, Psychology of Religion, Sociology of Religion, World Religions, Philosophy of Religion, Judaism, Islam, Hinduism, Buddhism, Eastern Religions, and Ethical, Theological Reflection on Current Issues. For: pastors, priests, rabbis. Submissions must be in English. Accepts unsolicited articles, unsolicited reviews, dot-matrix printing (if double-spaced), simultaneous submissions; does not publish research notes; publishes review-articles; accepts advertising--books, educational and church institutions, classifieds. Seeks articles that are lucid, non-technical reflections on issues and experiences of current importance. Especially looking for articles that shed fresh light on difficult issues in the society. Style of journal--University of Chicago style without footnotes (references incorporated). Length requirements--maximum, 3000 words; minimum, 800 words. Selection process--In most instances the four editors read all serious submissions, make independent judgments on acceptance and rejection, discuss editing needs if accepted, and determine which to use collectively. Responds in ten working days--maximum. Approximate proportion of submissions accepted for publication--one acceptance per six serious submissions. Indexed: P.A.I.S., Rel.Per., Hum.Ind., G.Soc.Sci.&Rel.Per.Lit., Rel.Ind.One.

228. CHRISTIANITY TODAY
Terry Muck, Executive Editor
Christianity Today, Inc.
465 Gunderson Dr.
Carol Stream, IL 60188

Subscription--18/yr.--$21. Description of subject matter--
social, political, theological commentary of concern to evangelicalism.
Publishes articles in Scripture, Ethics, Church History, Theology,
Evangelism, Pastoral Counseling, Missions, Psychology of Religion,
Sociology of Religion, World Religions, Philosophy of Religion, and
Religious Education. For: professors, laypersons, and pastors.
Submissions must be in English. Does not accept unsolicited articles,
unsolicited reviews, and simultaneous submissions; accepts dot-matrix
printing, does not publish research notes; publishes review-articles;
accepts advertising. Article styles include essay, personality profiles, straight news, interviews. Style of journal--Chicago Manual
of Style. One copy of manuscript required. Length requirements--
maximum, 3500 words. Selection process--Most articles are assigned--
"Many are submitted, few are chosen." Responds in approximately
3 weeks. Less than 1 percent of submissions are accepted for publication. Indexed: Chr.Per.Ind., Old Test.Abstr., Rel.Per., R.G.,
Biog.Ind., G.Soc.Sci.&Rel.Per.Lit., New Test.Abstr., Mag.Ind.,
PMR, Rel.&Theol.Abstr., Rel.Ind.One.

229. CLS QUARTERLY
Samuel E. Ericsson, Executive Editor
Christian Legal Society
Box 1492
Merrifield, VA 22116

Subscription--4/yr.--$15. Description of subject matter of
journal--some Ethics; topics affecting Christian lawyers who seek to
integrate their faith with their profession--could be legal theory of
First Amendment, legal aid, conciliation, recreation, money, civil
rights, putting Scripture into practice, education, etc. Accepts unsolicited articles, dot-matrix printing, simultaneous submissions; does
not accept unsolicited reviews; publishes research notes (if not too
extensive); publishes review-articles; accepts advertising--classified
and display. Address advertising correspondence to the attention
of Kathryn Sides. For: professors, students, lawyers, judges,
pastors. Submissions must be in English. Description of article that
is sought--generally not too scholarly. Quarterly is meant to be a
practical membership service, not a scholarly journal. Especially
seeking practical, thought-provoking pieces on being a Christian and
a lawyer. Requires one copy of manuscript. Length requirements--
maximum, 3000 words; minimum, 400 words. Selection process--
Themes selected ahead of time and articles often solicited. Unsolicited articles are circulated among CLS senior staff. Responds to
a submission in 4-6 weeks. Approximate proportion of submissions
accepted for publication--10 percent. Indexed: Leg.Per.

230. CRUX
    Klaus Bockmuehl, Ed.
    Regent College
    2130 Wesbrook Mall
    Vancouver, British Columbia V6T 1W6, Canada

Subscription--4/yr.--$10. Description of subject matter of journal--Seeks to expound the basic tenets of the Christian faith and to demonstrate that Christian truth is relevant to the whole of life. Publishes articles in Scripture, Ethics, Church History, Theology, Evangelism, Psychology of Religion, Sociology of Religion, Philosophy of Religion, Religious Education, and Christian Music. Accepts unsolicited articles and unsolicited reviews; does not accept advertising. Particularly interested in relating the teachings of Scripture to a broad spectrum of academic, social and professional areas of interest, to integrate them and to apply the insights gained to corporate and personal life and witness. Indexed: Old Test. Abstr., New Test.Abstr., Rel.&Theol.Abstr.

231. ETUDES
    Paul Valadier, Ed.
    Assas Editions
    14 rue d'Assas
    75006 Paris, France

Subscription--11/yr.--315 francs. Description of subject matter of journal--cultural and religious. Publishes articles in Ethics, Theology, Sociology of Religion, World Religions, Judaism, Islam, Hinduism, Buddhism, Eastern Religions, Religious Education, Literature, Arts, Foreign Affairs, Social Affairs. For: laypersons. Submissions must be in French. Accepts unsolicited articles, does not accept unsolicited reviews, dot-matrix printing, simultaneous submissions; publishes research notes and review-articles; accepts advertising. Seeks articles of reflexion. Requires one copy of manuscript. Length requirements--maximum, 12 pages; minimum, 6 pages. Selection process--Editorial Committee. Responds in 3 months. Approximate proportion of submissions accepted for publication--50 percent. Indexed: Cath.Ind., Hist.Abstr., M.L.A., Amer.Hist.&Life, CERDIC, New Test.Abstr., Phil.Ind., Pt.de Rep.

232. HERDER-KORRESPONDENZ
    Dr. David A. Seeber, Ed.
    Verlag Herder GmbH und Co. KG
    Hermann-Herder-Str. 4
    D-7800 Freiburg im Breisgau, West Germany (B.R.D.)

Subscription--12/yr.--DM 142.80. Description of subject matter of journal--Religion and society (church and world). For: laypersons. Sometimes accepts unsolicited articles, unsolicited reviews;

does not accept dot-matrix printing, simultaneous submissions; publishes research notes; does not publish review-articles; accepts advertising. Description of article that is sought--news stories, comments, documents, interviews. Style of journal--information on a high level. Most articles are written by the editors. Indexed: Cath.Ind.

233. JOURNAL OF CHRISTIAN NURSING
Ramona Cass, Ed.
5206 Main Street
P.O. Box 1650
Downers Grove, IL 60515

Subscription--4/yr.--$16. Description of subject matter of journal--articles that help Christian nurses integrate their faith with their personal and professional lives. Publishes articles in Bioethics, Counseling, Missions, Spiritual Care, Patient and Nurses' Personal Experiences, and Psychology and Religion. For: nurses. Submissions must be in English. Accepts unsolicited articles, dot-matrix printing; sometimes accepts unsolicited reviews; does not accept simultaneous submissions; publishes research notes (only related to nursing); does not publish review-articles; accepts advertising--Christian books, Christian Nursing Schools, mission agencies. Seeks articles that are personal and professional, aimed at nurses. Requires one copy of manuscript. Length requirements--maximum, 10 double-spaced pages; minimum--none. Selection process--Editor sends articles of a professional or technical nature to two reviewers for evaluation but makes final decision on these and all others. Responds in 3-4 months. Approximate proportion of submissions accepted for publication--5 percent. Indexed: Int.Nurs.Ind., CINAHL.

234. JOURNAL OF RELIGION AND HEALTH
Harry C. Meserve, Ed.
Box 1066
Southwest Harbor, ME 04679

Subscription--4/yr.--$30, individuals; $75, institutions. Description of subject matter of journal--interdisciplinary studies of the interrelationships of religion and the healing sciences. Publishes articles in Pastoral Counseling, Psychology of Religion, Sociology of Religion, and Philosophy of Religion. For: clergy, social workers, physicians, nurses, psychologists, and psychiatrists. Accepts unsolicited articles, simultaneous submissions (journal only publishes material that has not been published before); sometimes accepts unsolicited reviews; does not accept dot-matrix printing (unless very clear); does not publish research notes; publishes review-articles; accepts advertising--very selective (Publisher handles advertising.). Seeks scholarly studies, excellent in content and style, in the areas listed above. Style of manual--somewhat eclectic, mostly Chicago

Manual of Style. Requires 3 copies of manuscript. Length require-
ments--maximum, 40 typed pages--double-spaced; minimum, 8 pages
double-spaced. Selection process for publication of an article--cur-
rent interest, substance, and quality. Responds in 1-3 months.
Approximate proportion of submissions accepted for publication--50
percent. Indexed: Curr.Cont., Excerp.Med., Psychol.Abstr.,
SSCI, Arts&Hum.Cit.Ind., G.Soc.Sci.&Rel.Per.Lit., Past.Care&
Couns.Abstr., Rel.&Theol.Abstr., Rel.Ind.One.

235. MATURE YEARS
    John P. Gilbert, Ed.
    United Methodist Publishing House
    201 Eighth Ave., S.
    Nashville, TN 37203

    Subscription--4/yr.--$3.50. Description of subject matter of
journal--leisure reading for persons of retirement and beyond; it
also contains weekly Bible study for adults of this age. Seeks a
wide variety of subjects of interest for older adults such as fiction,
travel, hobbies, Bible study, theology, poetry, service opportunities,
health hints, etc. Accepts unsolicited articles, dot-matrix printing,
simultaneous submissions; sometimes accepts unsolicited reviews; does
not publish research notes or review-articles; does not accept advertising. Especially seeks articles that challenge or motivate older
adults. Style of journal--casual, informal, unsophisticated, easy-
reading. Requires one copy of manuscript. Length requirements--
maximum, 2500 words; minimum --. Selection process--Assistant
Editor and Editor review. Responds in about 6 weeks--varies. Approximate proportion of submissions accepted for publication--un-
solicited, 5 percent. Indexed: Meth.Per.Ind.

236. MODERN CHURCHMAN
    Prof. A.O. Dyson, Ed.
    Modern Churchmen's Union
    School House
    Leysters, Leominster
    Herefordshire HR6 OHB, England

    Subscription--4/yr.--$9. Publishes articles and reviews in
Ethics, Contemporary Theology, Pastoral Theology, Pastoral Counseling, Philosophy of Religion, Politics and Current Affairs. For:
professors, students, and laypersons. Submissions must be in English. Sometimes accepts unsolicited articles; does not accept unsolicited reviews; accepts dot-matrix printing, simultaneous submissions; does not publish research notes; publishes review-articles;
accepts advertising. Seeks original (no reprints), scholarly but un-
technical articles in the above fields. MC also publishes in each
essay a Re-Review of a notable book, and a Bibliography on a theme
of current interest. Especially looking for articles that deal with

19th- and 20th-century studies. Welcomes theological and ethical
reflection on topical societal themes. Requires one copy of manuscript. Style of journal--instructions to authors supplied to contributors. Requires one copy of manuscript. Length requirements--
maximum, 3500 words. Selection process--articles passed by Chief
Editor to Section Editor who has power of decision but may send to
outside referee. Responds within one month (normally). Approximate proportion of submissions accepted for publication--15 percent.
Comments--Many articles and most Re-reviews and Bibliographies are
commissioned. International authorship welcomed. Indexed: Rel.
Per., New Test.Abstr., Rel.Ind.One.

237. LE MONDE COPTE
    4, Rue du Général-Maunoury
    77165 St-Soupplets, France

Subscription--4/yr. Subject matter of journal--Scripture,
Church History, Theology, Sociology of Religion, Religion and Culture, The Coptic World. Submissions must be in French.

238. NEW BLACKFRIARS
    Rev. John Orme Mills, Ed.
    Blackfriars
    Oxford OX1 3LY, England

Subscription--11/yr.--$23. Description of subject matter of
journal--explores the relationship between Christianity and culture.
Publishes articles in Scripture, Ethics, Church History, Theology,
Psychology of Religion, Sociology of Religion, and Philosophy of
Religion. For: professors, laypersons, and church people. Submissions must be in French, German, Spanish, English, or Italian.
Sometimes accepts unsolicited articles; does not accept unsolicited
reviews, dot-matrix printing, or simultaneous submissions; does not
publish research notes; publishes review-articles; accepts advertis-
ing--publishers and conferences. Seeks articles of about 5000 words,
addressing an intelligent but not a highly specialized readership.
Especially looking for articles of good theology. Journal has a repu-
tation for focusing on provocative issues, for drawing attention to
new ideas. Length requirements--maximum, 6000 words; minimum,
2500 words. Selection process--Editorial Board and a team of readers. Responds in 2 weeks to 1 month. Approximate proportion of
submissions accepted for publication--10 percent. Parent Organiza-
tion--English Dominicans. Indexed: Br.Hum.Ind., Cath.Ind., Old
Test.Abstr., New Test.Abstr.

239. NEW CATHOLIC WORLD
    Laurie Felknor, Managing Ed.
    Paulist Press

997 MacArthur Blvd.
Mahwah, NJ   07430

Subscription--6/yr.--$10.00.   Description of subject matter of
journal--We treat current religious questions and thought.   Each issue is thematic.   For: professors, students, laypersons, clergy,
nuns.   Submissions must be in English.   Sometimes accepts unsolicited
articles; does not accept unsolicited reviews, dot-matrix printing,
simultaneous submissions; does not publish research notes, review-
articles; does not accept advertising.   Requires one copy of manuscript.   Generally all the articles are solicited from persons well
known in the fields of the subjects treated.   Length requirements--
maximum, 2500 words; minimum, 1500 words.   Responds in 2-3 weeks.
Comments: Our articles are solicited so far in advance of each issue that we very seldom can use an unsolicited article, unless one
just happens to fit in.   Parent Organization--Missionary Society of
St. Paul the Apostle in the State of New York.   Indexed: Cath.Ind.,
R.G., Access, G.Soc.Sci.&Rel.Per.Lit., Mag.Ind.

240.   ORIGINS NC DOCUMENTARY SERVICE
       Richard W. Daw, Ed.
       National Catholic News Service
       1312 Massachusetts Ave., N.W.
       Washington, DC 20005

Subscription--48/yr.--$79.   Material for publication in Origins
is selected on the basis of its interest and usefulness as documentation in reference to current issues.   The publication is sponsored
by the National Conference of Catholic Bishops.   Submissions must
be in English.   Does not accept unsolicited articles, unsolicited reviews; does not publish research notes; does not accept advertising.
Indexed: Cath.Ind.

241.   PRO MUNDI VITA BULLETIN
       Pro Mundi Vita
       Rue de La Science 7
       B-1040 Brussels, Belgium

Subscription--4/yr.--600 F (Belgium).   Description of subject
matter of journal--Topics of interest to Church leaders throughout
the world.   Explores the relation of the Catholic Church to the world
today.   Submissions must be in French, German, Spanish, English,
or Dutch.   Indexed: Rel.Ind.One.

242.   PRO MUNDI VITA DOSSIERS
       Pro Mundi Vita
       Centrum Informationis
       Rue de la Science 7
       B-1040 Brussels, Belgium

Subscription--4/yr.--600 F. Description of subject matter of journal--Topics which deal with problems of the relation of the Catholic Church to culture. Dossiers concerning Asia are published in English; those concerning Africa, North America and Europe in English and French; and those concerning Latin America in Spanish. Indexed: Rel.Per., Rel.Ind.One.

243. PROYECCION
Ildefonso Camacho, Ed.
Facultad de Teologia
Apartado 2002
18080 Granada, Spain

Subscription--4/yr.--$24.00. Description of subject matter--theology and today's society. Subject matter of journal--Scripture, Ethics, Church History, Theology, Pastoral Counseling, Sociology of Religion. For: students, laypersons, religious people. Submissions must be in Spanish. Sometimes accepts unsolicited articles; does not accept unsolicited reviews, dot-matrix printing, simultaneous submissions; does not publish research notes or review-articles; does not accept advertising. Requires 2 copies of manuscript. Length requirements--maximum, 20 pages; minimum, 10 pages. Selection process--Editorial Board. Indexed: Old Test.Abstr.

244. RELATIONS
Albert Beaudry, Ed.
Editions Beitarmin
8100 Bd. St.-Laurent
Montreal, Quebec, H2P 2L9, Canada

Subscription--monthly--$16 Canadian. Description of subject matter of journal--commentary on social and cultural issues from a Christian perspective. Publishes articles in Ethics, Social Analysis, Cultural Issues, Faith-Justice. For: laypersons, educators, pastors. Submissions must be in French. Sometimes accepts unsolicited articles, unsolicited reviews; does not accept dot-matrix printing, simultaneous submissions; publishes research notes, review-articles; accepts advertising--books, magazines. Seeks articles linking the Christian Tradition or the Teaching of the Church with a social issue interesting to Canadians. Especially looking for portrait of people (individuals or small groups) involved in the struggles for justice, human rights, helping the poor. Style of journal--for the well-informed non-specialist. Length requirements--maximum, 2000 words; minimum, 350 words. Requires one copy of manuscript. Selection process--Editorial Board meets twice a month; responds in 1 month. Approximate proportion of submissions accepted for publication--1/5 more or less. Parent Organization--Pères de la Compagnie de Jesus. Indexed: Cath.Ind., Can.Ind., CERDIC.

245. RELIGION IN COMMUNIST LANDS
      Dr. Paul Booth, Ed.
      Keston College
      Heathfield Rd.
      Keston, Kent BR2 6BA, England

Subscription--3/yr.--16 pounds; in USA--$30 from Keston Col-
lege, Box 1310, Framingham, MS 01701. Description of subject matter of journal--The theory and practice of religion in communist
countries; the relationship between religion and communism. Publishes articles in the following areas if within the context of communist states: Church History, Theology, Evangelism, Church Administration, Missions, Psychology of Religion, Sociology of Religion,
World Religions, Philosophy of Religion, Judaism, Islam, Buddhism,
and Eastern Religions. Sometimes accepts unsolicited articles, unsolicited reviews; accepts dot-matrix printing; accepts simultaneous
submissions, but not simultaneous publications in English; does not
publish research notes; publishes review-articles; accepts advertising--
books, other journals. For: professors, students, laypersons, others. Submissions must be in French, German, English, or Italian--
English is preferred; Russian and Eastern European languages and
any other language considered. Seeks well-researched "academic"
articles. Especially seeking short articles (up to 4000 words) on
philosophical, theological, political aspects of religion and communism.
Style of journal--British English (but articles submitted in American
English are acceptable and will be edited). Requires one copy of
manuscript. Length requirements for submissions--maximum, 10,000
words; minimum, 2500 words. Selection process--The Editor and
Editorial Board select primarily according to quality, but also bearing
in mind the balance and emphasis of each issue of the journal. Responds to a submission--1 week--2 months. Approximate proportion
of submissions accepted for publication--more than 50 percent (a
large proportion of the articles are solicited by the journal). Indexed: Abstr.Musl.Rel., Rel.Ind.One.

246. ST. MARK'S REVIEW
      Revd. P. M. Mendham, Ed.
      St. Mark's Cantena
      P.O. Box E67
      Queen Victoria Terrace, A.C.T. 2600, Australia

Subscription--4/yr.--$15.00 Australian. Description of subject
matter of journal--Articles of interest to church-related people--
general rather than specialized theological, cultural, church, Australian society types of material. Publishes articles in Scripture, Ethics, Church History, Theology, Evangelism, Pastoral Counseling,
Missions, Sociology of Religion, Religious Education, General Theo-
logical/Social Items of Interest to Clergy and Educated Laypeople.
For: professors, students, laypersons, and clergy. Submissions
must be in English. Accepts unsolicited articles, dot-matrix printing,

simultaneous submissions (but only by arrangement to co-publish); sometimes accepts unsolicited reviews; does not publish research notes; publishes review-articles; accepts advertising--usually only from Christian research or similar bodies. Seeking articles to bridge the gap between scholars and laypeople. Requires two copies of manuscript. Length requirements--maximum, 4000 words; minimum, 1000 words. Style of journal--footnoted (using either Harvard or endnote system). Selection process--try to present a theme two issues per year, otherwise choice is made on the basis of accessibility of the article by the general readership and relevance to the Australian church and society. Response to a submission--first response is immediate, then 2-6 months. Approximate proportion of submissions accepted for publication--50 percent. Comments: While Australian focus is a criterion (i.e., one of several) for publication, the journal is always looking for relevant overseas material. Indexed: Aus. P.A.I.S., Rel.Ind.One.

247. UTOPIAN CLASSROOM
Even Eve, Ed.
Kerista Commune Publications
543 Frederick St.
San Francisco, CA 94117

Subscription--4/yr.--$6; Utopian Philanthropists' Society Subscribing Membership--$36--12 publications/yr. including the Kerista book series. Description of subject matter of journal--describes religious equalitarian group living, positive future visions, global problems and innovative solutions with stories and comics about a new religious mythology. Publishes articles in Ethics, Theology, Psychology of Religion, Sociology of Religion, Philosophy of Religion, Religious Education, New Religions, Philanthropic Religious Service, Nonsexism and Equality in Religion, Religious Utopian Idealism, and New Mythologies. For: professors, students, laypersons, general audience. Submissions must be in English. Sometimes accepts unsolicited articles; does not accept unsolicited reviews; accepts dot-matrix printing, simultaneous submissions; publishes research notes and review-articles; accepts advertising--display and classifieds. Seeks articles concerning Scientific Utopian Theoretics and autonomous equalitarian Utopian communities. Especially seeking articles from people living in Religious Utopian Intentional Communities. Style of journal-- hip, intellectual, humorous, idealistic, informal. Requires one copy of manuscript. Length requirements--any length. Selection process-- Editors decide if article is particularly relevant to journal's unique focus. Responds in 2 weeks. Approximate proportion of submissions accepted for publication--vast majority of articles written by members of their collective. Indexed: New.Per.Ind.

248. VIDA RELIGIOSA
Buen Suceso, 22
Madrid, 8, Spain

Subscription--21/yr.--300 ptas. Description of subject matter of journal--practical and religious life after the II Vatican Council. For: professors, students, laypersons, etc. Submissions must be in Spanish. Does not accept unsolicited articles; accepts unsolicited reviews; publishes research notes; sometimes (only) publishes review-articles; does not accept advertising. Requires 2 copies of manu-script. Selection process--Editorial Board. Indexed: Canon Law Abstr.

OTHER JOURNALS THAT PUBLISH ARTICLES IN CULTURE AND RELIGION

11. SCIENCE AND RELIGION

249. AMERICAN SCIENTIFIC AFFILIATION JOURNAL
Wilbur L. Bullock, Ed.
American Scientific Affiliation
Box J
Ipswich, MA 01938

Subscription--4/yr.--$30. Description of subject matter of
journal--Any scientific issue or phenomenon that relates to evangelical Christian thought. For: professors, students, laypersons,
anyone interested in science and Christianity. Submissions must be
in English. Accepts unsolicited articles, unsolicited reviews, dot-
matrix printing; does not accept simultaneous submissions, does not
publish research notes; publishes review-articles; accepts advertising--
black and white camera ready, no graphics, editorial approval. Seeks
articles that can deal with an issue in an accurate and scholarly man-
ner and that can be understood by scientists in other disciplines as
well. Style of journal--academic. Requires 3 copies of manuscript.
Length requirements--maximum, 20-25 ms. pages; minimum--none.
Selection process--articles sent to 2 or more reviewers in field of
specialty of author. Responds in 2-6 months. Approximate proportion of submissions accepted for publication--50 percent. Indexed:
Chr.Per.Ind., G.Soc.Sci.&Rel.Per.Lit., Rel.&Theol.Abstr.

250. SCIENCE ET ESPRIT
Editions Bellarmin
c/o Sophie Desmarais
8100, Saint-Laurent
Montreal, Quebec, H2P 2L9, Canada

Subscription--3/yr.--$14 Canadian. Publishes articles in Scrip-
ture, Theology, Philosophy of Religion, and Philosophy. For: professors, students, and laypersons. Submissions must be in French
or English. Sometimes accepts unsolicited articles, unsolicited reviews; does not accept dot-matrix printing, simultaneous submissions;
does not publish research notes or review-articles; does not accept
advertising. Requires one copy of manuscript. Indexed: M.L.A.,
Old Test.Abstr., Rel.Per., CERDIC, New Test.Abstr., Pt.de Rep.,
Rel.Ind.One.

128 / Academic Journals in Religion

251. ZYGON
     Karl E. Peters, Ed.
     Joint Publication Board of Zygon
     Rollins College
     Winter Park, FL   32789

Subscription--4/yr.--$25, individuals; $34, institutions; $20, students. Description of subject matter of journal--Zygon provides a forum for exploring ways to unite values and knowledge, goodness and truth, religion and science. Zygon analyzes and reformulates the thinking and practice of all religions in light of contemporary scientific knowledge about the universe, human nature, and human society. Publishes articles in Religion and the Sciences. Seeks articles that are understandable outside the specific discipline from which they are written. Prefers articles relating religious thought and practice to cosmic, biological, and/or cultural evolution. Submissions must be in English. Seeks articles that join religious wisdom to recent discoveries about the world and human nature. Accepts unsolicited articles (Submit a one-page, typed, double-spaced abstract); sometimes accepts unsolicited reviews; accepts dot-matrix printing; does not accept simultaneous submissions; does not publish research notes; publishes review articles (inquire in advance); accepts advertising--books and journals dealing with subject matter related to our interests. (Correspondence concerning book reviews should be sent to Robert J. Russell; Center for Theology & the Natural Sciences; c/o The Graduate Theological Union; 246 Le Conte Avenue; Berkeley, CA 94709.) Style of journal--style exemplified by the Chicago Manual of Style and its author-date reference system. Style sheet available upon request. Requests 3 copies of manuscript. Length requirements--maximum, 30 pages; minimum, 15 pages typed double-spaced. Selection process--Blind referees with final decision by the editor. Responds to a submission--immediate acknowledgment. Six to twelve months to review and decide. Approximate proportion of submissions accepted for publication--20 percent. Parent Organization--Institute on Religion in an Age of Science. Indexed: Curr.Cont., Hist.Abstr., Hum.Ind., Old Test. Abstr., Psychol.Abstr., Rel.Per., SSCI, Arts&Hum.Cit.Ind., Amer. Hist.&Life, G.Soc.Sci.&Rel.Per.Lit., New Test.Abstr., Phil.Ind., Rel.&Theol.Abstr., Rel.Ind.One.

OTHER JOURNALS THAT PUBLISH ARTICLES
IN SCIENCE AND RELIGION

Documentation Catholique   450
Islamic Studies   475
Studies in Formative Spirituality
   352
Teilhard Review and Journal
of Creative Evolution   300

12. SOCIAL JUSTICE; SOCIAL CHANGE

252. CHRISTUS
Apartado Postal 21-272
Coyoacán, Coyoacán 0400, México D.F.

Subscription--$30, South America; $35, overseas. Subject
matter of journal--Sociology of Religion and Philosophy of Religion.
Accepts unsolicited articles; sometimes accepts unsolicited reviews,
accepts advertising. Submissions must be in Spanish.

253. CONSCIENCE ET LIBERTE
G. Rossi, Ed.
Schosshaldenstr. 17
CH-3006 Berne, Switzerland

Subscription--2/yr.--18 francs ($8). Subject matter of jour-
nal--Human Rights and Religious Liberty. For: professors, students,
laypersons, political and religious circles. Submissions must be in
French or English. Sometimes accepts unsolicited articles, unsolicited
reviews; sometimes publishes review-articles; does not accept advertising. Indexed: CERDIC.

254. THE CRITIC
John Sprague, Ed.
223 W. Erie St.
Chicago, IL 60610

Subscription--4/yr.--$16.00. Subject matter of journal--Ethics,
Church History, Theology, and Sociology of Religion. Accepts ad-
vertising. Submissions must be in English. Parent Organization--
Thomas More Association.

255. CROSS CURRENTS
Joseph E. Cunneen, Ed.
Mercy College
Dobbs Ferry, NY 10522

Subscription--4/yr.--$12.50, individuals; $15, libraries.

Description of subject matter of journal--Cross Currents explores
the implication of Christianity for our times. Publishes articles in
Scripture, Ethics, Church History, Theology, Evangelism, Missions,
Psychology of Religion, Sociology of Religion, World Religions, Religious Education, and Spirituality. For: professors, students,
laypersons, clergy. Submissions must be in English. Accepts unsolicited articles, unsolicited reviews; publishes review-articles; accepts advertising. Seeks articles that combine "true humanism"
with a deep interior life and profound compassion for the oppressed.
Especially seeking articles on the cutting edge of third-world Christianity. Selection process--Editorial Board makes final decision.
Indexed: Cath.Ind., Hum.Ind., G.Soc.Sci.&Rel.Per.Lit., Old Test.
Abstr., Rel.&Theol.Abstr.

256. CUADERNOS DE DERECHOS HUMANOS
     Juan Carlos Giacosa, Ed.
     Manuel A. Quintero, Ed.
     27, Chemin des Crêts-de-Pregny
     1218 Grand Sacconex
     Geneva, Switzerland

Subscription--4/yr. Subject matter of journal--Ethics and
Sociology of Religion. Submissions must be in Spanish. Accepts unsolicited articles.

257. E/S A
     Lee Ranck, Ed.
     United Methodist Church
     General Board of Church and Society
     100 Maryland Ave., N.E.
     Washington, DC 20002

Subscription--11/yr.--$10. Description of subject matter of
journal--Analysis of social issues from the perspective of Christian
faith and United Methodist stances. Publishes articles in Ethics and
Theology--Social Issues. For: laypersons and pastors. Submissions must be in English. Sometimes accepts unsolicited articles, unsolicited reviews; does not accept dot-matrix printing, simultaneous
submissions; does not publish research notes; publishes review-
articles; accepts advertising--book publishers, social service agen-
cies, etc. Seeks articles dealing with social issues from a Christian
perspective. Style of journal--nonscholarly. Requires one copy of
manuscript. Length requirements--maximum, 2000 words; minimum,
1200 words. Selection process--Production Editor reads manuscripts
and then passes possibilities on to the Editor who makes the selections. Responds in 1-2 months. Approximate proportion of submissions accepted for publication--1/10. Indexed: Rel.Per., Method.
Per.Ind., Rel.Ind.One.

258. ICUIS JUSTICE MINISTRIES
Clinton Stockwell, Director
Institute on the Church in Urban Industrial Society
5700 S. Woodlawn Ave.
Chicago, IL   60637

Subscription--4/yr. -$8, individuals; $12, institutions. Publishes articles in Ethics, Missions, Sociology of Religion, Urban Ministry, Social Justice, Community Organization. For: professors, laypersons, pastors, denominational officials. Submissions must be in English. Sometimes accepts unsolicited articles, unsolicited reviews. Seeks profiles of urban ministries, profiles of congregations, and resources on congregational ministries in urban contexts. Especially looking for essays on church-based community organizations at present. Requires one copy of manuscript. Length requirements-- maximum, 5 pages; minimum--1/2 to 1 page. Indexed: Rel.Ind.One.

259. LUCHA/STRUGGLE
New York Circus Collective
New York Circus
Box 37
Times Square Station
New York, NY   10108

Subscription--6/yr.--$10, individuals; $20, institutions. Description of subject matter of journal--Lucha includes material from Christians involved in social change movements in Latin America, involving the Theology of Liberation, analysis of the Church of the Poor, Biblical Exercises, etc. Publishes articles in Scripture, Theology, Evangelism, Sociology of Religion. For: professors, students, laypersons. Submissions must be in English or Spanish. Accepts unsolicited articles, unsolicited reviews, dot-matrix printing, simultaneous submissions; publishes research notes, review-articles; does not accept advertising. Style of journal--New York Times Style book. Requires one copy of manuscript. Length requirements--maximum, 15 pages; minimum --. Selection process--Evaluation by the New York Circus Collective. Responds in 3 weeks. Approximate proportion of submissions accepted for publication--30 percent. Indexed: Alt. Press Ind.

260. THE OTHER SIDE
Mark Olson, Ed.
300 W. Apsley St.
Philadelphia, PA   19144

Subscription- -10/yr.--$19.75. Description of subject matter of journal--the mission of The Other Side is to nurture and stimulate Christians in their commitment to and understanding of peace, justice, and Christian discipleship, challenging structures and values that contribute to poverty and oppression. We see our task as one of empowering followers of Jesus in the ministry of the cross. We also place a high value on building community between the magazine's readers and struggling sisters and brothers around the world. Publishes articles in Ethics, Social Justice, and Peace. For: professors, students, clergy, and laypersons. Submissions must be in English. The Other Side welcomes the following kinds of manuscripts: 1) Feature articles--We publish four to six major articles per issue; 2) two to four short profiles per issue; 3) offers life-style oriented articles celebrating and/or exploring responsible living; 4) offers essays on the arts and media; 5) publishes one or two poems per issue; 6) publishes 6-8 short-stories per year; 7) welcomes reviews of new non-fiction books, of mainline and alternative films, of records (especially Christian music). Accepts unsolicited articles, unsolicited reviews, dot-matrix printing; does not accept simultaneous submissions; does not publish research notes; publishes review-articles; accepts advertising--any kind, subject to editorial judgment. Style of journal--University of Chicago Manual of Style. Requires one copy of manuscript. Length requirements--maximum, 4000 words; minimum, 200 words. Selection process--manuscripts are reviewed and evaluated by the editorial staff in light of current interests and available space. Attention is given both to content and style. Responds to a submission--normally, 2-8 weeks. Approximate proportion of submissions accepted for publication--15 percent. Indexed: Chr.Per.Ind., Rel. Ind.One.

261. THE PEACEMAKER
     Bruce H. Barnitt, Ed.
     New Zealand Christian Pacifist Society
     29 McGregors Rd.
     Christchurch 6, New Zealand

Subscription--4/yr.--$5 New Zealand. Subject matter of journal--Pacifism and peace-related issues. For: laypersons, CPS members. Submissions must be in English. Accepts unsolicited articles, unsolicited reviews, dot-matrix printing, simultaneous submissions; does not publish research notes; publishes review-articles; does not accept advertising. Seeks articles--relating peace to scripture--theology to pacifism; news of peace groups; analysis of current affairs in Christian pacifist perspective. Requires one copy of manuscript. Length requirements--maximum, 2000 words; minimum, --. Selection process--Editor and Publishing Editor decide. Approximate proportion of submissions accepted for publication--99 percent. Indexed: CERDIC.

262. PHILIPPIANIANA SACRA
     Lucio Gutierrez, O.P., Ed.
     University of Santo Tomas
     Manila, Philippines

Subscription--3/yr.--P. 45.00; $18.00, overseas. Subject matter of journal--Ethics, Sociology of Religion, Social Justice, Liberation Theology, Religion in the Philippines. Submissions must be in English. Accepts unsolicited articles and unsolicited reviews.

263. PROBE
S. Judith Vaughan, Ed.
National Assembly of Religious Women
1307 S. Wabash, Rm. 206
Chicago, IL 60605

Subscription--4 or 5/yr.--$15. Description of subject matter--Justice for women in church and society. For: women, Roman Catholics. Submissions must be in English. Sometimes accepts unsolicited articles, reviews; accepts dot-matrix printing; does not accept advertising. Style of journal--8-page newsprint tabloid. Indexed: South.Bap.Per.Ind.

264. PUEBLA
Frei Gentil Avelino Titton, O.F.M., Dir.
Caixa Postal 90023
25689 Petrópolis
Rio de Janeiro, Brazil

Subscription--4/yr.--$35.00. Subject matter of journal--Ethics, Sociology of Religion, Social Justice, and Liberation Theology. Submissions must be in Spanish.

265. RECONCILIATION INTERNATIONAL
James H. Forest, Ed.
Cheryl Cayford, Managing Editor
International Fellowship of Reconciliation
Hof van Sonoy 15-17
1811 LD Alkmaar, Netherlands

Subscription--5/yr.--$20. Description of subject matter of journal--Nonviolent direct action for change--peace and justice issues--interviews with people who are involved in nonviolent direct action--different religious ways to nonviolence. Publishes articles in interreligious nonviolence, also articles in such areas as Ethics, Theology, Sociology of Religion, World Religions, Philosophy of Religion, Judaism, Islam, Hinduism, Buddhism, and Eastern Religions. For: professors, students, laypersons, and activists. Submissions must be in English. Sometimes accepts unsolicited articles; does not accept unsolicited reviews, dot-matrix printing; does not publish research notes; publishes review-articles; accepts advertising--usually exchanges with other journals/magazines. Seeks positive and human descriptions of nonviolent activity for peace and justice--from a religious or non-religious point of view; deals also with life-styles and consequences of nonviolent activity. Type of article especially seeking--interviews--mostly with people who would not receive attention in the mass media. Also information on different religious backgrounds to nonviolence. Style of journal--more colloquial, optimistic, up-beat; not too intellectual. Requires one copy of manuscript. Length requirements--maximum, 5000 words; minimum, 500 words. Selection process--Editorial Committee chooses themes for the coming issues, then each member of the committee can submit articles to be circulated among the committee members. The committee then discusses them, chooses what it wants to use, and seeks other material to fill gaps. Responds in 1-4 months. Comments--Journal is mostly an amateur effort; sometimes very in-house, but open to new ideas and criticisms--very informal. Indexed: Alt.Press Ind.

266. SOCIAL JUSTICE REVIEW
Rev. John H. Miller, C.S.C., S.T.D.
Catholic Central Union of America
3835 Westminster Pl.
St. Louis, MO 63108

Subscription--6/mo.--$15. Publishes articles in Social Science, Scripture, Ethics, Church History, Theology, Pastoral Counseling, Missions, Psychology of Religion, Sociology of Religion, and Religious Education. For: professors, students, laypersons. Submissions must be in English. Accepts unsolicited articles, simultaneous submissions; sometimes accepts unsolicited reviews; publishes review-articles; does not accept advertising. Style of journal--Webster's 9th Collegiate Dictionary. Requires one copy of manuscript. Seeks--intelligent, readable articles that contribute to the human condition, society, human dignity, written according to the authentic teaching of the Catholic Church. Responds in 2 weeks. Indexed: Cath.Ind., CERDIC.

267. SOCIAL WORK AND CHRISTIANITY
David A. Sherwood, Ed.
North American Association of Christians in Social Work
Box 90
St. Davids, PA 19087-0913

Subscription--2/yr.--$10, institutions; membership--individuals. Publishes articles in Ethics, Pastoral Counseling, Sociology of Religion, major issues concerning the relationship of social work and Christianity. For: professors, students, and social workers. Submissions must be in English. Accepts unsolicited articles, unsolicited reviews; accepts dot-matrix printing; publishes research notes and review-articles; accepts advertising--agency, school, publications, conferences, workshops. Seeks contributions that bring to light concerns of Christians in the ongoing integration of faith and practice, as well as professional concerns which have particular relevance to Christianity. Seeks articles whose content is relevant to major issues concerning the relationship of social work (human helping) and Christianity; literary merit; conciseness and clarity; inclusive language. Selection process--articles are reviewed anonymously by at least 3 members of the Editorial Board. Style of journal--in-text referencing. Requires 4 copies of manuscript. Length requirements--maximum, 20 pages; minimum, 2 pages. Comments: Include an abstract of not more than 150 words with submission. Responds to a submission--30 days, acknowledgment; 3-6 months for final decision. Approximate proportion of submissions accepted for publication--60-75 percent after appropriate revision. Indexed: Chr.Per.Ind.

268. SOJOURNERS
Jim Wallis, Ed.
Box 29272
Washington, DC   20017

Subscription--11/yr.--$15. Subject matter of journal--Justice and Peace Advocacy, Christian Spirituality and Community; Christian Feminism and Discipleship. For: professors, students, laypersons, and clergy. Submissions must be in English. Sometimes accepts unsolicited articles, unsolicited reviews; accepts dot-matrix printing; does not accept simultaneous submissions; does not publish research notes; publishes review-articles; accepts advertising--religious publishers, conference centers, colleges, and seminaries. Seeks news articles, poetry, and features. Type of article that is particularly sought--Christian feminism features by women. Style of journal--non-academic, accessible writing; inclusive language editing standard. Requires 1 copy of manuscript. Length requirements--maximum, 15-18 pages, typed; minimum, 1 page. Selection process--feature articles are sent to the manuscript editor for consideration and circulated to the editorial staff if deemed a possibility. After an evaluation by editors, articles are accepted or rejected. Poetry is handled the same way. News articles and cultural reviews are picked by Department head. Responds in 6-8 weeks. Approximate proportion of submissions that are accepted for publication--5 percent. Indexed: Rel. Per., Alt.Press Ind., Chr.Per.Ind., Rel.Ind.One.

269. WITNESS
Mary Lou Suhor, Ed.
Episcopal Church Publishing Co.
Box 359
Ambler, PA   19002

Subscription--11/yr.--$15. Description of subject matter of journal--justice and peace issues--racism, sexism, imperialism, classism--informed by liberation theologies. Publishes articles in Ethics,

Theology, Religious Education, Social Justice and Peace Issues confronting the church today; consciousness-raising. For: professors, students, laypersons, all interested in the Social Gospel Message. Accepts unsolicited articles, dot-matrix printing, simultaneous submissions; does not accept unsolicited reviews; does not publish research notes or review-articles; does not accept advertising. Submissions must be in English. We are an advocacy journal for justice issues. We serve a liberal to radical Christian constituency. Requires 1 copy of manuscript. Length requirements--maximum, 1500-2000 words; minimum--3-4 typewritten pages. Selection process-- Editorial Committee decides. Responds to a submission--immediate acknowledgment; time varies according to how backed up committee is. Indexed: Rel.Ind.One.

OTHER JOURNALS THAT PUBLISH ARTICLES IN SOCIAL JUSTICE; SOCIAL CHANGE

13. THEOLOGY

270. AMERICAN JOURNAL OF THEOLOGY & PHILOSOPHY
Dr. Larry Axel, Ed.
Purdue University
Department of Philosophy
West Lafayette, IN   47907

Subscription--3/yr.--$9, individuals; $15, libraries and organizations; $20, foreign subscription. Description of subject matter
of journal--Liberal religious thought in America; the "Chicago School"
of theology; the interface of theology and philosophy; naturalism in
theology. Publishes articles in Theology and Philosophy of Religion.
Accepts unsolicited articles, dot-matrix printing; does not accept unsolicited reviews, simultaneous submissions; does not publish research
notes or review-articles; does not accept advertising. For: professors, students, laypersons. Submissions must be in English.
Seeks scholarly articles, with no confessional stance assumed. Especially seeking articles that nourish an American dialogue between
theology and philosophy. Style of journal--scholarly format, footnotes using traditional "dissertation" format; usually 3-4 articles,
followed by Book Notes. Requires 3 copies of manuscript. Length
requirements--maximum, 25 pages. Selection process--peer review by
referees (30 members of our Editorial Board). Responds in 2-6
months. Approximate proportion of submissions accepted for publi-
cation--15 percent. Indexed: Chr.Per.Ind., Rel.&Theol.Abstr.

271. ANTONIANUM
Isaac Vázquez Janeiro, Ed.
Pontificio Ateneo Antonianum
Via Merulana 124
00185 Rome, Italy

Subscription--4/yr.--$30. Description of subject matter of
journal--religio-philosophical and theological arguments. Publishes
articles in Scripture, Ethics, Church History, Theology, Evangelism,
Church Administration, Pastoral Counseling, Missions, Psychology of
Religion, Sociology of Religion, World Religions, Philosophy of Religion, Judaism, Islam, Hinduism, Buddhism, Eastern Religions,
Religious Education. For: professors, students. Submissions must
be in French, German, Spanish, English, or Italian. Seeks researched,
scholarly articles. Style of journal--scientific style. Requires original

copy of manuscript. Length requirements--maximum, 40 pages; minimum, 15 pages. Selection process--The articles are submitted first to an expert and then to the Direction Council for the final decision. Responds in 2 months. Comments: the article must be accompanied with 1 summary. Indexed: Hist.Abstr., Old Test.Abstr., New Test. Abstr., Rel.&Theol.Abstr.

272. AUGUSTINIANUM
V. Grossi, Ed.
Institutum Patristicum Augustinianum
Via del S. Uffizio 25
00193 Rome, Italy

Subscription--3/yr.--45,000 lire. Publishes articles in Church History, Theology, Patristics. Submissions can be in any language. Sometimes accepts unsolicited articles; publishes research notes. Requires one copy of manuscript. Length requirements--maximum, 25 pages; minimum, 10 pages. Responds in 3 months. Approximate proportion of submissions accepted for publication--7/10. Indexed: Old Test.Abstr., New Test.Abstr.

273. AUSTRALASIAN CATHOLIC RECORD
Rev. F. Mecham, Ed.
Editorial Board
St. Patrick's College
Manly, New South Wales, Australia

Subscription--4/yr.--$20. Description of subject matter of journal--Theology, particularly in an Australasian context. For: laypersons. Submissions must be in English. Accepts unsolicited articles; does not accept unsolicited reviews, dot-matrix printing, and simultaneous submissions; does not publish research notes; publishes review-articles; accepts advertising--details from Advertising Manager, ACR St. Patrick's College mainly. Seeks articles in theology suitable for clergy. Style of journal--simple, reasonably short. Requires one copy of manuscript. Length requirements--maximum, 5000 words; minimum, none. Selection process--Editorial Board (6). Responds within six months. Approximate proportion of submissions that are accepted for publication--one in five. Indexed: Cath.Ind., Rel.&Theol.Abstr., Canon Law Abstr., New Test.Abstr.

274. CAHIERS DE JOSEPHOLOGIE
Roland Gauthier, Ed.
Oratoire Saint-Joseph du Mont-Royal
3800 Chemin Reine-Marie
Montreal H3V 1H6, Canada

Subscription--2/yr.--$20 Canadian. Description of subject

matter of journal--Everything in relation with St. Joseph, the spouse
of Mary, and in relation with the Holy Family (Jesus, Mary and
Joseph). Publishes articles in Scripture, Church History, and Theology. For: professors, students, and laypersons. Submissions
must be in English or French. Sometimes accepts unsolicited articles,
unsolicited reviews; does not accept dot-matrix printing; accepts
simultaneous submissions; publishes research notes and review-
articles; does not accept advertising. Seeks articles of scientific
research with complete footnotes. Requires 2 copies of manuscript.
Style of journal--that of a scientific journal with proofs in support
of each affirmation. Length requirements--maximum, 50 typed double-
spaced pages; minimum, 15 typed double-spaced pages. Selection
process--Each article is submitted to a committee of 3 persons. Responds in 1-2 years. Approximate proportion of submissions that
are accepted for publication--70 percent. Text in English and French.
Indexed: Cath.Ind., Old Test.Abstr., New Test.Abstr., Rel.&
Theol.Abstr.

275. CANON LAW ABSTRACTS
      Rev. Ivan Payne, Ed.
      Canon Law Society of Great Britain and Ireland
      Diocesan Offices
      Archbishop's House
      Dublin 9, Ireland

Subscription--2/yr.--5 pounds. Subject matter of journal--
Canon Law. For: professors, students, laypersons. Submissions
must be in English. Does not accept unsolicited articles, unsolicited
reviews, dot-matrix printing, simultaneous submissions; does not
publish research notes or review-articles; does not accept advertising. Seeks summaries of articles, documents, etc. relating to
Canon Law which are published in other journals. Requires one copy
of manuscript. Approximately 95 percent of all submissions are accepted for publication. Indexed: Old Test.Abstr.

276. CARMELUS
      Joachim Smet, Ed.
      Institutum Carmelitanum
      Via Sforza Pallavicini 10
      00193 Rome, Italy

Subscription--2/yr.--$25. Description of subject matter of
journal--Theology (especially spirituality and Mariology) and history
(especially Carmelite). Seeks original research or articles of permanent reference value. Especially seeking the above articles as related to the Carmelite Order. For: professors and students. Submissions must be in French, German, Spanish, English, Italian, Latin,
or Portuguese. Sometimes accepts unsolicited articles, unsolicited reviews; accepts dot-matrix printing; does not accept simultaneous

submissions; publishes research notes and review-articles; does not accept advertising. Style of journal--style sheet sent on request. Requires one copy of manuscript. Selection process--Editorial Board. Responds to a submission in 1-2 months. Approximate proportion of submissions accepted for publication--70-75 percent. Indexed: Cath.Ind.

277. CHICAGO STUDIES
     Rev. George J. Dyer, Ed.
     Civitas dei Foundation
     Box 665
     Mundelein, IL   60060

Subscription--3/yr.--$12.50. Description of subject matter--theology and allied topics. Publishes articles in Scripture, Ethics, Church History, Theology, Sociology of Religion, World Religions, and Religious Education. For: professors and students. Submissions must be in English. Accepts unsolicited articles; does not accept unsolicited reviews, dot-matrix printing, simultaneous submissions; does not publish research notes or review-articles; does not accept advertising. Seeks a non-technical presentation of research that has pastoral relevance. Style of journal--non-technical, no footnotes. Requires 1 copy of manuscript. Length requirements--maximum, 3000-5000 words; minimum, 3000 words. Selection process--Editorial Board review. Responds in about 6 weeks. Approximate proportion of submissions that are accepted for publication--10 percent. Indexed: Cath.Ind., New Test.Abstr., Old Test.Abstr., Canon Law Abstr. Parent organization--Faculty of St. Mary of the Lake Seminary.

278. CUESTIONES TEOLOGICAS MEDELLIN
     Gonzalo Soto Posado, Dir.
     Alberto Ramírez Zuluaga
     Faculdad de Teología U.P.B.
     Apartado Aéreo 1178
     Medellín, Colombia S.A.

Subscription--3/yr. Subject matter of journal--Scripture, Church History, and Theology. Submissions must be in Spanish. Parent Organization--Escuela de Ciencias Eclesiásticas de la Universidad Pontificia Bolivariana.

279. DIVINITAS
     Pontificia Accademia Teologica Romana
     Palazzo Canonici
     00120 Vatican City, Italy

Subscription--3/yr.--$24. Subject matter of journal--Scripture,

Ethics, Theology. Sometimes accepts unsolicited articles, unsolicited
reviews; does not accept dot-matrix printing, simultaneous submissions; does not publish research notes; publishes review-articles;
does not accept advertising. For: professors, students, and laypersons. Submissions must be in French, Spanish, Italian, or Latin.
Seeks articles on dogmatics. Especially seeking articles concerning
St. Thomas Aquinas. Style of journal--academic and orthodox. Requires one copy of manuscript. Length requirements--maximum, 20
pages; minimum --. Selection process--Selection based on quality
of the article, the good name of the author, originality, and orthodoxy. Responds to a submission in 14 days. Comments--always
send a query before submitting the manuscript. Indexed: New
Test.Abstr., Rel.&Theol.Abstr.

280. DIVUS THOMAS
     Perini Giuseppe, Ed.
     Collegio Alberoni
     Via Emilia Parmense 77
     29100 Piacenza, Italy

     Subscription--4/yr.--$14. Subject matter of journal--Philoso-
phy and Theology, especially Thomistic doctrine. For: professors,
students. Submissions must be in French, German, Spanish, English,
or Italian. Sometimes accepts unsolicited articles, unsolicited reviews;
does not accept dot-matrix printing, simultaneous submissions; publishes research notes, review-articles; does not accept advertising;
text appears in the above languages. Seeks scientific contributions
to the advancement of the doctrine in Theology, Philosophy, Ethics.
Especially seeking articles according to the Thomistic principles and
doctrine. Style of journal--scholarly. Length requirements--maxi-
mum, 50 typed pages; minimum, 10 pages. Selection process cri-
teria--scientific, plain, not opposite to the Catholic doctrine. Responds in 30 days. Approximate proportion of submissions accepted
for publication--60 percent. Indexed: Old Test.Abstr., New Test.
Abstr.

281. EPHEMERIDES MARIOLOGICAE
     Claretian Fathers
     Calle Buen Suceso no. 22
     28008 Madrid, Spain

     Subscription--3 or 4/yr.--$22. Description of subject matter
of journal--all the implications of Marian doctrine (Mariology): Biblical, patristic, historical, ecumenical, folk-traditional.... Sometimes
accepts unsolicited articles and unsolicited reviews; does not accept
dot-matrix printing or simultaneous submissions; publishes research
notes; does not publish review-articles; does not accept advertising.
For: professors. Submissions must be in French, German, Spanish,
English, or Italian. Seeks scientifically documented articles. Style

of journal--style "ideas." Requires one copy of manuscript. Length requirements--maximum, 30 pages; minimum, 10 pages. Selection process--Editorial Committee makes a decision. Indexed: New Test. Abstr.

282. EPHEMERIDES THEOLOGICAE LOVANIENSES

Administration:	Redaction:
Peeters	Universiteitsbibliotheek
B.P. 41	Ladeuzeplein 21
B-3000 Leuven, Belgium	B-3000 Leuven, Belgium

Subscription--4/yr. (issues 2-3 in one volume)--2000 Bfrancs; $50 USA. Seeks articles on biblical exegesis--scientific theology. Subject matter of journal--Scripture, Church History, Ethics, and Theology. For: professors and students. Submissions must be in French, English, or German. Sometimes accepts unsolicited articles; does not accept unsolicited reviews; accepts dot-matrix printing; does not accept simultaneous submissions, publishes research notes and review-articles; does not accept advertising. Requires two copies of manuscript, footnoted articles. Length requirements for submission--maximum--12,500 words; minimum--2500 words. Responds to a submission in 4 months. Approximate proportion of submissions accepted for publication--40 percent. Comments: Fasc. 1 and 4 include articles, notes and miscellaneous, book reviews, bulletin; Fasc. 2-3 (Elenchus Bibliographicus in one volume) a yearly (500 pages) bibliography of theological and canonical publications. Selection process--Editorial Board. Indexed: Old Test.Abstr., Rel.Per., New Test.Abstr., Rel.&Theol.Abstr., Rel.Ind.One.

283. ETUDES THEOLOGIQUES ET RELIGIEUSES
A. Gounelle, Ed.
D. Lys, Ed.
Institut Protestant de Theologie
13 rue Louis-Perrier
3400 Montpellier, France

Subscription--4/yr.--$20. Subject matter of journal--Scripture, Ethics, Church History, and Theology. For: students, laypersons, ministers, and priests. Submissions must be in French. Sometimes accepts unsolicited articles; does not accept unsolicited reviews, simultaneous submissions; accepts dot-matrix printing; publishes research notes, review-articles; accepts advertising. Seeks--theological articles putting the result of fundamental research at the disposal of the educated reader. Style of journal--not too technical, but with a fair amount of references. Requires one copy of manuscript. Length requirements--maximum, 12,000 words; minimum, 4000 words. Selection process--If the editor has any doubt, he submits the article to one or sometimes two specialists. Responds in 5-6 months. Approximate proportion of submissions accepted for

publication--1/3. Indexed: Bull.Signal, Curr.Cont., Old Test.
Abstr., Rel.Per., Arts&Hum.Cit.Ind., New Test.Abstr., Rel.Ind.
One.

284. GREGORIANUM
     Jacques Dupuis, S.J., Ed.
     Gregorian University Press
     Piazza della Pilotta, 35
     00187 Rome, Italy

Subscription--4/yr.--$45. Description of subject matter of
journal--theological and philosophical. Publishes articles in Scripture, Ethics, Theology, Evangelism, Missions, World Religions. For:
professors and students. Submissions must be in French, German,
Spanish, English, or Italian. Accepts unsolicited articles; does not
accept unsolicited reviews, dot-matrix printing, simultaneous submissions; publishes research notes and review-articles; does not accept
advertising. Requires 2 copies of manuscript. Length require-
ments--maximum, 40 pages; minimum, 15 pages. Selection process--
Editorial Board. Responds to a submission one month after receipt.
Approximate proportion of submissions accepted for publication--
50 percent. Parent Organization--Pontificia Università Gregoriana.
Indexed: Bull.Signal, Cath.Ind., Old Test.Abstr., Rel.Per., Canon
Law Abstr., New Test.Abstr., Phil.Ind., Rel.Ind.One, Rel.&Theol.
Abstr.

285. HEYTHROP JOURNAL
     Joseph Munitiz, Ed.
     Heythrop College (University of London)
     11 Cavendish Square
     London W1M 0AN, England

Subscription--4/yr.--$30. Description of subject matter of
journal--Theological and philosophical research. Publishes articles
in Scripture, Ethics, Church History, Theology, Psychology of Religion, Sociology of Religion, World Religions, Philosophy of Religion,
Philosophy--Metaphysics, Logic. For: professors, students. Submissions must be in English. Accepts unsolicited articles, dot-matrix
printing; does not accept unsolicited reviews, simultaneous submissions; publishes research notes and review-articles; accepts adver-
tising--mainly publishers. Seeking articles that are academically
sound, well researched and also original at a university level. Type
of article especially seeking--indispensable contribution that forwards
research. Manuscripts should be free from jargon, clear, precise.
One copy of manuscript is required. Length Requirements--maximum,
8000 words; minimum, 3000 words. Selection process--When in doubt
about accepting or rejecting, the editor consults two members of
staff; consultation always used before acceptance; criteria as above
but also subject to available space. Responds in 2 months.

Approximate proportion of submissions that are accepted for publication--30 percent. Comments--the journal is published by Heythrop College (Univ. of London), a Roman Catholic Institution run by Jesuits with the help of ecumenical lay staff. Indexed: Cath.Ind., Curr.Cont., Old Test.Abstr., Arts&Hum.Cit.Ind., Canon Law Abstr., Int.Z.Bibelwiss., New Test.Abstr., Phil.Ind., Rel.&Theol.Abstr.

286. HORIZONS
Walter E. Conn, Ed.
College Theology Society
c/o Villanova University
Villanova, PA 19085

Subscription--2/yr.--$12, nonmembers; $20, institutions. Description of subject matter--religious studies and theology. For: professors. Submissions must be in English. Accepts unsolicited articles, dot-matrix printing; does not accept unsolicited reviews, simultaneous submissions; does not publish research notes; publishes review-articles; accepts advertising--book publishers. Seeks articles that are scholarly, but general, not specialist--technical. Requires 4 copies of manuscript. Length requirements--maximum, c. 30 pages; minimum, c. 15 pages. Selection process--blind, refereed. Responds in 6-8 weeks (usually). Indexed: Cath.Ind., Old Test.Abstr., Rel.Per., SSCI, New Test.Abstr., Rel.Ind.One, Rel.&Theol.Abstr.

287. JOURNAL OF THEOLOGICAL STUDIES
Prof. M. D. Hooker, Ed.
The Revd. Professor M. F. Wiles, Ed.
Oxford University Press
Walton St.
Oxford OX2 6DP, England

Subscription--2/yr.--$80. Subject matter of journal--Detailed, research articles in Scripture, Church History, Theology, and Philosophy of Religion. For: professors and students. Submissions must be in English (occasionally in French or German). Accepts unsolicited articles; does not accept unsolicited reviews, simultaneous submissions; accepts dot-matrix printing; does not publish research notes or review-articles; accepts advertising. Requires one copy of manuscript. Length requirements--no specific limits. Selection process--Editorial decision on advice of reader. Indexed: Br.Hum.Ind., Curr.Cont., Old Test.Abstr., Rel.Per., Arts&Hum. Cit.Ind., New Test.Abstr., Rel.Ind.One, Rel.&Theol.Abstr.

288. MARIANUM
Ignazio M. Calabuig, OSM, Ed.
Pontificia Facolta Teologica Marianum

Viale Trenta Aprile 6
00153 Rome, Italy

Subscription--4/yr.--$24. Description of subject matter of journal--The journal is of a theological nature, focusing on the figure of Mary, Mother of Jesus, from a theological, historical, scientific viewpoint. For: professors and students. Submissions must be in French, German, Spanish, English, Italian, Latin, or Portuguese. Accepts unsolicited articles, unsolicited reviews; does not accept dot-matrix printing, simultaneous submissions; does not publish research notes; publishes review-articles; accepts advertising. Seeks articles that look at Mary from an academic viewpoint, reflecting current research and thought on Mary. Especially looking for--articles that are well-written, academic in tone, well researched, which focus on the thrust of the journal. Style of journal--academic. Requires 1 copy of manuscript. Length requirements--maximum, 60 pages; minimum, 5 pages. Selection process--the articles should be well written, reflecting research on the part of the author and falling within the scope of the journal. Approximate proportion of submissions accepted for publication--80 percent. Comments: We do ask that submissions be well presented--well typed and laid out. Indexed: New Test.Abstr.

289. METHOD: JOURNAL OF LONERGAN STUDIES
Mark D. Morelli, Ed.
Loyola Marymount University
Department of Philosophy
7101 W. 80 St.
Los Angeles, CA   90045

Subscription--Sept.-April--$12, individuals; $20, institutions. Description of subject matter of journal--Methodology, Interdisciplinary, Lonergan Studies. Publishes articles in Ethics, Theology, and Philosophy. For: professors and students. Submissions must be in English. Accepts unsolicited articles, dot-matrix printing; does not accept unsolicited reviews, simultaneous submissions, publishes research notes and review-articles; accepts advertising--conferences, new publications, journals. Seeks research articles, comparative studies. Submissions should be philosophically sophisticated and exhibit careful scholarship. Especially looking for articles which explore the relation of Lonergan's work to recent and contemporary philosophical and theological work. Style of journal--Chicago Manual of Style. Requires one copy of manuscript. Length requirements--maximum, 25 double-spaced pages. Selection process--All submissions are refereed. Final decision is the Editor's. Refereeing is blind. Comments are provided to those who submit articles. Responds in 1-2 months. Approximate proportion of submissions accepted for publication--15-20 percent. Indexed: Phil.Ind.

290. NEUE ZEITSCHRIFT FUER SYSTEMATISCHE THEOLOGIE UND
RELIGIONSPHILOSOPHIE
Prof. Dr. Oswald Bayer, Ed.
Universitaet Tuebingen
Institut fuer Christliche Gesellschaftslehre
Haelderlinstrasse 16
Tuebingen, West Germany (B.R.D.)

Subscription--3/yr.--$46.40. Publishes articles in Theology and
Philosophy of Religion. Submissions must be in German or English.
Accepts unsolicited articles; sometimes accepts unsolicited reviews;
accepts advertising. Selection process--Editorial Board makes a de-
cision based on the recommendation of readers. Indexed: Rel.Per.,
Rel.Ind.One, Rel.&Theol.Abstr.

291. THE NIGERIAN JOURNAL OF THEOLOGY
Rev. Fr. Theophilus Okere, Ed.
Seat of Wisdom Seminary
Box 2124
Owerri, Imo State, Nigeria

Subscription--2/yr.--$6.00. Subject matter of journal--Scrip-
ture, Ethics, Church History, Theology, Pastoral Counseling, Missions, Philosophy of Religion, Islam, Liturgy, Ecumenism, African
Traditional Religion, Religion and Culture. Accepts unsolicited articles and unsolicited reviews. Submissions must be in English.

292. PERSPECTIVA TEOLOGICA
Francisco Taborda, Ed.
Caixa Postal 5047
31611 Belo Horizonte-MG, Brazil

Subscription--3/yr.--$20. Subject matter of journal--Theology.
For: clergy. Sometimes accepts unsolicited articles and unsolicited
reviews; does not accept dot-matrix printing or simultaneous submissions; publishes research notes and review-articles; does not accept
advertising. Submissions must be in French, German, Spanish,
English, Italian or Portuguese. Seeks articles that are timely. Requires 2 copies of manuscript. Length requirements--maximum, 25
pages; minimum, 5 pages. Selection process--articles are reviewed
by a committee composed of professors from the School of Theology.
Responds to a submission in 2-3 months. Approximate proportion of
submissions accepted for publication--50 percent. Indexed: CERDIC.

293. REVISTA LATINOAMERICANA DE TEOLOGIA
I. Ellacuría, Dir.
Universidad Centroamericana José Simeón Cañas
Apartado 01-575
San Salvador, El Salvador

Subscription--3/yr.--$12.00. Subject matter of journal--Scripture, Church History, Theology, and Sociology of Religion. Accepts unsolicited articles and unsolicited reviews. Submissions must be in Spanish.

294. LA REVUE REFORMEE
Paul Wells, Ed.
Faculte de Theologie Réformée
33 av. Jules Ferry
13100 Aix en Provence, France

Subscription--4-5/yr.--120 francs. Description of subject matter of journal--Reformed theology addressing current issues. Publishes articles in Scripture, Ethics, Church History, Theology, and Evangelism. For: students, laypersons, and pastors. Submissions must be in French. Sometimes accepts unsolicited articles and unsolicited reviews; accepts dot-matrix printing and simultaneous submissions; does not publish research notes; publishes review-articles; does not accept advertising. Seeks popular articles on theological or ethical topics. Style of journal--reasonable, not technical. Requires one copy of manuscript. Length requirements--maximum, 5000 words; minimum, 2000 words. Selection process--articles are chosen according to their doctrinal value as contributions to the development of Reformed faith. Liberal, neo-orthodox or liberation theology not considered. Responds in 2-4 weeks. Approximate proportion of submissions accepted for publication--12-15 percent. Indexed: Old Test.Abstr., New Test.Abstr.

295. REVUE THOMISTE
Père Marie-Vincent Leroy, Ed.
Ecole de Theologie
1 av. Lacordaire
F 31078 Toulouse, France

Subscription--4/yr.--450 francs. Description of subject matter of journal--doctrinal review of theology and philosophy. Publishes articles in Scripture, Ethics, Church History, Theology, Philosophy of Religion, Judaism, and Islam. For: professors, students, laypersons. Submissions must be in French. Accepts unsolicited articles, simultaneous submissions; does not accept unsolicited reviews, dot-matrix printing; publishes research notes and review-articles; accepts advertising. Description of type of article that is sought--Biblical Theology, Patristic Theology, Speculative Theology, Philosophy, Doctrinal History. Especially seeking studies on the work and thought of St. Thomas Aquinas. Style of journal--well-referenced. Requires one copy of manuscript. Length requirements--40 double-spaced pages; minimum, 15 pages. Selection process--Editorial review; in consultation with special readers. Responds in about 3 months. Indexed: Bull.Signal, New Test.Abstr., Phil.Ind.

296. SCOTTISH JOURNAL OF THEOLOGY
A. I. C. Heron, Ed.
A. E. Lewis, Ed.
I. R. Torrance, Ed.
Scottish Academic Press Ltd.
33 Montgomery St.
Edinburgh EH7 5JX, Scotland

Subscription--4/yr.--$30, individuals; $70, institutions. Description of subject matter of journal--all aspects of systematic, Biblical and applied theology, of international and ecumenical significance.
Publishes articles in Scripture, Ethics, Church History, Theology,
and Philosophy of Religion. For: professors, students, laypersons,
and clergy. Submissions must be in English. Accepts unsolicited
articles, dot-matrix printing; does not accept unsolicited reviews,
simultaneous submissions; does not publish research notes; publishes
review-articles; accepts advertising--publications. Seeks articles
that are original and of relevance to the above. Requires three
copies of manuscript. Length requirements--maximum, 10,000 words;
average, 5000 words. Selection process--All submissions read and
adjudicated by all three editors; joint decision reached--sometimes
after guidance from consulting editors. Responds in 2-3 months.
Approximate proportion of submissions accepted for publication--50
percent. Indexed: Curr.Cont., Old Test.Abstr., Rel.Per., Arts&
Hum.Cit.Ind., New Test.Abstr., Rel.Ind.One, Rel.&Theol.Abstr.

297. SERVIR
Imprenta Venecia, S.A.
Mártires de la Conquista No. 20
Tacubaya, México 18, D.F.

Subscription--4/yr.--$15; overseas, $25. Subject matter of
journal--Ethics, Theology, and Sociology of Religion. Submissions
must be in Spanish.

298. STROMATA--EX CIENCIA Y FE
Jorge R. Seibold, Ed.
Asociacion Civil Loyola
Avda. Mitre 3226
1663 San Miguel, Argentina

Subscription--2 (double issues)/yr.--$20/ Latinamerica sub-
scribers--$15. Description of subject matter of journal--Theology,
Philosophy, Research articles and notes, Book reviews, Latin American published philosophy and theology reviews articles index. Sometimes accepts unsolicited articles and unsolicited reviews; accepts
dot-matrix printing; does not accept simultaneous submissions; publishes research notes and review articles; accepts advertising--Re-
ligion-Theology-Philosophy books, reviews, meetings, etc. Style of

journal--thorough research. For: professors, students, laypersons.
Submissions are usually in Spanish but may be in French, English,
or Italian. Requires 1 copy of manuscript. Length requirements--
none. Selection process--Review Council judges the quality and opportunity of publishing. Responds to a submission in 4-6 months.

299. STUDIA CANONICA
Francis G. Morrisey, Ed.
Saint Paul University
Faculty of Canon Law
223 Main St.
Ottawa, Ontario K1S 1C4, Canada

Subscription--2/yr.--$20 Canadian. Description of subject mat-
ter--commentaries on the Canon Law of the Roman Catholic Church;
Church Administration. For: professors and Canonists. Submissions must be in English or French. Sometimes accepts unsolicited
articles, unsolicited reviews; accepts dot-matrix printing (for manuscripts); does not accept simultaneous submissions; does not publish
research notes or review-articles; does not accept advertising. Type
of article that Studia Canonica seeks--studies on specific points of
Canon Law. Especially seeking--articles on 1983 Latin Code of Canon
Law and on proposed Oriental Code of Canon Law. Style of journal--
scholarly journal, footnoted articles. Requires 1 copy of manuscript.
Length requirements--maximum, about 75 double-spaced pages; minimum, 20 double-spaced pages. Selection process--Reading Committee. Responds in 4-5 months. Approximate proportion of submissions accepted for publication--if solicited, most; if unsolicited, 50
percent. Text in English, French, Latin. Indexed: Cath.Ind.,
Canon Law Abstr.

300. TEILHARD REVIEW & JOURNAL OF CREATIVE EVOLUTION
Michael Le Morvan, Ed.
Teilhard Centre for the Future of Man
23 Kensington Square
London W83 5HN, England

Subscription--3/yr.--$12. Description of subject matter of
journal--articles within our fields of interest which are well written
for generally intelligent but largely nonspecialist readership. Publishes articles in Theology, research material on Teilhard de Chardin,
special interests in Religion and Science, Ecology and Conservation,
Liberation Theology. For: wide spectrum. Submissions must be in
English. Seeks generally well-written articles, which fall within the
journal's areas of concern and which will inform and provoke its
readers. Accepts unsolicited articles; does not accept unsolicited
reviews and simultaneous submissions; publishes research notes and
review-articles; does not accept advertising. Especially looking for
articles in the areas of Science and Religion; Philosophical/

Theological/Spiritual Basis of Ecology/Conservation. Style of journal--straight forward--mainly essay style. Occasionally poems are published. Two copies of manuscript are required. Length requirements--maximum, 6000 words; minimum, 2000 words--however, shorter "notes" would be acceptable. Selection process--Editor reads the articles; some are rejected at this point. Otherwise if doubtful, they will be sent to one or more referees for their comments before a decision is made. Responds in 6-9 months, unless article is borderline. Comments--The title of the journal may be changed in the next 12 months. Indexed: Cath.Ind.

301. THEOLOGIA EVANGELICA
     Prof. J. A. Loader, Ed.
     University of South Africa
     Faculty of Theology
     Box 392
     Pretoria 0001, South Africa

Subscription--3/yr.--R.7.20. Publishes articles in Theology. For: professors and students. Submissions must be in English or Afrikaans (with English abstracts). Accepts unsolicited articles, dot-matrix printing; sometimes accepts unsolicited reviews; does not accept simultaneous submissions; publishes research notes and review-articles; does not accept advertising. Seeks original research articles; articles on currently topical religious/ecclesiastical issues (primarily in South Africa but not exclusively); preferably accessible to students. Style of journal--scholarly but accessible. Selection process--Editorial Board consists of representatives of different disciplines in theology--Each selects those contributions appropriate for publication. Editor has final say in cases of doubt/differences of opinion. Responds in 6 months (in ideal circumstances). Approximate proportion of submissions accepted for publication--75 percent. Indexed: New Test.Abstr., Rel.Ind.One.

302. THEOLOGIAI SZEMLE
     Dr. Kalman Tarr, Editor-in-Chief
     Magyarországi Egyhazak Ökumenikus Tanácsa
     Szabadság tér 2
     1054 Budapest, Hungary

Subscription--12/yr. Description of subject matter of journal--academic material on theology. Publishes articles in Scripture; Ethics; Church History; Theology; Psychology of Religion; Sociology of Religion; Philosophy of Religion; Literary Criticism (secular and sacred literature). For: professors, students, and pastors. Submissions must be in German or English. Accepts unsolicited articles, unsolicited reviews, dot-matrix printing, simultaneous submissions; publishes research notes and review-articles. Accepts advertising. Seeks new publications in above themes. Especially looking for articles in ecclesiology. Style of journal--academic. Requires 2 copies of manuscript. Length requirements--maximum, 25 pages; minimum, 4 pages. Selection process--Editor-in-Chief, Dr. Kalman Tarr, makes a final decision in consultation with a board of advisors. Responds in 3 months. Approximate proportion of submissions accepted for publication--70 percent. Indexed: Hist.Abstr.

303. THEOLOGICAL STUDIES
Walter J. Burghardt, Ed.
Theological Studies, Inc.
Georgetown University
37th and "O" Sts., N.W.
Washington, DC 20057

Subscription--4/yr.--$14, U.S.; $17, Canada and foreign. Description of subject matter--Scholarly research relating to Scripture, theology, religious studies, ethical and moral issues, world religions. Publishes articles in Scripture, Ethics, Church History, Theology, Psychology of Religion, Sociology of Religion, World Religions, Philosophy of Religion, Judaism, Islam, Hinduism, Buddhism, Eastern Religions and Religious Education. For professors, students, and laypersons. Submissions must be in English. Accepts unsolicited articles; sometimes accepts unsolicited reviews; does not accept simultaneous submissions; publishes research notes and review-articles; accepts advertising--related to theology/religion in some way. Seeking articles that make a contribution to the development of theology. Type of article, especially looking for--Biblical, historical, systematic, pastoral. Style of journal--Style booklet, available on request. Requires that 2 copies be submitted. Length requirements--maximum, 20,000 words; minimum, 500 (for notes). Selection process--evaluation by competent scholars. Length of time to respond to a submission--varies, depending on return of evaluations; c. 3 months. Approximate proportion of submissions accepted for publication--10 percent. Comments- all material must be in double space; endnotes, not footnotes; clean manuscripts. Indexed: Cath.Ind., Curr.Cont., Hum.Ind., Old Test.Abstr., Rel.Per., Arts&Hum.Cit.Ind., Canon Law Abstr., New Test.Abstr., Rel.Ind.One, Rel.&Theol.Abstr.

304. THEOLOGIE UND GLAUBE
Wendelin Knoch, Ed.
Winifried Schulz, Ed.
Ferdinand Schoeningh
Juehenplatz 1
4790 Paderborn, West Germany (B.R.D.)

Subscription--4/yr.--48 DM. Description of subject matter--academic articles pertaining to all aspects of Theology. For: professors, people interested in Theology. Submissions must be in German. Sometimes accepts unsolicited articles, unsolicited reviews;

does not accept dot-matrix printing, simultaneous submissions; does not publish research notes; publishes review-articles; does not accept advertising. Style of journal--academic. Requires one copy of manuscript. Length requirements--maximum, 15 pages (with exceptions); minimum, --. Selection process--expert opinion of professors of own faculty. Responds in 1-2 weeks. Approximate proportion of submissions accepted for publication--75 percent. Indexed: Old Test.Abstr., Rel.Per., Rel.&Theol.Abstr., Canon Law Abstr., New Test.Abstr.

305. THEOLOGIE UND PHILOSOPHIE
Hermann Josef Sieben, Ed.
Verlag Herder GmbH und Co. KG
Hermann-Herder-Str. 4
D-7800 Freiburg im Breisgau, West Germany (B.R.D.)

Subscription--4/yr.--DM 162. Description of subject matter of journal--Theology and Philosophy. Publishes articles in Scripture, Ethics, Church History, and Theology. For: professors and students. Submissions must be in German. Accepts unsolicited articles, dot-matrix printing, simultaneous submissions; sometimes accepts unsolicited reviews; publishes research notes and review-articles; does not accept advertising. Seeks contributions to research. Style of journal--academic. Requires one copy of manuscript. Length requirements--maximum, 30 pages; minimum, 10 pages. Selection process--Editorial Board decides, if out of their field--outside specialists competent in that area make the decision. Responds in 2-3 weeks. Approximate proportion of submissions accepted for publication--50 percent. Indexed: Rel.&Theol.Abstr., Canon Law Abstr., New Test.Abstr.

306. THEOLOGISCH-PRAKTISCHE QUARTALSCHRIFT
Oberoesterreichischer Landesverlag GmbH
Landstr. 41
A-4010 Linz, Austria

Subscription--4/yr.--S.288. Subject matter of journal--Any subject of Theology, when of general interest. For: professors, students, laypersons, others who are interested in Theology. Submissions must be in German. Accepts unsolicited articles; does not accept unsolicited reviews, dot-matrix printing, simultaneous submissions; does not publish research notes; publishes review-articles; accepts advertising--yes, when paid for. Style of journal--high level, but generally understandable. Requires 2 copies of manuscript. Length requirements--maximum, 14 manuscript pages; minimum, --. Selection process--Each editor reads the manuscript. Approval/rejection is made through a conference of the editors. Responds in 1-2 months. Comments: About 30 articles per annum can be printed, most of them are solicited. Parent Organization--Theologische

Hochschule der Dioezese Linz. Indexed: Canon Law Abstr., New Test.Abstr.

307. THEOLOGISCHE ZEITSCHRIFT
Prof. Dr. Klaus, Ed.
Theology Faculty of the University Basel
CH-4051 Nadelberg 10 Basel, Switzerland

Subscription--4/yr.--95 Swiss francs SFR. Description of subject matter of journal--integrated ecumenical theology. Publishes articles in Scripture, Ethics, Church History, and Theology. For: professors, students, and clergymen. Submissions must be in French, German, or English. Accepts unsolicited articles, unsolicited reviews, dot-matrix printing; does not accept simultaneous submissions; publishes research notes and review-articles; does not accept advertising. Seeks studies on important theological subjects--historical and ecumenical relation to the theological tradition of Basel. Style of journal--academically trained, scientific. Requires one copy of manuscript. Length requirements--maximum, 25 pages; minimum, 5 pages. Selection process--scientific quality--theological subject--interesting to at least two of the classical theological disciplines--chosen by a committee of experts. Responds in 3-4 weeks. Approximate proportion of submissions accepted--50 percent. Parent Organization--Universitaet Basel, Theologische Fakultaet. Indexed: Old Test.Abstr., New Test.Abstr., Rel.Ind.One, Rel.&Theol.Abstr.

308. THEOLOGY
The Rt. Revd. Peter Coleman, Ed.
The Revd. Leslie Houlden, Ed.
Dr. Grace Jantzen, Ed.
Society for Promoting Christian Knowledge
Holy Trinity Church
Marylebone Road
London NW1 4DU, England

Subscription--6/yr.--$20. Subject matter of journal--primarily in Theology; however, articles are published in the following areas: Scripture, Ethics, Church History, Evangelism, Church Administration, Pastoral Counseling, Missions, Psychology of Religion, Sociology of Religion, World Religions, Philosophy of Religion, Judaism, Islam, Hinduism, Buddhism, Eastern Religions, Religious Education. Accepts unsolicited articles; does not accept unsolicited reviews, dot-matrix printing, simultaneous submissions; does not publish research notes; publishes review-articles; accepts advertising--mainly from publishers, but other advertisers accepted. Especially seeking academic articles that can be read by the non-specialist. Interested in current issues. Welcomes ecumenical and international contributions. Requires one copy of manuscript. Length requirements--maximum, 4500 words; minimum, 1500 words except reviews of books (shorter).

Selection process--the three editors see each submission independently and then decide jointly at regular Editorial meetings (bimonthly).
Responds in 2-3 weeks. Approximate proportion of submissions accepted for publication--25 percent. Indexed: Br.Hum.Ind., New
Test.Abstr., Rel.Ind.One, Rel.&Theol.Abstr.

309. THEOLOGY DIGEST
     Bernhard Asen, Ed.
     Theology Digest, Inc.
     3634 Lindell Blvd.
     St. Louis, MO 63108-3395

Subscription--4/yr.--$9. Subject matter of journal--English
digests of foreign language theology. Publishes articles in Scripture,
Ethics, Church History, Theology, Missions, and Eastern Religions.
For: professors, students, and laypersons. Does not accept unsolicited articles, unsolicited reviews, dot-matrix printing, simultaneous submissions; does not publish research notes, review-articles;
does accept advertising. Seeks previously published foreign language articles. Selection process--an editorial board reviews articles
summarized from foreign language theological journals. If accepted,
they are digested and printed under the original author's name upon
their approval of the manuscript. Indexed: Cath.Ind., Old Test.
Abstr., Int.Z.Bibelwiss., Rel.&Theol.Abstr.

310. THEOLOGY TODAY
     Hugh T. Kerr, Ed.
     Craig Dykstra, Ed.
     P.O. Box 29
     Princeton, NJ 08542

Subscription--4/yr.--$16. Description of subject matter of
journal--The critical interpretation of Christian faith for today's
church, culture, and society. Publishes articles in Theology, Arts,
Science. For: professors and ministers. Submissions must be in
English. Accepts unsolicited articles; does not accept unsolicited
reviews, dot-matrix printing, simultaneous submissions; does not publish research notes; publishes review-articles; accepts advertising--
mostly book publishers. Seeking articles that are innovative and
creative rather than comparative or analytic discussions. Style of
journal--Chicago Manual. Requires one copy of manuscript. Length
requirements--maximum, 3500-5000 words; minimum, 1500 words. Selection process for publication of an article--According to the chosen
theme or symposium for each issue and after at least two editors
read and report. Responds in 2 weeks. Approximate proportion of
submissions that are accepted for publication--10-20 percent. Comments: Circulation over 14,000. Payment for articles--50-100 dollars.
Indexed: Curr.Cont., Hum.Ind., Old Test.Abstr., Bk.Rev.Ind.,
Arts&Hum.Cit.Ind., Bk.Rev.Mo., New Test.Abstr., G.Soc.Sci.&Rel.
Per.Lit., Rel.Ind.One, Rel.&Theol.Abstr.

311. THOMIST
Rev. Joseph A. DiNoia, Ed.
Thomist Press
487 Michigan Ave., NE
Washington, DC   20017

Subscription--4/yr.--$15.   Description of subject matter of
journal--covers a broad range of contemporary philosophical and theological questions.   The purpose of the journal is to cultivate fruitful
dialogue between modern and contemporary philosophical systems and
the classical tradition of philosophy and Christian theology.   History
of philosophy, historical theology and textual studies as they bear
on enduring speculative questions or as they illumine the intellectual
setting of Thomistic thought also come within the scope of the journal.   Publishes articles in Ethics, Theology, Philosophy of Religion,
World Religions, and Philosophy.   For: professors, students, and
laypersons.   Submissions must be in English.   Accepts unsolicited
articles, dot-matrix printing, simultaneous submissions; sometimes accepts unsolicited reviews; does not publish research notes; publishes review-articles, accepts advertising--ads pertaining to the
philosophical-theological scene--i.e., books, journals, publishing com-
panies.   Seeks articles which discuss central issues in the various
subfields of philosophy and systematic theology.   Type of article especially seeking--especially, though not exclusively, those in which
the discussion can be advanced by creative use of the thought of
Aquinas and significant authors in the Thomist tradition.   Style of
journal--The Chicago Manual of Style.   Requires 2 copies of manuscript.   Length requirements--maximum, 40 pages; minimum, 10
pages.   Selection process--several readers separately assess an article, and a decision is made based on all of their thoughts and reflections.   Responds to a submission in 3-4 months.   Approximate
proportion of submissions accepted for publication--40 percent.   Indexed: Cath.Ind., Curr.Cont., Arts&Hum.Cit.Ind., New Test.
Abstr., Phil.Ind., Rel.&Theol.Abstr.

312. TIJDSCHRIFT VOOR THEOLOGIE
T. M. Schoof, Ed.
Studia Catholica Foundation
Postbus 35
6500 AA Nijmegen, Netherlands

Subscription--4/yr.--75 fl.   Description of subject matter of
journal--actual Christian problems in theological interpretation.   Publishes articles in Scripture, Ethics, Church History, Theology, Missions, and Philosophy of Religion.   For: professors, students, and
laypersons.   Submissions must be in Dutch.   Accepts unsolicited articles; does not accept unsolicited reviews; does not accept simultaneous submissions; publishes research notes, review-articles; accepts
advertising--for theological books.   Seeks articles 7500 to 12,500
words, notes included.   Style of journal--readable; compatible with

academic approach. Requires one copy of manuscript. Selection process--decision by Editorial Board, on the basis of at least two reports by specialists. Responds to a submission in one to three months. Approximate proportion of submissions accepted for publication--varies considerably. Comments: We accept translated articles (into Dutch, that is) if they are not easily accessible otherwise in our language area. Summaries in English are added to all articles. Indexed: New Test. Abstr., Old Test.Abstr.

313. ZEITSCHRIFT FUER KATHOLISCHE THEOLOGIE
P. Hans Bernh Meyer, Director   Editor: Theologische Fakultaet
Verlag Herder   Universitaet Innsbruck
Wollzeile 33   Redaction: Sillgasse 6
A-1010 Vienna, Austria   A-6020 Innsbruck, Austria

Subscription--4/yr.--S.H. 654-. Description of subject matter--research on Christian theology and philosophy. Publishes articles in Scripture, Ethics, Church History, Theology, Missions, Psychology of Religion, Sociology of Religion, World Religions, Philosophy of Religion, Judaism, Islam, Hinduism, Buddhism, Eastern Religions, Religious Education and Philosophy. For: professors, students, and laypersons. Submissions must be in German, (sometimes) in French and English. Seeks research articles. Style of journal--scholarly. Accepts unsolicited articles, dot-matrix printing; sometimes accepts unsolicited reviews; does not accept simultaneous submissions; publishes research notes, review-articles; accepts advertising--books, periodicals. Length requirements--maximum, 30 pages; minimum, 5 pages. Selection process--critical examination by at least 2 professors. Responds in one month. Approximate proportion of submissions accepted for publication--60 percent. Parent Organization--Universitaet Innsbruck, Theologische Fakultaet. Indexed: Old Test. Abstr., Canon Law Abstr.

OTHER JOURNALS THAT PUBLISH
ARTICLES IN THEOLOGY

AFER 501
Africa Theological Journal 502
AJS Review 479
Alliance Life 314
America 448
American Baptist Quarterly 1
American Benedictine Review 315
Andrews University Seminary Studies 2
Angelicum 3

Anglican Theological Review 4
Asbury Theological Journal 5
Bangalore Theological Forum 513
Banner 6
Baptist Quarterly N.S. 112
Benedictines 316
Berliner Theologische Zeitschrift 7
Bibbia E Oriente 163
Bibel und Liturgie 165

14. RELIGIOUS NURTURE; MINISTRY; RELIGIOUS LIFE

314. ALLIANCE LIFE
Maurice R. Irvin, Ed.
Christian and Missionary Alliance
350 North Highland Ave.
Nyack, NY 10960-0992

Subscription--every 2 weeks--$9.50. Description of subject
matter of journal--articles on Christian living, various forms of
Christian service and Christian work, particularly missions. Publishes articles in Scripture, Ethics, Theology, Evangelism, and Missions. For: laypersons. Submissions must be in English. Seeks
articles on Christian living, first person experiences. Style of jour-
nal--moderately popular. Requires one copy of manuscript. Length
requirements--maximum, 1500-1800 words; minimum, --. Selection
process--read and evaluated by two or three editors, final selection
by Editor. Responds in 1-3 months. Approximate proportion of submissions accepted for publication--15 percent. Indexed: Chr.Per.
Ind., G.Soc.Sci.&Rel.Per.Lit.

315. AMERICAN BENEDICTINE REVIEW
Rev. Terrence Kardong, Ed.
American Benedictine Review, Inc.
St. Benedict's Abbey
Atchison, KS 58652

Subscription--4/yr.--$10. Subject matter of journal--mostly
monastic studies but also other material on religion and humanities.
For: monks/nuns/laymen. Submissions must be in English. Accepts unsolicited articles, dot-matrix printing; does not accept unsolicited reviews, simultaneous submissions; does not publish research
notes; publishes review-articles; does not accept advertising. Seeks
research articles on the theology and history of monasticism. Style
of journal--MLA but not "works cited"--new form. One copy of
manuscript required. Length requirements--maximum, 30-40 pages;
minimum, 5-6 pages. Selection process--three readers evaluate and
recommend. Editor makes final decision. Improvements are usually
requested. Responds in 4-5 months. Approximate proportion of
submissions that are accepted for publication--50 percent. Indexed:
Cath.Ind., Rel.Per., New Test.Abstr.

161

316. BENEDICTINES
Sister Mary Alice Guilfoil, Ed.
Mount St. Scholastica, Inc.
Atchison, KS 66002

Subscription--2/yr.--$8, U.S.A.; $10, surface foreign; $13, airmail foreign. Description of subject matter--Monastic life--mainly Benedictine, but not exclusively; contemporary interpretations; experiments--evaluations, etc. Publishes articles (from some perspectives, mainly monastic) in--Church History, Theology, Psychology of Religion, Sociology of Religion, Philosophy of Religion; Contemporary application of Monastic life, values, issues. For: monks and nuns. Submissions must be in English. Sometimes accepts unsolicited articles, unsolicited reviews; accepts dot-matrix printing; does not publish research notes; publishes review-articles; does not accept advertising. Type of article sought--open to variety--but focus on today's expression of monastic life, values, questions or relationship to broader religious questions, groups--issues. Style of journal--relatively "scholarly"--reflects some research, not just "essay reflections." Descriptions of processes or experiments in monastic living, work, new issues, etc. Length requirements-- maximum, 15 pages; minimum, 10 pages. Selection process--generally a thematic selection--articles that complement a focus. Responds to a submission--try for immediate acknowledgment, then depending how close it is to publishing time, it depends--ordinarily 6 weeks ... frequently, much faster--especially if article is "easily inappropriate" for the journal. Indexed: Bull.Signal. Parent Organization--Mount St. Scholastica Convent.

317. THE CHICAGO THEOLOGICAL SEMINARY REGISTER
Perry D. LeFevre, Ed.
Chicago Theological Seminary
5757 University Avenue
Chicago, IL 60637

Subscription--3/yr.--$2.00. Publishes articles in Church Administration and Religious Education. Submissions must be in English.

318. CHRISTIAN MINISTRY
Alfred P. Klausler, Ed.
Christian Century Foundation
407 S. Dearborn St.
Chicago, IL 60605

Subscription--bimonthly--$8.50. Describe subject matter of journal--clergy professional. A journal in Scripture, Ethics, Evangelism, Church Administration, Pastoral Counseling, Psychology of Religion, Sociology of Religion, and Religious Education. For:

clergy. Articles appear in English. Sometimes accepts unsolicited articles; does not accept unsolicited reviews, dot-matrix printing, simultaneous submissions. Does not publish research notes; publishes review-articles. Accepts advertising--books (church related). Seeks "how-to" articles for and by clergy and seminary teachers. Submit one copy of manuscript. Length requirements--maximum, 3000 words; minimum, 250 works. Selection of material by Editorial Board consensus. Responds in 1 month. Indexed: G.Soc.Sci.& Rel.Per.Lit., Rel.Ind.One.

319. CHRISTIAN STANDARD
Sam E. Stone, Ed.
Standard Publishing
8121 Hamilton Ave.
Cincinnati, OH   45231

Subscription--52/yr.--$14.00. Description of subject matter-- essays and news relating to the restoration of New Testament Christianity. Publishes articles in Scripture, Evangelism, and Church Administration. For: professors, students, laypersons, church staff/leaders. Articles appear in English. Accepts unsolicited articles; does not accept unsolicited reviews, dot-matrix printing, simultaneous submissions. Does not publish research notes or review-articles. Does not accept advertising. Submit one copy of manuscript. Length requirements--maximum, 2500 words; minimum, 500 words. Selection process--read all submitted and select the most suitable for our needs at the time. Respond in 4-6 weeks. Accepts approximately 1/3 of all submissions. Indexed: G.Soc.Sci.&Rel.Per.Lit.

320. CURRENTS IN THEOLOGY AND MISSION
Ralph W. Klein, Ed.
Christ Seminary-Seminex
539 N. Grand
St. Louis, MO   63103

Subscription--6/yr.--$13.50. Description of subject matter-- professional journal for pastors. Publishes articles in Scripture, Ethics, Church History, Theology, Evangelism, Church Administration, Pastoral Counseling, Missions, and Religious Education. For: professors, students, laypersons, primarily clergy. Submissions must be in English. Accepts unsolicited articles, dot-matrix printing; does not accept unsolicited reviews, simultaneous submissions; does not publish research notes; publishes review-articles; accepts advertising--publishers. Seeks articles--in-depth, readable, relevant to people in active ministry. Style of journal--Chicago Manual of Style, Journal of Biblical Literature, footnotes at the end of the manuscript. Requires 1 copy of manuscript. Length requirements-- maximum, 20 pages. Selection process--Review Board of Professors and Pastors. Responds in 4 months. Approximate proportion of

submissions accepted for publication--50 percent. Indexed: Old
Test.Abstr., Rel.Per., Int.Z.Bibelwiss., New Test.Abstr., Rel.Ind.
One, Rel.&Theol.Abstr.

321. THE DEACON
    Southern Baptist Convention
    Sunday School Board
    127 Ninth Ave., N.
    Nashville, TN 37234

    Subscription--4/yr.--$8.50. Description of subject matter of
journal--"Helps" for the layperson who has been selected as a min-
ister to the needs of others in the congregation. Publishes articles
in Theology, Evangelism, Missions, and Lay Ministry. For: laypersons and pastors. Submissions must be in English. Accepts unsolicited articles, unsolicited reviews, dot-matrix printing--near letter quality required; does not accept simultaneous submissions; does
not publish research notes; publishes review-articles; does not accept advertising. Seeks practical "how to" articles which address
ministry needs. Style of journal--informal, 8th grade reading level.
Requires 2 copies of manuscript. Length requirements--maximum,
2100 words; minimum, 400 words. Articles are selected on the basis
of: issue theme, readers' needs, applicability to other deacon groups,
readability, clarity of expression and concepts. Responds in 2 to
8 weeks. Accepts approximately 2/3 of all submissions for publication. Indexed: South.Bap.Per.Ind.

322. DECISION
    Roger C. Palms, Ed.
    Billy Graham Evangelistic Association
    1300 Harmon Place
    Minneapolis, MN 55403

    Subscription--Monthly--$5. Publishes articles in Scripture,
Church History, Evangelism, Missions, Personal Conversion Testimonies, Christian Growth and Nurture. For laypersons and clergy.
Submissions must be in English. Accepts unsolicited articles; does
not accept unsolicited reviews, dot-matrix printing, simultaneous submissions; does not publish research notes or review-articles; does not
accept advertising. Seeks article--personal experience--showing the
way in which biblical principles were applied to everyday living or
crisis experiences; conversion testimonies; teaching articles dealing
with spiritual growth, Bible doctrine, implications of the Christian
faith for one's life and work--preferably by pastors, teachers, those
mature in faith. Requires 1 copy of manuscript. Length require-
ments--maximum, 2000 words; minimum, 100 words. Selection pro-
cess--we commission a few; unsolicited mss. which have potential
are circulated among the members of our staff with a space for comment by them. Our editor makes the final decision as to whether or

not the article is accepted for publication. Responds in 2 months.
Under 5 percent of all submissions are accepted for publication.
Comments--We look for articles which are positive--we do not carry
controversial or issues-oriented material. Indexed: Chr.Per.Ind.

323. DIACONATE MAGAZINE
Rev. Albert J. Nevins, Ed.
Vincent Giese, Pub.
P.O. Box 19113
Tampa, FL 33686

Subscription--6/yr.--$18. Publishes articles in Scripture,
Ethics, Church History, Theology, Evangelism, Church Administration, Pastoral Counseling, Missions, Psychology of Religion, Sociology
of Religion, Religious Education--related to permanent deaconate.
For: permanent deacons, priests. Submissions must be in English.
Accepts unsolicited articles, dot-matrix printing; does not accept unsolicited reviews, simultaneous submissions; publishes research notes;
does not publish review-articles; accepts advertising--related to magazine. Requires one copy of manuscript. Length requirements--
maximum, no maximum as we have run articles in parts over several
issues; minimum, 2000 words. Responds usually the day manuscript
is received. Approximate proportion of submissions that are accepted
for publication--50-60 percent. Payment on publication.

324. DIAKONIA
Helmut Erharter, Ed.
Stephansplatz 313
A-1010 Vienna, Austria

Subscription--6/yr.--78 DM. Description of subject matter
of journal--theological, anthropological and practical contributions for
pastoral workers. Publishes articles in Scripture, Ethics, Theology,
Evangelism, Church Administration, Pastoral Counseling, Missions,
Psychology of Religion, Sociology of Religion, Philosophy of Religion,
Judaism, Religious Education, Pastoral Activities. For: laypersons,
priests, pastoral assistants. Sometimes accepts unsolicited articles,
simultaneous submissions; does not accept unsolicited reviews, dot-
matrix printing; does not publish research notes or review-articles;
does not accept advertising. Seeks short, profound informative
articles. Style of journal--academic but clear. Requires 2 copies
of manuscript. Length requirements--maximum, 8 pages; minimum,
4 pages. Selection process--Editorial Board meets 2 times a year.
Indexed: Cath.Ind.

325. DISCOVERY
Pam Toplisky, Ed.
John Milton Society for the Blind

Rm. 249
475 Riverside Dr.
New York, NY 10115

Subscription--11/yr.--free. Description of subject matter--
religious material for children and youth. For: blind clergy and lay.
Submissions must be in English. Does not accept unsolicited articles
or simultaneous submissions; sometimes accepts unsolicited reviews;
accepts dot-matrix printing; does not publish research notes; sometimes publishes review-articles; and does not accept advertising.
Seeks--articles and materials for religious magazine for young readers
ages 8 through 18. This interdenominational agency sends Christian
literature in braille, on records and in large type form, free on request to any person who cannot see to read. The program of Christian Service to the blind and visually handicapped persons is made
possible by the generous support of many people who send their contributions to the John Milton Society for the Blind at the above address. (Braille) Indexed: South.Bap.Per.Ind. for children 8 through
18.

326. DOCTRINE AND LIFE
Rev. Austin Flannery, Ed.
Dominican Publications
St. Saviour's
Dublin 1, Ireland

Subscription--10/yr.--$18. Description of subject matter--
Christian life and Christian belief today, Liturgy, The Social Gospel. Publishes articles in Scripture, Ethics, and Theology. For:
clergy and religious. Submissions must be in English. Sometimes
accepts unsolicited articles; does not accept unsolicited reviews,
simultaneous submissions; accepts dot-matrix printing, does not publish research notes; publishes review-articles; accepts advertising--
books and courses in religious/theological field. Seeks articles that
range from 2500-3000 words concerning significant developments in
Christian life and belief today. Requires 1 copy of manuscript.
Length requirements--maximum, 3000 words; minimum, 1000 words.
Selection process--Editor reads and decides. Responds--from one
day to two months. Approximate proportion of submissions accepted
for publication--25 percent. Indexed: Cath.Ind., Old Test.Abstr.,
New Test.Abstr.

327. DOMINICAN ASHRAM
Paul Kuruvilla, Ed.
St. Charles' Seminary
Seminary Hill
Nagpur 440 006, India

Subscription--4/yr. Subject matter of journal--Dominican Life.
Accepts unsolicited articles. Submissions must be in English.

328. EAST ASIAN PASTORAL REVIEW
Rev. Felipe Gomez, Ed.
East Asian Pastoral Institute
Box 1815
Manila, Philippines

Subscription--4/yr.--$12. Subject matter--Theology, Evan-
gelism, Church Administration, Pastoral Counseling, Missions, Psychology of Religion, Sociology of Religion, World Religions, Religious
Education--All with "pastoral" viewpoint. For: professors, students,
laypersons, pastoral agents. Submissions must be in English. Sometimes accepts unsolicited articles; does not accept unsolicited reviews;
accepts dot-matrix printing, simultaneous submissions; does not publish research notes; publishes review-articles; does not accept advertising. Seeks articles which can help the local Churches of Asia
to grow, to become more "Asian," or that can help all kinds of ministry to become more efficient. Articles especially seeking--articles
on inculturation, theological reflection from Asian point of view.
Style of journal articles--not scholarly--but rather practical, though
good theology is welcome. Requires one copy of manuscript. Length
requirements--maximum, 20 pages; minimum, 7-8 pages. Selection
process--articles are read by members of the Editorial Board, then
recommended, finally accepted. Approximate proportion of submissions that are accepted for publication--about 80 percent. Comments--
Articles are written from a Catholic point of view, but ecumenical
articles of other origins are also considered. Indexed: Cath.Ind.

329. GROUP
Joani Schultz, Editorial Director
Thom Schultz Publications, Inc.
2890 N. Monroe Avenue
Box 481
Loveland, CO 80539

Subscription--8/yr.--$19.50. Description of subject matter in
journal--Articles aimed at leaders of high-school-age interdenominational Christian youth groups. Group needs articles that tell about
successful youth groups or youth group projects. Groups involved
in music, drama, art, helping others, missionary work, etc. are regularly featured. How-to articles for membership building, worship
planning, handling specific group problems, and improving as a
leader are welcomed. Leadership tips are also welcomed--how to
lead effective discussions, how to increase enthusiasm. Ideas for
group use are needed--games, crowdbreakers, discussion starters,
role plays, worship ideas, fund raisers. For: professional youth
leaders and volunteer youth leaders. Sometimes accepts unsolicited
articles; does not accept unsolicited reviews, dot-matrix printing,
simultaneous submissions; publishes research notes (as statistics);
does not publish review-articles; accepts advertising--Christian-
oriented products that apply to youth leaders or high-school age

young people. Seeks articles concerning--membership building, worship planning, handling specific group problems, and improving as
a leader. Style of journal--conversational, how-to, non-preachy.
One copy of manuscript required. Length requirements--maximum,
1,700 words; minimum, 500 words. Manuscripts should be typewritten, double-spaced, on one side of paper. Name and address
should appear on upper right corner of first page. Each page should
be numbered and include title or your name. Include stamped, self-
addressed envelope for return of unaccepted manuscript. Selection
process--Group plans from 6 months to a year ahead and assigns
many articles to fit that criterion. Responds to a submission in 2-4
weeks. Approximate proportion of submissions that are accepted
for publication--most of assigned submissions; maybe one in 10 unsolicited submissions. Comments--we only purchase with all-rights
copyright. Payment for articles. Indexed: Biol.Abstr.

330. HIS DOMINION
     Dr. Franklin A. Pyles, Ed.
     Faculty of Canadian Theological Seminary
     Regina, Saskatchewan, Canada

Subscription--4/yr.--$7 U.S. in the U.S.; $7 Canadian in Canada. Description of subject matter of journal--Matters of special interest to ministerial personnel covering topics of worldwide content
pertaining to the thought and practice of Christianity. Publishes
articles in Church History, Theology, Evangelism, Church Administration, Pastoral Counseling, Missions, and Religious Education. For:
professors, students, pastors. Submissions must be in English.
Sometimes accepts unsolicited articles, unsolicited reviews; accepts
dot-matrix printing; does not accept simultaneous submissions; does
not publish research notes or review-articles; does not accept advertising. Seeks articles that are scholarly writings, with a practical purpose. Each issue has a theme, and a query letter is recommended to discover what new subjects will be explored in the following year. Especially seeking any new research or discoveries in the
subject of themes we explore. Requires 2 copies of manuscript.
Length requirements--maximum, 2500 words; minimum, 1000 words.
Selection process--The editor selects such articles as he deems fit
to cover the theme of the issue. Usually he contacts writers ahead
of time--even a year in advance. Responds to a submission in 2-3
weeks. Comments: We do not receive many unsolicited articles. A
query letter is highly recommended.

331. LEADERSHIP
     John Tros, Ed.
     Leadership Publications
     Box 2522
     Kampala, Uganda

Subscription--Monthly--$16 (surface); $40 (airmail). Publishes articles in Scripture, Ethics, Church History, Theology, Evangelism, Church Administration, Religious Education. For: professors, students, laypersons, others. Submissions must be in French, Spanish, English, or Italian. Accepts unsolicited articles, dot-matrix printing, simultaneous submissions; does not accept unsolicited reviews; does not publish research notes or review-articles; does not accept advertising. Seeks short, lively, concrete articles. Requires 1 copy of manuscript. Length requirements--maximum, 4 pages; minimum, --. Selection process--Editor's choice. Responds in 1 month. Approximate proportion of submissions accepted for publication--1/3. Parent Organization--Comboni Missionaries. Indexed: Rel.&Theol.Abstr.

332. MILITARY CHAPLAINS' REVIEW
      Chaplain (Maj.) William Noble
      Army Chaplain Board
      Fort Monmouth, NJ   07703

Subscription--4/yr. Description of subject matter of journal--Subjects of interest to military chaplaincy. Publishes articles in Ethics, Theology, Evangelism, Pastoral Counseling, Psychology of Religion, etc. For: military chaplains. Submissions must be in English. Accepts unsolicited articles, unsolicited reviews, dot-matrix printing, simultaneous submissions; does not publish research notes; publishes review-articles, does not accept advertising. Requires 1 copy of manuscript. Length requirements for a submission--maximum, 20 pages; minimum, 12 pages. Selection process--Editor's judgment. Approximate proportion of submissions accepted for publication--80 percent. Indexed: Ind.U.S.Gov.Per.

333. MOODY MONTHLY
      Michael Umlandt, Ed.
      Moody Bible Institute of Chicago
      820 N. LaSalle St.
      Chicago, IL   60610

Subscription--11/yr.--$16.95. Description of subject matter--Articles that encourage evangelical Christians to think and live biblically. A journal in Scripture, Church History, Theology, Evangelism, Missions, and Religious Education. For: laypersons. Submit articles in English. Does not accept unsolicited articles, unsolicited reviews, or simultaneous submissions; accepts dot-matrix printing; does not publish research notes; publishes review-articles; accepts advertising--books, products related to church buildings, CE curriculum, etc. Seeks practical Christian living articles about the Bible, Christians, and Christian experience. Style of manual--anecdotal, popular writing. Require 1 copy of manuscript. Length requirements--maximum, 2000 words; minimum, 750 words. Selection process--Editorial staff evaluates each manuscript that makes it past an initial screening of the managing editor. Responds--6 weeks to 2 months. Accepts approximately 5 percent of the submissions for publication. Indexed: Chr.Per.Ind., R.G., G.Soc.Sci.&Rel.Per.Lit.

334. THE NAVY CHAPLAIN
     Chaplain Resource Board
     United States Navy
     6500 Hampton Blvd.
     Norfolk, VA 23508-1296

Subscription--6/yr.--Free. Description of subject matter of journal--ministry in a variety of Navy, Marine Corps, Coast Guard settings. For: active, reserve, and retired chaplains. Submissions must be in English. Does not accept unsolicited articles, dot-matrix printing, simultaneous submissions; accepts unsolicited reviews; does not publish research notes; publishes review-articles; does not accept advertising. Subject areas are established by the Navy Chief of Chaplains. Authors are selected by the Chaplain Resource Board. Style of journal--magazine format. Requires one copy of manuscript. Length requirements--maximum, 3000 words; minimum, 1200 words. Indexed: CERDIC.

335. PASTORAL LIFE
     Rev. Jeffrey Mickler, SSP
     Society of St. Paul
     Canfield, OH 44406

Subscription--11/yr.--$15. Description of subject matter-- Ministry--any aspect. Scripture outlooks or study. Publishes articles in Scripture, Ethics, Theology, Evangelism, Church Administration, Pastoral Counseling, Psychology of Religion, and Religious Education. For: priests/religious men and women. Submissions must be in English. Accepts unsolicited articles; sometimes accepts unsolicited reviews; does not accept dot-matrix printing or simultaneous submissions; does not publish research notes; publishes review-articles; and accepts advertising--ministerial/educational. Seeks long in-depth articles--well researched on any aspect of ministry. Requires 1 copy of manuscript. Length requirements--maximum, 20 pages, double spaced; minimum, 10 pages double spaced. Selection process--Three man editorial board with editor make final decision. Responds in one month (longer, during holidays and summer). Accepts approximately 75-90 percent of all submissions for publication. Indexed: Cath.Ind.

336. PENDLE HILL PAMPHLETS
     Rebecca K. Mays, Ed.
     Pendle Hill Publications
     338 Plush Mill Road
     Wallingford, PA 19086

Subscription--6/yr.--$10. Description of subject matter of journal--The spiritual journey and how it leads to work--academic and lay--in the world. Publishes articles in Scripture, Ethics, Church History, Theology, Quaker Evangelism, Church Administration, Pastoral Counseling, Quaker Missions, Psychology of Religion, Sociology of Religion, World Religions, Philosophy of Religion, Judaism, Islam, Hinduism, Buddhism, Eastern Religions, Religious Education, The Inward Journey, Religion and Art, Social Activism, Nonviolence. For: professors, students, laypersons, others. Submissions must be in English. Accepts unsolicited articles, dot-matrix printing; does not accept unsolicited reviews, simultaneous submissions; does not publish research notes or review-articles; does not accept advertising. Seeks essays that speak from an author's concern about a topic of contemporary relevance that show a familiarity with Quaker faith and practice. Especially seeking articles that bridge the current cultural gap between academic and lay readerships on any of the above topics. Style of journal--Chicago Manual of Style. Requires 3 copies of manuscript. Length requirements--maximum, 9000 words; minimum, 7200 words. Selection process--Editor screens all incoming manuscripts with help of a preview committee in borderline cases. Selected manuscripts (3-4) go to each of 4 meetings annually for full review of Publications Committee (20 members) who make all final decisions about what is published using Quaker concensus to reach unity. Responds to a submission--6 months for full committee review; 3 months for editorial screening. Approximate proportion of submissions accepted for publication--10 percent. Parent Organization-- Pendle Hill, a Quaker Center for Study and Contemplation. Indexed: Vert.File Ind.

337. PRIESTS & PEOPLE
     Bernard Bickers, Ed.
     Tablet Publishing Co.
     48 Great Peter St.
     London SW1 2HB, England

Subscription--10/yr.--$23. Description of subject matter of journal--content is varied, wide-ranging. Publishes articles in Scripture, Ethics, Church History, Theology, Evangelism, Church Administration, Pastoral Counseling, Missions, Psychology of Religion, Sociology of Religion, Philosophy of Religion, and Religious Education For: clergy and laity. Submissions must be in English. Accepts unsolicited articles, unsolicited reviews, dot-matrix printing, simultaneous submissions (occasionally); does not publish research notes; publishes review-articles; accepts advertising--mainly to do with books/courses/church materials, etc. Seeks articles that are clear, concise, interesting, provocative, informative on any aspect of Christian life. Requires 1 copy of manuscript. Length requirements-- maximum, 5000 words; minimum, 1500 words. Selection process--depends on the issue--special or not--otherwise tries to achieve a balance. Responds to a submission--immediate acknowledgment but if unsolicited length varies. Approximate proportion of submissions accepted for publication--commissioned, 95 percent; unsolicited, 20 percent. Parent Organization--Catholic Church. Indexed: Cath.Ind., Old Test.Abstr., Canon Law Abstr., New Test.Abstr., Rel.&Theol. Abstr.

338. QUARTERLY REVIEW: JOURNAL FOR REFLECTION ON MIN-
ISTRY
Charles E. Cole, Ed.
Box 871
Nashville, TN 37202

Subscription--4/yr.--$15, individuals and libraries. Descrip-
tion of subject matter--academic disciplines as they relate to ministry. Publishes articles in Scripture, Ethics, Church History, Theology, Church Administration, Pastoral Counseling, Religious Educa-
tion--emphasizing their relevance for ministry. For professors, students, laypersons, and ministers. Submissions must be in English.
Seeks articles that instruct, advocate positions or courses of action,
and converse with opposing views. Style of manual--Chicago Manual
of Style, Webster's Third Dictionary. Requires 3 copies of manuscript. Length Requirements--maximum, 25 pages; minimum, 8 pages.
Selection process--First review by editors. Acceptable manuscripts
are reviewed by 1 or 2 outside readers. Manuscripts are then either
accepted, rejected, or returned for revision. Revisions usually reviewed only by editors. Responds in 3 months. Approximately 15
percent of all unsolicited submissions are accepted for publication.
Indexed: Hum.Ind., Old Test.Abstr., Rel.Per., Rel.&Theol.Abstr.,
G.Soc.Sci.&Rel.Per.Lit., Rel.Ind.One.

339. REVIEW FOR RELIGIOUS
Daniel F. X. Meenan, Ed.
3601 Lindell Blvd., Rm. 428
St. Louis, MO 63108

Subscription--6/yr.--$11. Description of subject matter--Inter-
disciplinary treatment of topics relating to personal life and commitment of Roman Catholic sisters, brothers and priests: theology,
spirituality, psychology, etc. Publishes articles in Scripture, Theology, Counseling and above. For: Religious sisters, brothers, and
priests. Submissions must be in English. Accepts unsolicited articles; does not accept unsolicited reviews, dot-matrix printing, simultaneous submissions; publishes research notes; does not publish
review-articles; does not accept advertising. Seeking articles which
bear on the personal rather than professional lives of the readership;
studies related to the living out of their vowed commitment; prayer;
practicalia related to their life-circumstance (community living, etc.).
Style of journal--standard thesis format with end notes. Requires 1
copy of manuscript. Length requirements--maximum, 5000 words;

minimum, 1500 words. Responds in 6-8 weeks. Approximately 60 percent of all submissions are accepted for publication. Indexed: Cath.Ind., Bk.Rev.Ind., New Test.Abstr.

340. SISTERS TODAY
Mary Anthony Wagner, Sr. Ed.
Liturgical Press
Saint John's Abbey
Collegeville, MN 56321

Subscription--10/yr.--$10. Description of subject matter--
Goal: exploring the vision of the Church and women in our time.
Publishes articles in Scripture (spirituality), Ethics (social justice issues), and Theology (practical). For: laypersons and religious men/women. Submissions must be in English. Articles sought--publish some poetry and art/graphics; articles reflecting new thinking on prayer, spirituality, the Church, application of the gospel to social issues: the role of women and other minorities. Sometimes accepts unsolicited articles; does not accept unsolicited reviews, simultaneous submissions; does not publish research notes or review-articles; accepts advertising--especially relative to retreats, education, spiritual institutes, etc. Type of article especially looking for--new thinking, new approach to above article topics--not old things rehashed. Style of journal--substantial in content but not theoretically speculative. 1 copy of manuscript is required. Length requirements--maximum, 10-12 double spaced pages; minimum, 1 or 2 pages, if developed. Selection process--staff determines themes for each volume in advance in accord with mss. received and selects in accord with the theme and quality. Key contributions are also invited. Responds in approximately 1-2 months. Approximately 10 percent of all submissions are accepted for publication. This percentage is less for submitted poetry. Indexed: Cath.Ind.

341. WORD & WORLD
Arland J. Hultgren, Ed.
Luther Northwestern Seminary
2481 Como Ave., West
St. Paul, MN 55108

Subscription--4/yr.--$15. Description of subject matter--Theology for Christian ministry. Publishes articles in Scripture, Ethics, Church History, Theology, Evangelism, Church Administration, Pastoral Counseling, Missions, and Religious Education. For: professors, students, laypersons, and clergy. Submissions must be in English. Sometimes accepts unsolicited articles, unsolicited reviews; accepts dot-matrix printing; does not accept simultaneous submissions; publishes research notes and review-articles; accepts advertising--publishers (book ads). Seeks articles in all branches of Christian theology which communicate to a general, but theologically educated, audience (mostly clergy). Especially looking for articles which draw upon theological research and communicate their significance for the church and its ministry. Style of journal--footnotes according to AAR/SBL style. Requires 2 copies of manuscript. Length requirements--maximum, 20 pages (double spaced); minimum, 10 pages (double spaced). Selection process--most are solicited by the editor in consultation with the Editorial Board in relation to the theme of each issue. Unsolicited articles are evaluated in terms of forthcoming themes or general appeal to readership. Responds in about 30 days to unsolicited submissions. Approximate proportion of submissions accepted for publication--nearly 100 percent for solicited articles; about 20 percent--unsolicited. Comments--the journal seeks to serve an ecumenical readership. Indexed: Old Test.Abstr., New Test. Abstr., Rel.Ind.One, Rel.&Theol.Abstr.

OTHER JOURNALS THAT PUBLISH ARTICLES IN RELIGIOUS NURTURE; MINISTRY; RELIGIOUS LIFE

15. SPIRITUALITY; MYSTICISM; CONTEMPLATIVE LIFE

342. CONFER: REVISTA DE VIDA RELIGIOSA

Núñez de Balboa, 99   Núñez de Balboa, 115 bis
28006 Madrid, Spain   28006 Madrid, Spain
(Confer, masculine)   (Confer, feminine)

Subscription--3/yr.--4,000 ptas. Subject matter of journal--
Church History, Theology, Spirituality, and Monasticism. Accepts
unsolicited articles, accepts advertising--publications. Submissions
must be in Spanish. The journal is organized around a theme.

343. ENVOY
Fr. Adrian van Kaam, C.S.Sp., Ph.D., Ed.
Duquesne University
Institute of Formative Spirituality
600 Forbes Ave.
Pittsburgh, PA 15282

Subscription--6/yr.--$6. Description of subject matter of jour-
nal--Simple, yet profound reflections encourage the reader to seek
God's direction and message through spiritual reading, meditative
reflection, prayer, and contemplation. For: students, laypersons,
religious. Submissions must be in English. Seeks practical, inspirational articles by authors who possess a deep appreciation and understanding of ongoing formation. Their writings should exhibit the
goals of the Institute of Formative Spirituality to present in a living
way the teachings of the Christian formation tradition. Accepts unsolicited articles, dot-matrix printing, simultaneous submissions; does
not accept unsolicited reviews; does not publish research notes or
review-articles; does not accept advertising. Style of journal--
spiritual articles; reflective poetry; classical corner; questions of
the month. Requires 2 copies of manuscript. Indexed: Cath.Ind.

344. GEIST UND LEBEN
Echter-Verlag
Juliuspromenade 64
Postfach 5560
8700 Wuerzburg 1, West Germany (B.R.D.)

Subscription--6/yr.--48 DM. Description of subject matter--

Christian spirituality, Mysticism. Submissions must be in German.
Accepts unsolicited articles, unsolicited reviews, dot-matrix printing;
does not accept simultaneous submissions; publishes research notes,
review-articles; does not accept advertising. Seeks articles concerning ancient and modern mysticism and the spirituality of the Society
of Jesus. Style of journal--scientific. Requires one copy of manuscript. Length requirements--maximum, 15 pages; minimum, 1 page.
Selection process--by 3 experts. Responds in 2 weeks. Approximate proportion of submissions accepted for publication--1/8. Indexed: New Test. Abstr.

345. GRANDE SINAL
     Ephraim Ferreira Alves, Sec.
     Rua Frei Luís, 100
     25689 Petrópolis
     Rio de Janeiro, Brazil

Subscription--10/yr.--$50.00. Subject matter of journal--
Scripture, Ethics, Sociology of Religion, and Spirituality. Submissions must be in Portuguese. Accepts unsolicited articles and advertising.

346. HAELAN
     Paul W. Mikels, Ed.
     Ecumenical Theological Center
     8425 West McNichols
     Detroit, MI 48221

Subscription--$5.00/yr. Description of subject matter of jour-
nal--The art of worship, prayer and meditation practice. Publishes
articles in Church Administration, Philosophy of Religion, Judaism,
Islam, Hinduism, Buddhism, Eastern Religions, and Religious Education. Submissions must be in English.

347. MANRESA
     Casa de Escritores S.J. (CESI)
     Pablo Aranda 3
     28006 Madrid, Spain

Subscription--4/yr.--$22. Description of subject matter of
journal--Jesuit spirituality. Publishes articles in Scripture, Theology,
Pastoral Counseling, and Spirituality. For: professors, religious.
Submissions must be in French, Spanish, or English. Accepts unsolicited articles, simultaneous submissions; publishes research notes;
accepts advertising--on topics of theology, spirituality. Seeks ar-
ticles--good quality, academic level. Especially seeking articles--
Ignatian spirituality for today. Requires 1-2 copies of manuscript.
Length requirements--maximum, 16 pages; minimum, 8-10 pages.

Selection process--sometimes articles are solicited; others are unsolicited. Responds in 3 weeks to a submission. Parent Organization--
Loyola, Centro de Espiritualidad. Indexed: New Test.Abstr.

348. ORTHODOX WORD
     Fr. Herman Podmoshensky, Ed.
     St. Herman of Alaska Brotherhood
     Platina, CA 96076

Subscription--6/yr.--$12. Description of subject matter--Chris-
tian orthodoxy, universal mysticism, spiritual life, martyrology. Publishes articles in Scripture, Ethics, Church History, Theology, Evangelism, Pastoral Counseling, Missions, Psychology of Religion, Sociology of Religion, World Religions, Philosophy of Religion, Religious
Education, Hagiography, Monography. For: monastics, clergymen,
professors, students, and laypersons. Submissions must be in English. Seeks articles concerning Christian mystics and new martyrs.
Especially looking for book reviews from patristic viewpoint. Style
of journal--patristic thought. Requires 1 copy of manuscript. Length
requirements--maximum, 10 pages; minimum, 2 pages. Responds in
one month. Indexed: Rel.Per.

349. PARACLETE
     David Bundrick, Ed.
     Gospel Publishing House
     1445 Boonville Ave.
     Springfield, MO 65802

Subscription--4/yr.--$4.50; $8.50, 2 yrs. Description of subject matter of journal--Pneumatology--Paraclete is a journal concerning the person and work of the Holy Spirit. Publishes articles in
Scripture, Church History, and Theology. For: professors, students, ministers. Submissions must be in English. Accepts unsolicited articles, unsolicited reviews, dot-matrix printing, simultaneous submissions; does not publish research notes; publishes review-
articles; does not accept advertising. Seeks articles dealing with
Bible exposition, exegesis, theology, or history related to Pentecostal studies. Reviews of books dealing with the Holy Spirit are
considered. Type of article especially seeking--generally, the
articles should be favorable to the Pentecostal doctrinal positions.
Style of journal--Kate L. Turablan, A Manual for Writers. Requires
1 copy of manuscript. Length requirements--maximum, 2400 words
+ documentation; minimum, 1200 words + documentation. Selection
process--criteria: 1) readability, 2) contribution to Pentecostal
scholarship, and 3) suitability to editorial needs, e.g. theme of issue. Responds in about 2 weeks. Approximate proportion of submissions accepted for publication--50 percent. Parent Organization--
General Council of the Assemblies of God, Inc. Indexed: CERDIC.

350. REVISTA DE ESPIRITUALIDAD
Secundino Castro Sanchez, Ed.
Padres Carmelitas Descalzados
Triana 9
28016 Madrid, Spain

Subscription--4/yr.--1,300 ptas. Publishes articles in Church
History, Theology, Psychology of Religion, Spirituality, and Worship.
Submissions must be in Spanish. Sometimes accepts unsolicited arti-
cles and unsolicited reviews; accepts advertising. Indexed: New
Test.Abstr.

351. SPIRITUALITY TODAY
Rev. Richard Woods, O.P.
Spirituality Today Journal, Inc.
7200 W. Division St.
River Forest, IL 60305

Subscription--4/yr.--$11. Description of subject matter of
journal--Aspects of spiritual life--not restricted to but largely focused
on Christian spirituality, especially Roman Catholic, but ecumenical
in scope. For: professors, laypersons. Submissions must be in
English. Sometimes accepts unsolicited articles, unsolicited reviews
(rarely); accepts dot-matrix printing; does not accept simultaneous
submissions; does not publish research notes, review-articles; accepts
advertising--publishers, special educational programs. Type of article journal seeks--thoughtful assessment and evaluation of contemporary trends and figures in spirituality. Articles especially
looking for--those of third-world concerns. Style of journal--Uni-
versity of Chicago Manual of Style. Requires one manuscript.
Length requirements--maximum, 20 double-spaced pages (pica);
minimum, 12 pages. Selection process--1st and 2nd readers--Editor's
final choice based on excellence in writing, content, and focus. Responds to submission--card on receipt; evaluation may take up to
4 months. Approximate proportion of submissions accepted for pub-
lication--30-40 percent. Comments: A stipend is paid based on the
rate of $5 per printed page for first North American serial rights
only. Parent Organization--Dominicans, Province of St. Albert the
Great. Indexed: Cath.Ind., Old Test.Abstr.

352. STUDIES IN FORMATIVE SPIRITUALITY
Fr. Adrian Van Kaam, C.S.Sp., Ph.D., Ed.
Duquesne University
Institute of Formative Spirituality
600 Forbes Ave.
Pittsburgh, PA 15282

Subscription--3/yr.--$16. Description of subject matter of
journal--Studies address the dimension of dynamic spiritual unfolding

from the point of view of the science of formative spirituality and its
auxiliary disciplines. Publishes articles in Psychology of Religion.
For: professors, students, laypersons, religious. Submissions must
be in English. Accepts unsolicited articles, dot-matrix printing,
simultaneous submissions; does not accept unsolicited reviews; does
not publish research notes or review-articles; does not accept advertising. Seeks studies which offer a systematic approach to physio-
logical, psychological, emotional and spiritual formation. Especially
seeking thematic articles by contemporary experts in their areas of
concentration. Style of journal--articles, reprints, translations; summaries and bibliographies; Glossary of the Science of Formative Spirituality; book annotations. Requires 2 copies of manuscript. Indexed: Cath.Ind., Curr.Cont., Hum.Ind., Arts&Hum.Cit.Ind., Rel.
&Theol.Abstr.

353. VIE CONSACREE
      Léon Renwart, s.j. Business Manager
      Rue de Bruxelles   61
      B-5000 Namur, Belgium

Subscription--6/yr.--BEF 400.- Description of subject matter
of journal--Doctrinal and practical study of the implications of the
consecration to God by religious and other persons. Publishes
articles in Theology of the Religious Life. For: religious men and
women. Manuscripts may be submitted in French, German, Spanish,
English, Italian, or Dutch. Articles are published only in French.
Requires one copy of manuscript. Length requirements--maximum,
20 pages; minimum--2-3 pages. Selection process--advice of a publisher's readers' committee. Responds to a submission--acknowledg-
ment--immediately; advice--plus or minus 2 months. Indexed: Canon
Law Abstr.

354. THE WAY
      Rev. Philip Sheldrake, Ed.
      Rev. David Lonsdale, Ed.
      Heythrop College
      11 Cavendish Square
      London W1M 0AN, England

Subscription--4/yr.--$25. Description of subject matter of
journal--mainly Christian Spirituality with interests in theology, pastoral concerns in ecumenical context. For: professors, students,
laypersons, clergy, and religious. Submissions must be in French,
German, Spanish, English, or Italian. Sometimes accepts unsolicited
articles; does not accept unsolicited reviews, simultaneous submissions; accepts dot-matrix printing; does not publish research notes
or review-articles; does not accept advertising. Requires one copy
of manuscript. Length requirements--maximum, 4000 words; minimum, 3000 words. Responds to a submission in one month.

Comments: We usually commission articles on particular themes selected by Editorial Committee. Parent Organization--Society of Jesus. Indexed: Cath.Ind., Old Test.Abstr., New Test.Abstr.

OTHER JOURNALS THAT PUBLISH ARTICLES
IN SPIRITUALITY; MYSTICISM; CONTEMPLATIVE LIFE

355. CHRIST TO THE WORLD/CRISTO AL MUNDO
Basil M. Arthadeva, Ed. Fr.
Via di Propaganda 1-C
00187 Rome, Italy

Subscription--5/yr.--$20. Description of subject matter of
journal--Doctrinal questions (Christian), approach to other religions,
experiences of conversion to the Catholic faith. Publishes articles in
Scripture, Ethics, Theology, Evangelism, Pastoral Counseling, Missions, Philosophy of Religion, Judaism, Islam, Hinduism, and Buddhism.
For: professors, students, laypersons, priests, and nuns. Submissions must be in French, Spanish, or English. Seeking articles
concerning conversion experiences of individuals or groups to the
Catholic faith. Requires 2 copies of manuscript. Length require-
ments--maximum, 20 pages (450 words per page); minimum, 5 pages
(450 words per page). Selection process--seeks unity and coherence
of Christian doctrine on the foundation Christ established which is
the preservation of Peter from error (i.e., papal infallibility). Responds in 2 weeks to a month (maximum). Approximate proportion
of submissions accepted for publication--50 percent. Comments--we
publish nothing that could damage the integrity of the faith Christ
taught and continues to teach through His church. Indexed: Cath.
Ind.

356. DISCIPLESHIP JOURNAL
Susan Maycinik, Ed.
Navigators
Box 6000
Colorado Springs, CO 80934

Subscription--6/yr.--$12. Description of subject matter--
Strives to instruct about and promote obedience to Scripture; also
to equip the growing disciple to win others to Christ and help them
grow to maturity. Publishes articles in Scripture, Evangelism, and
Missions. For: laypersons. Submissions must be in English. Accepts unsolicited articles, dot-matrix submissions; does not accept
unsolicited reviews, simultaneous submissions; does not publish research notes or review-articles; accepts advertising. Seeks articles--
exposition of Scripture, essay, "how-to" regarding aspects of Christian

life and ministry. Especially looking for articles that give practical instruction in disciplining others. Requires 1 manuscript. Length requirements--maximum, 3000 words; minimum, 600 words. Selection process--Editor screens articles for Selection Committee. Responds in 2-6 weeks. Approximate proportion of submissions that are accepted for publication--8 percent. Indexed: Chr.Per.Ind.

357. GLOBAL CHURCH GROWTH
     Dr. Kent R. Hunter
     c/o Church Growth Center
     Corunna, IN 46730

Subscription--4/yr.--$11.50. Description of subject matter of journal--We are the spokespiece for the worldwide Church Growth Movement and our passion is for world evangelization. Publishes articles in Evangelism, Missions, and Church Growth. For: professors, students, laypersons, missionaries. Submissions must be in English. Sometimes accepts unsolicited articles and unsolicited reviews; accepts dot-matrix printing, simultaneous submissions (if notified); publishes research notes and review articles; accepts advertising--any advertising that is compatible to our mission and would be a service to our readership. Seeks articles that are timely and practical insights in Church Growth or dealing with the growth of God's kingdom through world evangelization. Especially seeking material that is informative and preferably not limited by cultural bounds. Style of journal--2 column format. Requires one copy of manuscript. Length requirements--maximum, 2000 words; minimum, 1500 words. Selection process--First, if the article fits within the theme for a particular issue to be published; second, if the information would be of great benefit to our readers at this time; third, if it demonstrates the author's ingenuity and originality in the field. Responds to a submission in 1 month. Approximate proportion of submissions accepted for publication--65 percent. Indexed: Chr.Per.Ind.

OTHER JOURNALS THAT PUBLISH
ARTICLES IN EVANGELISM

AFER 501
Africa Theological Journal 502
Alliance Life 314
America 448
American Baptist Quarterly 1
Antonianum 271
Asbury Theological Journal 5
Banner 6
Baptist Program 442
Berliner Theologische Zeit-

schrift 7
Bibbia E Oriente 163
Bibel und Kirche 164
Boletín Teológico 524
Brethren Life and Thought 455
Calvin Theological Journal 11
Catalyst: Social Pastoral Magazine for Melanesia 223
Christian Medical Society Journal 226

17. MISSIONS

358. COMMISSION
Leland F. Webb, Ed.
Southern Baptist Convention
Foreign Mission Board
3806 Monument Ave.
Box 6767
Richmond, VA 23230

Subscription--9/yr.--$6.50. Description of subject matter--
Foreign missions, primarily by Southern Baptists and associated
Baptist groups abroad. For: laypersons and pastors. Submissions must be in English. Sometimes accepts unsolicited articles and
unsolicited reviews; does not accept dot-matrix printing, simultaneous
submissions; does not publish research notes; publishes review-
articles; does not accept advertising. Seeks articles that relate to
foreign missions--activity, strategy, biblical basis, development, some
biography. One copy of manuscript required. Length requirements
--varies, space is limited. Selection process--determined by subject,
relation to other content and available space. Responds in about 3
weeks. Approximate proportion of submissions accepted for publica-
tion--15 percent. A schedule for securing direct coverage by reporting teams provides most content. Magazine currently is about
45 percent photographic.

359. DANSK MISSIONSBLAD
Jakob Rönnow, Ed.
Danske Missionsselskab-Danish Missionary Society
Strandagervej 24
DK-2900 Hellerup, Denmark

Subscription--12/yr.--112 Kr. Subject matter of journal--
Mission work and background. Publishes articles in Evangelism,
Missions, World Religions, Philosophy of Religion, Islam, Hinduism,
Buddhism, and Eastern Religions. For: students, laypersons, and
pastors. Submissions must be in English or Nordic languages. Accepts unsolicited articles, unsolicited reviews, dot-matrix printing,
simultaneous submissions; sometimes publishes research notes; publishes review-articles; does not accept advertising. Type of article
especially seeking--This is the most important condition--Christianity

and indigenous religion in Madagaskar, Japan, India, Tanzania, Taiwan, Muslim countries. Requires 1 copy of manuscript. Length requirements--maximum, 4 pages; minimum--none. Responds in 2 months. Approximate proportion of submissions that are accepted for publication--one third. Indexed: Abstr.Musl.Rel.

360. EVANGELICAL MISSIONS QUARTERLY
     James W. Reapsome, Ed.
     Evangelical Missions Information Service
     Box 794
     Wheaton, IL 60189

Subscription--4/yr.--$14.95. Subject matter--Missions. Description of subject matter--successful missionary work, practical ideas, new strategies, trends in church planning and nurture, medicine, literature, education, relief, and development. For: professors, students, laypersons, and missionaries (primary audience). Submissions must be English. Accepts unsolicited articles, unsolicited reviews, dot-matrix printing; does not accept simultaneous submissions; does not publish research notes or review-articles; accepts advertising--schools, publishers, missions service agencies, travel agencies, etc. Seeks articles which outline practical strategies and trends in missions and which discuss missions issues, describing successful work (case studies). Especially looking for articles by missionaries or missions professors, writing from experience. 1 copy of manuscript is required. Length requirements--maximum, 3500 words; minimum, 1500 words. Selection process of article--on basis of relevance to audience, good quality of content and writing, presents new and useful material. Responds in 2 weeks. One in 15 submissions is accepted for publication. Indexed: Chr.Per.Ind., Rel.&Theol.Abstr.

361. EXTENSION
     Bradley Collins, Ed.
     Catholic Church Extension Society of the United States
     35 E. Wacker Dr.
     Chicago, IL 60601

Subscription--10/yr.--Free to Extension Society supporters. Description of subject matter--Stories about home missions in the U.S. helped by Extension Society and topics involved in our funding needs, primarily of rural America. Publishes articles in Missions. For: laypersons, clergy, and religious. Submissions in English. Sometimes accepts unsolicited articles; does not accept unsolicited reviews; accepts dot-matrix printing, simultaneous submissions; publishes research notes; does not publish review-articles; accepts advertising. Seeks articles where evangelization or religious education are primary subjects: What does it mean to be a missionary in the U.S. today? Always searching for new trends. All articles must focus on missions in areas supported by Extension Society (currently 90 dioceses across the U.S.). Style of journal--short articles focused on people and places--human interest feature--style. One copy of manuscript required. Length requirements--maximum, 2000 words; minimum, 800 words. Selection process--topics selected for year's issues. Commissions articles that cannot be done in-house. Responds in 1-2 months. Approximate proportion of submissions that are accepted for publication--5 percent, unsolicited; 100 percent commissioned articles. Comments--Query first required. Very few unsolicited manuscripts fit needs of journal. Photos also used with articles. Indexed: Cath.Ind.

362. INDIAN MISSIOLOGICAL REVIEW
Sebastian Karotemprel, Ed.
Sacred Heart College
Shillong 793 008, India

Subscription--4/yr.--$10.00. Subject matter of journal--Evangelism and Missions. Accepts unsolicited articles; sometimes accepts unsolicited reviews; accepts advertising. Submissions must be in English.

363. INTERNATIONAL REVIEW OF MISSION
Eugene Stockwell, Ed.
World Council of Churches
Commission on World Mission and Evangelism
150 Route de Ferney
1211 Geneva 20, Switzerland

Subscription--4/yr.--$17.50. Description of subject matter of journal--all aspects of the Church's missionary effort. Publishes articles in Evangelism, Missions, Sociology of Religion, and Ecumenism. For: professors, students, and laypersons. Submissions must be in English. Accepts unsolicited articles and unsolicited reviews. Selection process--Editorial Board. Indexed: Br.Hum.Ind., Abstr.Musl.Rel., Chr.Per.Ind., Rel.&Theol.Abstr., Rel.Per., Rel.Ind.One.

364. MARYKNOLL
Moises Sandoval, Ed.
Maryknoll Society
Maryknoll, NY 10545

Subscription--Monthly--$1 (or any amount sent). Subject matter of journal--Missions. Accepts unsolicited articles; sometimes accepts unsolicited reviews; publishes review-articles; does not accept advertising. For: professors, students, laypersons, others. Submissions must be in Spanish or English. Requires one copy of manuscript. Co-sponsor--Catholic Foreign Mission Society of America. Indexed: Cath.Ind.

365. MISSIOLOGY
Ralph R. Covell, Ed.
600 Walnut Ave.
Scottsdale, PA 15683

Subscription--4/yr.--$15, individuals; $20, institutions. Publishes articles with a Missiological Focus in Scripture, Church History, Theology, Evangelism, Missions, Sociology of Religion, World Religions, Judaism, Islam, Hinduism, Buddhism, and Eastern Religions. For: professors, students, laypersons, missionaries. Accepts unsolicited articles, unsolicited reviews, dot-matrix printing; does not accept simultaneous submissions; publishes review-articles (short ones); sometimes publishes research notes; accepts advertising--books, programs, conferences. Seeks articles which give new data, new approaches, or a new interpretation. Style of journal--Chicago style. Requires 1 copy of manuscript. Length requirements--maximum, no more than 40 double-spaced pages; minimum, none. Selection process--three-person Editorial Board--one Roman Catholic, one conciliar Protestant, and one evangelical Protestant. Responds in 3 months. Approximate proportion of submissions accepted for publication--50 percent. Indexed: Hist.Abstr., Rel.Per., Chr.Per.Ind., Amer.Hist.&Life, CERDIC, Rel.Ind.One, Rel.&Theol. Abstr.

366. MISSION STUDIES
Dr. Thomas Kramm, Ed.
Postfach 1110
D-5100 Aachen, West Germany (B.R.D.)

Subscription--2/yr.--$12.00. Description of subject matter of journal--The study of theological, historical, and practical questions relating to mission. Publishes articles in Church History, Theology, Evangelism, Missions, World Religions, Philosophy of Religion, Islam, and Eastern Religions. Submissions must be in English.

367. WORLD MISSION JOURNAL
Bill Banghann, Ed.
Jim Burton, Ed.
Southern Baptist Convention
Brotherhood Commission
1548 Poplar Ave.
Memphis, TN 38104

Subscription--12/yr.--$6.60. Description of subject matter--The World Mission Journal is the men's mission magazine of the

Southern Baptist Convention--it tells the story of contemporary
Southern Baptist missions and the involvement of lay persons in missions and ministry. Publishes articles in Evangelism and Missions.
For: laypersons and pastors. Submissions must be in English. Accepts unsolicited articles; does not accept unsolicited reviews, accepts dot-matrix printing, simultaneous submissions; does not publish research notes, review-articles; does not accept advertising.
Seeks articles on SBC missions focusing on SBC missionaries at home
and overseas; laymen who have discovered a call to be a missionary
in their own communities or elsewhere. Style of journal--literary
journalism--upbeat, visual orientation. One copy of manuscript is
required. Length requirements--maximum, 700 words; minimum, 500
words. Selection process--quality journalism, contemporary in focus,
which appeals to a general reading audience. Responds--up to 6
months. Approximate number of submissions accepted for publica-
tion--20 percent. Comments--Find it difficult to accept articles which
are not accompanied by professional quality black-and-white pho-
tography. Indexed: South.Bap.Per.Ind.

368. ZEITSCHRIFT FUER MISSIONSWISSENSCHAFT UND RELIGIONS-
    WISSENSCHAFT
    Thomas Kramm, Ed.
    Postfach 1110
    D-5100 Aachen, West Germany (B.R.D.)

Subscription--4/yr.--DM 42. Subject matter of journal--Church
History, Evangelism, Missions, Psychology of Religion, Sociology of
Religion, World Religions, Philosophy of Religion, Judaism, Islam,
Hinduism, Buddhism, and Eastern Religions. Submissions must be
in German, French, or English. Accepts unsolicited articles; ac-
cepts advertising. Indexed: Rel.Per., Canon Law Abstr., Rel.Ind.
One, Rel.&Theol.Abstr.

OTHER JOURNALS THAT PUBLISH
ARTICLES IN MISSIONS

Africa Theological Journal 502
Alliance Life 314
America 448
American Baptist Quarterly 1
Annals Magazine 222
Antonianum 271
Asbury Theological Journal 5
Banner 6
Baptist Program 442
Bibliotheca Sacra 8
Brethren Life and Thought 455

Bulletin of the Christian Institute
 of Sikh Studies 467
Calvin Theological Journal 11
Caribbean Journal of Religious
 Studies 525
Catalyst: Social Pastoral Maga-
 zine for Melanesia 223
Centre for the Study of Islam and
 Christian Muslim Relations
 Newsletter 472
China Study Project Journal 514

18. CHURCH ADMINISTRATION

369. IUS CANONICUM
      Tomás Rincón, Ed.
      Ediciones Universidad de Navarra, S.A.
      Apdo. 396
      31080 Pamplona, Spain

Subscription--2/yr.--$27. Description of subject matter of
journal--The journal has different sections: Studies in Church Administration; Book Reviews; Commentaries on Specific Laws of the
Church; and Commentaries on Canonical Judicial Decisions. Publishes research articles in Church Administration, Canon Law, and
Civil Law dealing with Ecclesiastical Matters. For: professors. Submissions must be in Spanish (at times other languages are accepted).
Sometimes accepts unsolicited articles, unsolicited reviews; does not
accept dot-matrix printing, simultaneous submissions; publishes research notes and review-articles; does not accept advertising. Style
of journal--UNESCO Norms. Requires 2 copies of manuscript. Length
requirements--maximum, 50 pages; minimum, 5 pages (book reviews).
Selection process--Editorial Board decides which articles will be published according to scientific quality. Responds in one month (approximately). Approximate proportion of submissions accepted for
publication--40 percent (last four years). Indexed: Canon Law
Abstr.

370. PRESCHOOL LEADERSHIP
      Amy Ashworth, Ed.
      Southern Baptist Convention
      Sunday School Board
      127 Ninth Avenue, North
      Nashville, TN 37234

Subscription--4/yr.--$7.25. Description of subject matter--
Preschool Leadership is a quarterly publication for administering
preschool work in Sunday School and Church Training. Publishes
articles in Church Administration and Religious Education. For:
laypersons and ministers of Childhood Education. Submissions must
be in English. Does not accept unsolicited articles or unsolicited reviews; accepts dot-matrix printing; does not accept simultaneous
submissions; does not publish research notes; publishes review-

articles; does not accept advertising. Seeks articles that assist preschool leaders in planning and implementing preschool work in local
churches. Especially looking for articles relating to characteristics
and needs of preschoolers, training sessions, and personal development helps for teachers and teaching tips/seasonal suggestions. Style
of journal--52 pages at 32 or 38 characters per line. Requires 2
copies of manuscript. Length requirements--maximum, 180 lines;
minimum, 90 lines. Selection process--Editor enlists 99 percent of
the writers who have experience in preschool work in Southern Baptist
Churches. Responds in 2-4 weeks. Approximately 5 percent of the
submissions are accepted for publication. Indexed: South.Bap.Per.
Ind.

371. TODAY'S PARISH
     Mary Carol Kendzia, Ed.
     Twenty-Third Publications
     Box 180
     Mystic, CT 06355

Subscription--7/yr.--$15. Description of subject matter--guide
to effective management and ministry for the contemporary parish.
Subject matter of journal--Church Administration. For: laypersons
and parish professionals. Submissions must be in English. Accepts
unsolicited articles, unsolicited reviews, dot-matrix printing; does
not accept simultaneous submissions; does not publish research notes;
and accepts advertising--pertinent to parish needs. Especially looking for practical ideas, programs and suggestions for parish use; human interest-type stories of parish life. Style of journal--"magazine"
style of writing, no interviews. Length requirements--maximum,
1800 words; minimum, none. How an article is chosen for publica-
tion--how well the article is written, whether it is appropriate subject
matter. Also, timeliness is a consideration. Responds in 4-6 weeks.
Approximately 30 percent of all submissions are accepted for publication. Indexed: Cath.Ind.

OTHER JOURNALS THAT PUBLISH ARTICLES IN CHURCH ADMINISTRATION

America 110
American Baptist Quarterly 1
Antonianum 271
Banner 6
Baptist Program 442
Berliner Theologische Zeit-
   schrift 7
Bibliotheca Sacra 8
Calvin Theological Journal 11

Caribbean Journal of Religious
   Studies 525
The Chicago Theological Seminary
   Register 317
Christian Century 224
Christian Education Journal 374
Christian Medical Society Journal
   226
Christian Ministry 318

19. RELIGIOUS EDUCATION

372. ASSOCIATION OF BRITISH THEOLOGICAL AND PHILOSOPHICAL
LIBRARIES. BULLETIN. N.S.
John V. Howard, Ed.
Association of British Theological and Philosophical Libraries
Edinburgh University Library
George Square
Edinburgh EH8 9LJ, Scotland

Subscription--3/yr.--$15. Description of subject matter of
journal--Bibliography and Librarianship of Religion and Philosophy.
For: librarians. Submissions must be in English. Accepts unsolicited articles, unsolicited reviews; does not accept dot-matrix printing, simultaneous submissions; publishes research notes and review-
articles; accepts advertising--camera-ready copy and flyers for in-
sertion. Seeks--results of original work, literature surveys, history
of religious and philosophical libraries. Style of the journal--associa-
tion news, reference section, articles. Requires one copy of manuscript. Length requirements--maximum, 4000 words; minimum, 400
words. Selection process--Editor's judgment, supported when necessary by reference to subject specialists. Responds to a submission
in one month. Approximate proportion of submissions accepted for
publication--75 percent. Indexed: LISA

373. BRITISH JOURNAL OF RELIGIOUS EDUCATION
Dr. J. M. Hull, Ed.
Faculty of Education
University of Birmingham
P.O. Box 363
Birmingham B15 2TT, England

Subscription--3/yr.--7.50 pounds. Subject matter of journal--
Religious Education as taught in the State schools of Britain together
with studies of the relationship between religions and education in
Britain and internationally. For: professors, students, and laypersons. Submissions must be in English. Accepts unsolicited articles, dot-matrix printing; does not accept unsolicited reviews,
simultaneous submissions; publishes research notes and review-
articles; accepts advertising--advertisements relevant to the interests of British Religious Education teachers in State schools. Articles

should be double-spaced with wide margins using one side of paper only. A style sheet indicating other necessary information for preparation of an article may be obtained from the journal. BJRE has an equal opportunities policy. Contributors should avoid sexist language. A leaflet giving advice is available, on request, from the Editor. Requires one copy of manuscript. Length requirements-- maximum, 2000-5000 words. Selection process--Editorial discretion with professional consultation. Responds in one week to three months. Approximate proportion of submissions accepted for publication--1/3. Indexed: Br.Educ.Ind., Rel.&Theol.Abstr., Abstr. Musl.Rel.

374. CHRISTIAN EDUCATION JOURNAL
Wesley R. Willis, Ed.
Scripture Press Ministries, Inc.
Box 513
Glen Ellyn, IL   60318

Subscription--2/yr.--$7. Description of subject matter--theological/philosophical articles in Christian education and education research material. For: professors, students, and church leaders. Submissions must be in English. Accepts unsolicited articles, dot-matrix printing, simultaneous submissions; sometimes accepts unsolicited reviews; publishes research notes and review-articles; does not accept advertising. Seeks articles--theoretical and empirical research. Consideration will be given to topics directly related to Christian education, including church ministry and church leadership, and to reactions to current or past journal articles. Style of journal--A Manual of Style by the University of Chicago Press. Requires 2 copies of manuscript. Length requirements--maximum, 20 pages; minimum, 8 pages. An abstract of 50 words or less summarizing the main points of the article should accompany the manuscript. Selection process--a review panel reads and evaluates. Responds in 3-6 months. Approximately 25-50 percent of all submissions are accepted for publication. Indexed: Chr.Per.Ind., Rel. Ind.One.

375. CHRISTIAN SCHOLAR'S REVIEW
William Hasker, Ed.
Huntington College
Huntington, IN   46750

Subscription--4/yr.--$12, individuals; $15, libraries. Description of subject matter of journal--Publication has as its main objective the integration of Christian faith and learning on both the intra- and interdisciplinary levels. As a secondary purpose, CSR seeks to provide a forum for the discussion of the theoretical issues of Christian higher education. Publishes articles in Religious Education. Accepts unsolicited articles; publishes book reviews and review-

articles; accepts advertising--new book releases. Welcomes articles
of high standards of original scholarship and of general interest
dealing with all aspects of Christian thought and the interrelationship
of Christian thought with all areas of scholarly interest. Style of
journal--University of Chicago Manual of Style. Additional information in the first issue of each volume. Requires 2 copies of manuscript. Indexed: Bibl.Engl.Lang.&Lit., Chr.Per.Ind., G.Soc.Sci.&
Rel.Per.Lit., New Test.Abstr., Rel.&Theol.Abstr., Rel.Ind.One.

376. CHRISTLICH-PAEDAGOGISCHE BLAETTER
     Edgar Josef Korherr, Ed.
     Verlag Herder
     Wollzeile 33
     A-1010 Vienna, Austria

Subscription--6/yr.--288 S. Description of subject matter of
journal--Paedagogical, catechetical subjects and models. Publishes
articles in Religious Education. For: professors, students, laypersons, and priests. Submissions must be in German. Seeks articles that are practical (Catholic) oriented. Sometimes accepts unsolicited articles, unsolicited reviews; does not accept dot-matrix
printing, simultaneous submissions; publishes research notes and
review-articles. Type of article especially seeking--articles concerning inculturation in Europe. Articles must be clear, vivid, and ex-
pressive. Requires one copy of manuscript. Length requirements--
maximum, 8 pages; minimum, one page. Selection process--Chief
Editor is responsible for selection. Responds in 3 months. Approximate proportion of submissions accepted for publication--12 percent.
Indexed: Canon Law Abstr.

377. CHURCH AND SYNAGOGUE LIBRARIES
     William H. Gentz, Ed.
     Church and Synagogue Library Association
     Box 19357
     Portland, OR   97219

Subscription--6/yr.--$15. Description of subject matter of
journal--Everything related to the world of libraries in local churches
and synagogues. For: laypersons and librarians. Submissions
must be in English. Accepts unsolicited articles, dot-matrix printing, simultaneous submissions; does not accept unsolicited reviews;
does not publish research notes; publishes review-articles; accepts
advertising--books and other materials for library use. Description
of type of article that is sought--how to, inspiration for library work.
Bibliographies do not apply. Style of journal--Univ. of Chicago Style
manual. Requires one copy of manuscript. Length requirements for
submissions--maximum, 1500 words. Selection process--Editor and
Executive Secretary decide. Occasional reports and suggestions from
national board. Responds in 2 weeks to 1 month. Indexed: Chr.
Per.Ind., CERDIC.

378. DIALOGUE ON CAMPUS
George W. Jones, Ed.
Association for the Coordination of University Religious Affairs
Executive Committee
Office of Religious Programs
Ball State University
Muncie, IN 47306

Subscription--4/yr.--$5. Description of subject matter--the
practice of religion in college; information on college campuses; information on religious groups and program resources. Publishes articles in Religious Education, Religion in Higher Education--practice,
administration of. For: administrators and campus ministers. Articles appear in English. Accepts unsolicited articles, unsolicited reviews, dot-matrix printing, simultaneous submissions. Publishes research notes and review-articles. Accepts advertising--if it provides
a service to members. Seeks news stories, book reviews, editorials,
and program descriptions. Type of article especially looking for--
Pluralism. Style of journal--none. Submit one copy of manuscript.
Length requirements--maximum, 1200 words. Selection of material by
editor on basis of probable interest and value to college administrators. Responds in 1 month. Approximately 95 percent of submissions are published. Comments--Dialogue is essentially a newsletter.
Carries articles up to 1200 words, especially presentations at
annual meetings. Indexed: ERIC

379. HUMAN DEVELOPMENT
Linda Amadeo, Executive Editor
42 Kirkland Street
Cambridge, MA 02138

Subscription--4/yr.--$18. Description of subject matter of
journal--Designed for persons involved in the tasks of religious
leadership and formation, spiritual direction of pastoral care, and education. For: professors, clergy, educators. Submissions must be
in English. Publishes articles in Church Administration, Pastoral
Counseling, Psychology of Religion, and Religious Education. Accepts
unsolicited articles, unsolicited reviews; does not accept simultaneous
submissions; does not accept advertising. Seeks articles which pertain to issues and problems related to human growth and development.
Requires 2 copies of manuscript. Length requirements--maximum,
4500 words with not more than 10 listings in the Bibliography. Selection process--Editorial Board. Comments: Will consider filler items
of between 500 and 1000 words. Parent Organization--Jesuit Educational Center for Human Development. Indexed: Cath.Ind., Educ.
Ind., C.I.J.E., Lang.&Lang.Behav.Abstr.

380. INTERACTION
Martha Jander, Ed.

Concordia Publishing House
1333 S. Kirkwood Rd.
St. Louis, MO   63122

Subscription--monthly--$8.75.   Subject matter of journal--a
magazine for church school teachers, giving practical and inspirational advice.   Publishes articles in Religious Education.   For laypersons and church school teachers.   Submissions must be in English.   Sometimes accepts unsolicited articles; does not accept unsolicited reviews; accepts dot-matrix printing; does not accept simultaneous submissions; does not publish research notes or review-
articles; does not accept advertising.   Requires 1 copy of manuscript.   Parent Organization--Lutheran Church--Missouri Synod,
Board for Parish Services.   Indexed: Curr.Cont.

381.   JEWISH EDUCATION
       Dr. Alvin I. Schiff, Ed.
       Board of Jewish Education of Greater New York
       426 W. 58th St.
       New York, NY   10019

Subscription--4/yr.--$12.50.   Description of subject matter of
journal--History, Philosophy, Psychology, Ethics, Sociology of Jewish
Education; research on curriculum and methodology; articles about curriculum and methodology; comparative Jewish education.   For: professors, students, laypersons, principals, administrators, teachers,
rabbis.   Submissions must be in English.   Accepts unsolicited articles, unsolicited reviews; does not accept simultaneous submissions;
does not publish research notes; publishes review-articles; accepts
advertising--educational materials and events.   Requires 2 copies
of manuscript.   Length requirements--maximum, 6000 words; minimum,
2000 words.   Selection process -sent to 3 readers (members of Editorial Board) for comment; decision made by Editor.   Responds to a
submission--immediate acknowledgment, final response within 3-4
months.   Approximate proportion of submissions accepted for publica-
tion--25-35 percent.   Comments: Jewish Education is the major pub-
licaton on Jewish Education.   Indexed: Educ.Ind., Psychol.Abstr.,
Ind.Jew.Per., Rel.&Theol.Abstr.

382.   JOURNAL OF CHRISTIAN EDUCATION
       Nell Holm, Ed.
       Australian Teachers' Christian Fellowship
       120 Chalmers St.
       Surry Hills
       New South Wales 2010, Australia

Subscription--3/yr.--$18, individuals; $24, institutions.   Publishes articles in Education/Christianity Interface.   The purpose of
this journal is to consider the implications of the Christian faith for

the entire field of education and to examine its contribution to the
solution of educational problems. It seeks to present and to examine
philosophically Christian views on education, to publish reports of
experiments in curriculum and method based on Christian principles
and to discuss in the light of such principles some of the more important developments in modern education around the world. Seeks
articles that have an evangelical basis of faith, acceptable by authors
of other persuasions. Accepts unsolicited articles, dot-matrix printing;
sometimes accepts unsolicited reviews; does not accept simultaneous
submissions; publishes research notes and review-articles; does not
accept advertising. For: professors, school teachers, others. Submissions must be in English. Style of journal--scholarly, academic
style that tries to link theory and practice. Style sheet for contributors may be obtained. Requires 2 copies of manuscript. Selection
process--articles received are sent to referees for comment. Responds
to a submission in 2 months. Approximate proportion of submissions
accepted for publication--80 percent, although many articles are returned with many helpful suggestions for revision that authors usually
accommodate and resubmit. Indexed: Educ.Ind., Aus.P.A.I.S.,
Aus.Educ.Ind., Chr.Per.Ind., Rel.&Theol.Abstr., Rel.Ind.One.

383. KEY TO CHRISTIAN EDUCATION
      Virginia Beddow, Ed.
      Standard Publishing
      8121 Hamilton Ave.
      Cincinnati, OH 45231

      Subscription--4/yr.--$4. Description of subject matter of
journal--ideas that are working in the field of Christian Education.
Publishes articles in Religious Education. For: professors, laypersons, and staff members. Submissions must be in English. Accepts
unsolicited articles; does not accept unsolicited reviews, dot-matrix
printing, simultaneous submissions; does not publish research notes
or review-articles; does not accept advertising. Seeks success
stories, useable ideas, seasonal articles, contemporary topics, and
"how to" articles. Style of journal--most readers will be selective;
department pages are included as well as general interest articles.
Requires one copy of manuscript. Length requirements--maximum,
2000 words; minimum, 800 words. Selection process--Is it practical?
Is it written in a readable style? Does it fit an upcoming theme?
Responds in 1-2 months. Approximate proportion of submissions accepted for publication--15 percent. Indexed: CERDIC, Chr.Per.Ind.

384. LIVING LIGHT
      Berard L. Marthaler, Ed.
      United States Catholic Conference
      1312 Massachusetts Ave. N.W.
      Washington, D.C. 20005

Subscription--4/yr.--$15. Description of subject matter of journal--
interdisciplinary review of Christian education, catechesis and pastoral
ministry. Primarily for Catholics with an ecumenical thrust. Publishes articles in Religious Education and Pastoral Ministry. Accepts
unsolicited articles, dot-matrix printing; sometimes accepts unsolicited
reviews; publishes review-articles; accepts advertising--books, conferences, workshops of interest to religious educators and church
workers. For: professors, graduate students, DREs/DCEs. Submissions must be in English. Seeks articles of interest to professional religious educators. Especially seeking--reports on developments
in the field and research. Style of journal--Chicago Manual of Style.
Length requirements--maximum, 4000 words; minimum, 1000 words.
Selection process--Editor does first screening, then consults one or
more advisors. Final decision made on basis of how well an article
fits with the theme of a particular issue. Responds in 1-2 months.
Approximate proportion of submissions accepted for publication--un-
solicited mss. 1 in 5. Parent Organization--United States Catholic
Conference, Department of Education. Indexed: Old Test.Abstr.,
Cath.Ind.

385. LUMEN VITAE
Pierre Mourlon Beernaert, Ed.
Lumen Vitae Press
186 rue Washington
1050 Brussels, Belgium

Subscription--4/yr.--$25. Subject matter of journal--Scripture,
Church History, Theology, Pastoral Counseling, Missions, Psychology
of Religion, Sociology of Religion, World Religions, Religious Education. Submissions must be in French or English. Accepts unsolicited
articles, unsolicited reviews; does not accept dot-matrix printing,
simultaneous submissions; does not publish research notes; publishes
review-articles; accepts advertising--books, periodicals, courses (religion). Seeks articles dealing with religious formation (for children
and adults). Especially looking for catechetics and pastoral studies.
Requires one copy of manuscript. Length requirements--maximum,
4000 words; minimum, -- words. Selection process--First, screening
by the editor or assistant editor who passes the article on to two
other members of the board or of the Institute. Responds in approximately 2 months. Parent Organization--International Centre for Religious Education. Editions are in English and French. Indexed:
Cath.Ind., Educ.Ind., New Test.Abstr., Rural Recreat.Tour.Abstr.,
Rel.&Theol.Abstr., World Agri.Econ.&Rural Sociol.Abstr.

386. LUTHERAN EDUCATION
Merle L. Radke, Ed.
Concordia College
7400 Augusta St.
River Forest, IL 60305

Subscription--5/yr.--$8. Publishes articles in Religious Education. For: teachers. Submissions must be in English. Accepts unsolicited articles, unsolicited reviews; does not accept dot-matrix printing; does not publish research notes; publishes review-articles; accepts advertising--related to education. Seeks articles useful to teachers in Lutheran schools. Style of journal--MLA. Requires one copy of manuscript. Length requirements--maximum, 3000 words. Seeks timely, interesting, scholarly articles. Responds to a submission in 3 weeks. Approximate proportion of submissions accepted for publication--25 percent. Indexed: Educ.Ind., CERDIC.

387. MINISTERIAL FORMATION
World Council of Churches
Programme in Theological Education
P.O. Box 66
150 Route de Ferney
1211 Geneva 20, Switzerland

Subscription--4/yr. Description of subject matter of journal--Ecumenical journal supported by the World Council of Churches. Publishes articles in Religious Education and Ministerial Formation. Submissions must be in English. Accepts unsolicited articles. Seeks articles which encourage and inform the renewal of the churches through programs of ministerial formation. Indexed: Rel.Ind.One.

388. NATIONAL CATHOLIC EDUCATIONAL ASSOCIATION MOMENTUM
Patricia Feistritzer, Ed.
National Catholic Educational Association
1077 30 St., NW
Washington, DC 20007

Subscription--4/yr.--$16. Subject matter of journal--Religious Education, General Education, Educational Research. For: Catholic educators, all levels. Submissions must be in English. Accepts unsolicited articles, unsolicited reviews, dot-matrix printing; does not accept simultaneous submissions; does not publish research notes; publishes review-articles; accepts advertising--display--no classified. Seeks articles that are practical and theoretical. Requires one copy of manuscript. Responds in 3 months. Approximate proportion of submissions accepted for publication--1/4 to 1/3. Indexed: Cath. Ind., Curr.Cont., Educ.Ind.

389. ORIENTATION
Mrs. Rita Swanepoel, Ed.
Prof. B. J. Van Der Walt, Ed.
The Institute of Reformational Studies
Potchefstroom University for CHE
Potchesfstroom, 25201 Republic of South Africa

Subscription--free. Description of subject matter of journal--Christian higher education. Publishes articles in Sociology of Religion and Religious Education. Submissions must be in English.

390. RELIGION TEACHER'S JOURNAL
     Gwen Costello, Ed.
     Twenty-Third Publications
     Box 180
     Mystic, CT   06355

Subscription--7/yr.--$14. Description of subject matter--articles that assist catechists/teachers in their role as religious educators. Publishes articles in Scripture, Theology, Religious Education, and all facets of religious learning that involve catechists. For: laypersons, DRE's and catechists, principals, and teachers. Submissions must be in English. Accepts unsolicited articles; does not accept unsolicited reviews, dot-matrix printing, simultaneous submissions; does not publish research notes or review-articles; accepts advertising--products or services that directly relate to religious education/catechetical ministry. Seeks--practical, feasible articles about programs, inspirational articles about growing spirituality, and informative articles that explain theological issues. Submit one copy of manuscript. Length requirements--maximum, 7 pages; minimum--none. Selection process--each issue has a general theme. We look for these articles first. Then we choose those most helpful to catechists in general. Themes: beginning of year, All Saints, Advent/Christmas, sacraments, Lent, prayer, Summer Bible School program. Responds in 2-4 weeks. Approximately 10 percent are accepted for publication. Indexed: Cath.Ind.

391. RELIGIONSUNTERRICHT AN HOEHEREN SCHULEN
     Roman Mensing, Ed.
     Patmos Verlag
     Am Wehrhahn 100
     Postfach 6213
     4000 Dusseldorf 1, West Germany (B.R.D.)

Subscription--6/yr.--DM.38. Description of subject matter of journal--Religious Education in high schools and colleges. For: professors, students, teachers. Submissions must be in German. Sometimes accepts unsolicited articles; does not accept unsolicited reviews, simultaneous submissions; does not publish research notes or review-articles; accepts advertising--new editions on themes of Religious Education. Description of type of article that is sought--explanations, discussions, essay. Requires one copy of manuscript. Length requirements--maximum, 10 pages; minimum, 2 pages. Responds in 1-2 months. Parent Organization: Bundesverband der Katholischen Religionslehrer an Gymnasien e.V. Indexed: CERDIC.

392. RELIGIOUS EDUCATION
John Westerhoff, Ed.
Jack Spiro, Ed. elect (1988)
Randolph Crump Miller, Managing Ed.
Religious Education Association
409 Prospect St.
New Haven, CT   06510

Subscription--4/yr.--membership. Description of subject mat-
ter--all aspects of education in relation to religion. Publishes articles in Scripture, Ethics, Church History, Theology, Church Administration, Pastoral Counseling, Missions, Psychology of Religion, Sociology of Religion, World Religions, Philosophy of Religion, Judaism,
and Religious Education. For: professors, students, laypersons,
clergy--rabbis--priests. Submissions must be in English. Accepts
unsolicited articles; does not accept unsolicited reviews, dot-matrix
printing; publishes review-articles; accepts advertising. Seeks--
scholarly article, but not too technical. Style of journal--Standard
Chicago. Requires one copy of manuscript. Length requirements--
maximum, 7000; minimum, 2000 words. Selection process--Editor's
choice--peer review--invitation. Responds in 1-4 months. Approximately 10 percent of the submissions are accepted for publication.
Indexed: Curr.Cont., Educ.Ind., Psychol.Abstr., Rel.Per., Adol.
Ment.Hlth.Abstr., Arts&Hum.Cit.Ind., G.Soc.Sci.&Rel.Per.Lit., Ind.
Jew.Per., Rel.Ind.One, Rel.&Theol.Abstr.

393. SEARCH
Southern Baptist Convention
Sunday School Board
127 Ninth Ave. N.
Nashville, TN   37234

Subscription--4/yr.--$11.50. Description of subject matter--
primarily contemporary issues in the areas of religious education,
church music, administration, practical theology, preaching/worship.
Publishes articles in Ethics, Church History (limited), Theology (practical), Evangelism, Church Administration, Pastoral Counseling, Missions, Psychology of Religion, Sociology of Religion, Philosophy of
Religion, and Religious Education. For: professors, pastors, and
church staff. Submissions must be in English. Accepts unsolicited
articles, unsolicited reviews, dot-matrix printing; does not accept
simultaneous submissions; rarely publishes research notes; publishes
review-articles; does not accept advertising. Seeks articles that are
contemporary but not controversial, scholarly but readable. Requires
2 copies of manuscript. Length requirements--maximum, 5000 words;
minimum, 2000 words. Selection process (choosing an article for publication)--articles which seem to the editors to meet readers' interests
and needs, which provide some kind of new or interesting perspective,
thought provoking. Responds in 6 weeks. Approximately 40 percent
of all submissions are accepted for publication. Indexed: South.Bap.
Per.Ind.

394. THE SOUTHERN BAPTIST EDUCATOR
Arthur L. Walker, Jr., Ed.
Southern Baptist Convention
Education Commission
901 Commerce, Suite 600
Nashville, TN   37203-3620

Subscription--12/yr.--$6. Description of subject matter--Articles that concern higher education, particularly those which relate to private, church-related institutions. Publish articles concerning higher education and Baptist colleges. For: professors, college administrators, and trustees. Submissions must be in English. Sometimes accepts unsolicited articles; does not accept unsolicited reviews, dot-matrix printing; accepts simultaneous submissions; does not publish research notes or review-articles; does not accept advertising. Requires 1 copy of manuscript to be submitted. Length requirements--varies. Selection process--manuscript is reviewed by the publications editorial body. Responds in 2-4 weeks. Approximately 50 percent of all submissions are accepted for publication. Indexed: South. Bap.Per.Ind.

395. THEOLOGICAL EDUCATION
David S. Schuller, Ed.
Association of Theological Schools
Box 130
Vandalia, OH   45377

Subscription--2/yr.--$5. Theological Education is the journal of the Association of Theological Schools. Publishes articles in Religious Education and Theological Education. Submissions must be in English. For: professors. Seeks articles that concern the education of candidates for ordination by Christian Churches. Does not accept unsolicited articles (The journal is organized around a theme following papers that have been presented before the Association or reports commissioned by the Association); does not accept advertising. Indexed: Curr.Cont., Rel.Per., Rel.Ind.One.

396. TODAY'S CATHOLIC TEACHER
Ruth A. Matheny, Ed.
Peter Li, Inc.
2451 E. River Rd.
Dayton, OH   45439

Subscription--8/yr.--$14.95. Description of subject matter of journal--articles of academic and professional interest to Catholic school administrators and teachers. For: professors and administrators. Submissions must be in English. Accepts unsolicited articles; does not accept unsolicited reviews, dot-matrix printing, simultaneous submissions; does not publish research notes or review-

articles; accepts advertising--pertinent to education and Catholic
schools. Seeks good curricular articles. Style of journal--non-
technical language. Requires one copy of manuscript. Length re-
quirements--maximum, 1500 words; minimum, 750 words. Selection
process--Issues are thematic in nature. Special articles deal with
current educational concern. Responds in about 6 weeks unless immediately rejected. Approximate proportion of submissions accepted
for publication--30 percent. Indexed: Cath.Ind., CERDIC.

397. VERBUM
     Hoger Katechetisch Instituut
     Nijmegen
     Postbus 38083
     6503 AB Nijmegen, Netherlands

Subscription--8/yr.--38.50 fl., individuals; 30.00 fl., students.
Description of subject matter of journal--religious education for 12-
16 year-olds--Catechesis (school). For: professors, students, and
laypersons. Submissions must be in Dutch. Sometimes accepts unsolicited articles, unsolicited reviews; does not accept dot-matrix
printing, simultaneous submissions; does not publish research notes;
publishes review-articles; accepts advertising--books, materials, etc.
concerning religious education. Seeks practical articles that can be
used by religious teachers. Requires one copy of manuscript.
Length requirements--maximum, 10 pages; minimum, 2 pages. Selection process--we have an Editorial Team; issues are planned. Responds to a submission--some, months; others, weeks. Parent Or-
ganization--Centraal Bureau voor het Katholiek Onderwijs. Indexed:
CERDIC.

OTHER JOURNALS THAT PUBLISH ARTICLES IN
RELIGIOUS EDUCATION

20. COMMUNICATIONS (HOMILETICS; SPEECH; BROADCASTING; REPORTING)

398. THE CATHOLIC JOURNALIST
James A. Doyle, Ed.
Catholic Press Association
119 North Park Ave.
Rockville Center, NY   11570

Subscription--12/yr.--$10.   Description of subject matter of
journal--news and features about Catholic publishing.   Subject matter of journal--Religious Journalism and Publishing.   For: publishers and journalists.   Submissions must be in English.   Accepts
unsolicited articles; does not accept unsolicited reviews, dot-matrix
printing, simultaneous submissions; does not publish research notes;
publishes review-articles; accepts advertising--books, equipment,
graphic suppliers, list houses.   Style of journal--newspaper format.
Requires one copy of manuscript.   Length requirements--maximum,
1500 words; minimum, 500 words.   Selection process--Editor decides
and responds quickly.   Responds in 1 week.   Approximate proportion of submissions accepted for publication--5 percent.   Indexed:
Cath.Ind.

399. ETERNITY
William J. Petersen, Ed.
Evangelical Ministries, Inc.
1716 Spruce St.
Philadelphia, PA   19103

Subscription--Monthly--$17.50.   Eternity is a news-oriented
monthly aimed at providing coverage and Biblical perspective on the
news and cultural trends of the day.   We are looking for journalists,
rather than theologians, as writers.   Indexed: Chr.Per.Ind., G.
Soc.Sci.&Rel.Per.Lit.

400. HOMILETIC AND PASTORAL REVIEW
Rev. Kenneth Baker, Ed.
Catholic Polls, Inc.
86 Riverside Dr.
New York, NY   10024

Subscription--11/yr.--$20. Description of subject matter of journal--a journal that strives to serve the interests of Catholic parish priests. Each issue contains sermonic aids. For: laypersons and clergy. Publishes articles in Scripture, Ethics, Church History, Theology, Evangelism, Church Administration, Pastoral Counseling, Missions, and Religious Education. Accepts unsolicited articles; sometimes accepts unsolicited reviews; publishes sermons; accepts advertising. Seeks sermons or outlines that draw on conservative Catholic theology. Most contributions come from priests. Style of journal--popular. Indexed: Cath.Ind., Rel.&Theol.Abstr., Old Test.Abstr., Canon Law Abstr., New Test.Abstr.

401. MEDIA DEVELOPMENT
      Dr. Michael Traber, Ed.
      122 Kings Road
      London, SW3 4TR England

Subscription--4/yr.--$25. Description of subject matter of journal--The theory and practice of mass and alternative communications worldwide. For: communicators. Sometimes accepts unsolicited articles, unsolicited reviews; accepts dot-matrix printing; does not accept simultaneous submissions; does not publish research notes or review-articles; does not accept advertising. Submissions should be in French, German, Spanish, or English. Requires one copy of manuscript. Length requirements--maximum, 3000 words; minimum, 2000 words. Responds in 2 weeks. Indexed: CERDIC, Commun.Abstr.

402. PROCLAIM
      James E. Hightower, Jr., Ed.
      Southern Baptist Convention
      Sunday School Board
      127 9th Ave. N.
      Nashville, TN 37234

Subscription--4/yr.--$9.50. Description of subject matter--Biblical preaching. For: pastors and associates. Submissions must be in English. Publishes articles in Preaching and Worship. Type of article sought--query for specifications. Accepts unsolicited articles, dot-matrix printing; does not accept unsolicited reviews, simultaneous submissions; accepts dot-matrix printing, does not publish research notes or review-articles; does not accept advertising. Style of Journal--Chicago Manual of Style. Length requirements--query. Responds in 8-12 weeks. Indexed: South.Bap.Per.Ind.

403. RELIGIOUS BROADCASTING
      Dr. Ben Armstrong, Ed.
      National Religious Broadcasters, Inc.
      CN 1926
      Morristown, NJ 07960

Subscription--11/yr.--$18. Description of subject matter of journal--Helpful articles of religious broadcasting nature. For: religious broadcasters and program producers. Submissions must be in English. Accepts unsolicited articles, unsolicited reviews, dot-matrix printing, simultaneous submissions; publishes research notes, review-articles, accepts advertising--paid. Seeks educational, how to, helpful hints on religious broadcasting. Style of journal--request style guide from journal. Requires one copy of manuscript. Length requirements--maximum, 7 double-spaced pages; minimum, 2 double-spaced pages. Selection process--individually reviewed by Editorial Board. Responds to a submission in 6 weeks. Indexed: Chr.Per. Ind.

OTHER JOURNALS THAT PUBLISH ARTICLES IN
COMMUNICATIONS (HOMILETICS; SPEECH;
BROADCASTING; REPORTING)

Concordia Theological Quarterly
   24
Epiphany Journal   30
Expository Times   181
The Other Side   260
Search   393
Southwestern Journal of The-
   ology   193

404. HYMN
Paul Westermeyer, Ed.
Hymn Society of America
National Headquarters
Texas Christian University
Fort Worth, TX 76129

Subscription--4/yr.--membership. Hymn is a journal of congregational song for church musicians, clergy, scholars, poets, and others with varied backgrounds and interests. A journal of research and opinion, containing practical and scholarly articles. Hymn reflects diverse cultural and theological identities, and also provides exemplary hymn text and tunes in various styles. Accepts unsolicited articles, unsolicited reviews, dot-matrix printing, simultaneous submissions; publishes research notes and review-articles; accepts advertising--in keeping with the standards of the publication. Requires 3 copies of manuscript. Length requirements--maximum, 2000 words; minimum, 500 words. Selection process--chosen by an Editorial Advisory Board. Responds in 6 weeks. Approximate proportion of submissions accepted for publication--40 percent. Indexed: Chr.Per. Ind., Music Ind., Rel.Ind.One, Rel.&Theol.Abstr.

405. MUSICAE SACRAE MINISTERIUM
M. Pierre Blanchard, Sec.
Via Di Torre Rosia, 21
I-00165 Rome, Italy

Subscription--$20/yr. Subject matter of journal--Sacred Music. Submissions must be in French, German, English, Italian, or Latin.

406. VANGUARD
Editor
P.O. Box 549
Station A
Vancouver, British Columbia V6C 2N3 Canada

Subscription--6/yr.--$24. Description of subject matter of journal--Essays, Reviews and Information on Historical and Contemporary

Art. Accepts unsolicited articles and unsolicited reviews; accepts advertising. Publishes articles in Religious Art. Indexed: CERDIC, RILA.

OTHER JOURNALS THAT PUBLISH ARTICLES IN SACRED MUSIC; ARTS

22. WORSHIP; LITURGY

407. FEU NOUVEAU
rue de l'Ange 34
B 6001 Marcinelle, Belgium

Subscription--12/yr.--850 FB; $54.00, overseas. Subject matter of journal--Scripture and Worship.

408. LITURGISCHES JAHRBUCH
Eduard Nagel, Ed.
Liturgisches Institut
Jesuitenstrasse 13 C
D-5500 Trier, West Germany (B.R.D.)

Subscription--4/yr.--DM 44. Publishes articles in Church History, Theology, Liturgy, Worship, and Hermeneutics. Submissions must be in German. Accepts unsolicited articles; sometimes accepts unsolicited reviews; accepts advertising. Selection process--Editorial Board makes a decision on the recommendation of assigned readers. Indexed: Rel.Ind.One.

409. MODERN LITURGY
Kenneth E. Guentert, Ed.
Resource Publications, Inc.
160 E. Virginia St.
San Jose, CA 95112

Subscription--9/yr.--$36. Description of subject matter of journal--Worship; especially as impacted by the musical, lively, visual, and architectural arts. Publishes articles in Liturgy/Worship. Accepts unsolicited articles, dot-matrix printing; sometimes accepts unsolicited reviews; does not accept simultaneous submissions; publishes review-articles; accepts advertising--liturgical goods and services. For: professionals, academics, laity involved in worship. Submissions must be in English. Seeks articles that are helpful to the business of planning worship in keeping with the principles of Vatican II. Especially looking for challenging articles on sacramental theology, symbology, scripture as pertaining to worship, preaching theory. Style of journal--practical, helpful, not usually footnoted. Requires

one copy of manuscript. Length requirements--maximum, 3000 words;
minimum, --. Selection process--reviewed by two Editors. Responds
in one month. Approximate proportion of submissions accepted for
publication--25 percent. Indexed: Cath.Ind., Music Artic.Guide.,
Music Ind.

410. WORSHIP
     R. Kevin Seasoltz, O.S.B. (general editor)
     Liturgical Press
     St. John's Abbey
     Collegeville, MN 56321

     Subscription--6/yr.--$18. Description of subject matter--litur-
gical studies and related subjects (e.g. theology, arts, behavioral
sciences, culture). For: professors, students, and laypersons.
Submissions must be in English. Accepts unsolicited articles, dot-
matrix printing; does not accept unsolicited reviews, simultaneous
submissions; publishes review-articles; does not publish research
notes; accepts advertising--no camera-copy; academic programs,
serious publishers. Seeks theoretical articles in which implications for
contemporary worshiping communities are drawn out. Type of article
particularly looking for--pastoral liturgy. Style of journal--docu-
mented articles; footnotes. Worship follows its own style manual.
Requires 1 copy of manuscript. Length requirements--maximum, 6000
words; minimum, 3000 words. Selection process--reviewed by Editorial Committee. Worship is a juried periodical. Responds in 3
weeks. Approximate proportion of submissions accepted for publica-
tion--10 percent. Indexed: Cath.Ind., Old Test.Abstr., Rel.Per.,
Canon Law Abstr., New Test.Abstr., Rel.Ind.One, Rel.&Theol.
Abstr.

OTHER JOURNALS THAT PUBLISH ARTICLES IN
WORSHIP; LITURGY

Bangalore Theological Forum   513
Bibel und Liturgie   165
Catholica   12
Doctrine and Life   326
The Furrow   37
Group   329
Lutheran Forum   443
Melita Theologica   58
The Nigerian Journal of
     Theology   291
Orthodox Tradition   460
Proclaim   402
Revista de Espiritualidad   350
Search   393

23. HISTORY OF RELIGIONS; COMPARATIVE RELIGIONS; WORLD RELIGIONS

411. BUDDHIST-CHRISTIAN STUDIES
David W. Chappell, Ed.
East-West Religions Project
University of Hawaii
2530 Dole Street
Honolulu, Hawaii, U.S.A.   96822

Subscription--1/yr.--$5.00, individuals; $8.00, institutions.
Subject matter of journal--Ethics, Theology, Psychology of Religion,
Sociology of Religion, World Religions, Philosophy of Religion,
Buddhism, Eastern Religions.   Accepts unsolicited articles; some-
times accepts unsolicited reviews.   Submissions must be in English.
Style of journal--typed, double-spaced, with notes at the end.   Re-
quires 2 copies of manuscript.

412. BULLETIN OF THE AMERICAN SCHOOLS OF ORIENTAL RE-
SEARCH
Prof. Walter E. Rast, Ed.
Valparaiso University
Department of Theology
Valparaiso, IN   46383

Subscription--4/yr.--$28.00, members; $35.00, nonmembers;
$45.00, institutions.   Subject matter of journal--World Religions.
Accepts unsolicited articles; sometimes accepts unsolicited reviews;
accepts advertising.   Submissions must be in English.

413. HISTORY OF RELIGIONS
J. M. Kitagawa, Ed.
F. E. Reynolds, Ed.
W. D. O'Flaherty, Ed.
L. E. Sullivan, Ed.
University of Chicago Press
5801 S. Ellis Ave.
Chicago, IL   60637

Subscription--4/yr.--$12.70, individuals; $45, institutions.

Description of subject matter of journal--Systematic and comparative
studies of religion(s). Publishes articles in History of Religions.
For: professors, students, and laypersons. Submissions should be
in English (we have a policy of translating accepted manuscripts in
major languages into English). Sometimes accepts unsolicited articles, unsolicited reviews, accepts dot-matrix printing (if of sufficient
quality to be photocopied, etc.); does not accept simultaneous submissions; does not publish research notes; publishes review-articles;
accepts advertising--academic/scholarly. Articles especially looking
for--articles which are responsibly comparative and/or which advance
the state of knowledge and of thinking on their topics. Style of
journal--University of Chicago Press style. Refer to journal issues
for samples. Requires 1 copy of manuscript (prefers 2). Length
requirements--maximum, 45 pages (unless so excellent that editors
decide to publish it in 2 or more parts serially). Selection process--
distribution to editors, who meet periodically to discuss and evaluate
submissions; when desirable, the opinion of an outside reader is
sought. Responds in 4 weeks to 1 year--depends on schedule of
board meeting and outside reader response. Approximate proportion
of submissions that are accepted for publication--10-20 percent. Indexed: Curr.Cont., Hum.Ind., Old Test.Abstr., Rel.Per., Amer.
Hist.&Life, Arts&Hum.Cit.Ind., G.Soc.Sci.&Rel.Per.Lit., Int.Z.
Bibelwiss., New Test.Abstr., Rel.Ind.One, Rel.&Theol.Abstr.

414. ISTINA
     Centre d'Etudes Istina
     45 rue de la Glacière
     75013 Paris, France

Subscription--4/yr.--230 francs. Description of subject matter
of journal--Judaism and Christianity; Western and Eastern Christianity; Ecumenism. For: professors, students, and laypersons.
Submissions must be in French. Accepts unsolicited articles and
unsolicited reviews. Affiliate--Centre National de la Recherche Sci-
entifique, Paris. Indexed: Bull.Signal, Rel.Per., New Test.Abstr.,
Rel.Ind.One.

415. JOURNAL OF DHARMA
     Thomas Kadankavil, Ed.
     Dharmaram College
     Centre for the Study of World Religions
     Bangalore 560029, India

Subscription--4/yr.--$18. Description of subject matter--a
quarterly on world religions. Publishes articles in World Religions,
Philosophy of Religion, Judaism, Islam, Hinduism, Buddhism, Eastern
Religions, Religious Education. For: professors, students, those in-
terested in comparative study of religions. Submissions must be in
English. Accepts unsolicited articles, unsolicited reviews; does not

accept dot-matrix printing, simultaneous submissions; publishes research notes; does not publish review-articles; does not accept advertising. Each issue is on a particular theme. Articles appropriate
to a title that has already been announced will be the only ones accepted for publication. Seeking articles which promote interreligious
dialogue. Style of journal--MLA Handbook. Requires 1-2 copies of
manuscript. Length requirements--maximum, 6000 words; minimum,
3200 words. Selection process--scientifically prepared, useful from
an interreligious perspective, original contributions. Responds in
6 months. Parent Organization--Dharma Research Assoc. Indexed:
Curr.Cont., Phil.Ind., Arts&Hum.Cit.Ind., Rel.Ind.One.

416. KAIROS
      Dr. Kurt Schubert, Ed.
      Zeitschrift fuer Religionswissenschaft und Theologie
      Otto Mueller Verlag
      Ernest Thun Strasse 11
      A-5020 Salzburg, Austria

      Subscription--4/yr.--S 300. Publishes articles in Church His-
tory, Sociology of Religion, World Religions, Philosophy of Religion,
Judaism, Islam, Hinduism, Buddhism, Eastern Religions. Submissions must be in German. Accepts unsolicited articles, unsolicited
reviews; accepts advertising. Indexed: Rel.Per., New Test.Abstr.,
Rel.Ind.One.

417. NUMEN
      Prof. Dr. M. Heerma van Voss, Ed.
      E. J. Brill
      Oude Rijn 33a-35
      2312 HB Leiden, Netherlands

      Subscription--2/yr.--84 fl. Subject matter of journal--Church
History, World Religions, Judaism, Islam, Hinduism, Buddhism,
Eastern Religions (history of religions, comparative religions). For:
professors, students, and laypersons. Submissions must be in French,
German, English, or Italian. Text in the above languages. Sometimes accepts unsolicited articles; does not accept unsolicited reviews,
simultaneous submissions; does not publish research notes; publishes
review-articles. Requires 2 copies of manuscript. Indexed: Curr.
Cont., Rel.Per., New Test.Abstr., Rel.Ind.One.

418. RELIGION
      Stuart Mews, Ed.
      Ivan Strenski, Ed.
      Academic Press Inc. (London) Ltd.
      111 Fifth Ave.
      New York, NY 10003

Subscription--4/yr.--$28 (individuals). Description of subject
matter of journal--religion in all its manifestations, including modern
world views such as the many humanisms, fascisms, Marxisms, and
traditionalisms. Publishes articles in Psychology of Religion, Sociol
ogy of Religion, World Religions, Philosophy of Religion, Judaism,
Islam, Hinduism, Buddhism, Eastern Religions, and Religious Education. For: professors. Submissions must be in English. Accepts
unsolicited articles, unsolicited reviews, dot-matrix printing; does
not accept simultaneous submissions; publishes research notes and
review-articles; accepts advertising. Seeks methodologically sophisticated articles, attuned to religious pluralism, with a cross-cultural
and transhistorical comparative perspective. Especially looking for
articles that are interdisciplinary, comparative, and original--articles
that make waves! Style of journal--Academic standard style. Requires 3 copies of manuscript. Length requirements--maximum, 40
pages; minimum, 20 pages. Selection process--Editorial Board and
outside referees. Responds in 3 months. Approximate proportion
of submissions that are accepted for publication--20 percent. Indexed:
Curr.Cont., Old Test.Abstr., Arts&Hum.Cit.Ind., New Test.Abstr.,
Rel.Ind.One.

419. RELIGIOUS TRADITIONS
Dr. Arvind Sharma, Ed.
The University of Sydney
Department of Religious Studies
New South Wales 2006, Australia

Subscription--1/yr.--$15. Subject matter of journal--Sociology
of Religion, World Religions, Philosophy of Religion, Judaism, Islam,
Hinduism, Buddhism, and Eastern Religions. Submissions must be
in English. Accepts unsolicited articles, unsolicited reviews; does
not accept simultaneous submissions. Style of journal- style sheet
appears on the back cover of the journal. Each article-length
manuscript should contain a brief abstract of 50 to 75 words on a
separate sheet.

420. REVUE DE L'HISTOIRE DES RELIGIONS
Presses Universitaires de France
108 bd. Saint Germain
75279 Paris Cedex 6, France

Subscription--4/yr.--290 francs. Description of subject matter
of journal--history of religions. Publishes articles in Scripture,
Psychology of Religion, Sociology of Religion, World Religions,
Philosophy of Religion, Judaism, Islam, Hinduism, Buddhism, and
Eastern Religions. For: professors, students, and laypersons. Sub-
missions must be in French, Spanish, English, Italian, or Portuguese.
Accepts unsolicited articles, unsolicited reviews, dot-matrix printing,
simultaneous submissions; publishes research notes and review-articles;

does not accept advertising. Seeks articles that show original scientific research and that are well expressed. Style of journal--suc-
cinct and clear. Requires 2 copies of manuscript. Length require-
ments--maximum, 35 pages; minimum, --. Selection process--sub-
mitted articles are read by a committee who give their decision on
content and style. Responds in 1-2 months. Approximate proportion of submissions accepted for publication--65 percent. Indexed:
Curr.Cont., Rel.Per., Arts&Hum.Cit.Ind., New Test.Abstr., Rel.
Ind.One.

421. STUDIES IN COMPARATIVE RELIGION
      Editorial Board--Peter Hobson, Ralph Smith, Olive Clive-Ross
      Perennial Books Ltd.
      Pates Manor
      Bedfont, Middlesex TW14, 8JP, England

      Subscription--2/yr.--$19.50. Description of subject matter--
Studies in Comparative Religion is devoted to the exposition of the
teachings, spiritual methods, symbolism and other facets of the great
religious traditions of the world. It provides a forum where out-
standing contemporary authors give the traditional theses underlying
the different religions of both East and West. Since it is not tied
to the interests of any religious tradition to the exclusion of others,
its perspective is not sectarian. Studies in Comparative Religion
therefore lays particular stress on the timeless elements in any given
religion. It voices the common traditional spirit behind the different
world religions and thus serves as a corrective to the mutually con-
flicting approaches to religion in the modern world. Publishes articles in Theology, Philosophy of Religion, World Religions, Judaism,
Islam, Hinduism, Buddhism, and Eastern Religions. For: professors, students, laypersons. Requires 1 copy of manuscript. Responds in 2-3 months (or less). Approximate proportion of submissions accepted for publication--50 percent. Indexed: Curr.Cont.,
Hum.Ind., Arts&Hum.Cit.Ind.

422. WORLD FAITHS INSIGHT
      K. L. S. Rao, Ed.   Distributor:
      Marcus Braybrooke, Ed.   Anima Publications
      University of Virginia   1053 Wilson Ave.
      Department of Religion   Chambersburg, PA 17201
      Charlottesville, VA   22903

      Subscription--3 issues per year--1 year--$10; 2 yrs.--$19; 3
yrs.--$28. Subject matter of journal--Theology, Psychology of Re-
ligion, Sociology of Religion, World Religions, Eastern Religions,
Judaism, Islam, Hinduism, and Buddhism. For: professors. Submissions must be in English. Sometimes accepts unsolicited articles
and unsolicited reviews; accepts dot-matrix printing; does not accept
simultaneous submissions; sometimes publishes research notes;

publishes review-articles; accepts advertising--at the discretion of the editor. Indexed: Chr.Per.Ind.

OTHER JOURNALS THAT PUBLISH ARTICLES IN HISTORY OF RELIGIONS; COMPARATIVE RELIGIONS; WORLD RELIGIONS

America 448
Anglican Theological Review 4
Anima 423
Antonianum 271
Asbury Theological Journal 5
Asian Issues 512
Bangalore Theological Forum 513
Banner 6
Bijdragen 9
Bulletin of the Christian Institute of Sikh Studies 467
The Bulletin of the Henry Martyn Institute of Islamic Studies 471
Caribbean Journal of Religious Studies 525
Catalyst: Social Pastoral Magazine for Melanesia 223
Centre for the Study of Islam and Christian Muslim Relations Newsletter 472
Cercle Ernest Renan. Cahiers 13
Chicago Studies 277
China Study Project Journal 514
The Chinese Theological Review 515
Ching Feng 468
Christian Century 224
Christian Jewish Relations 424
Christian Orient 426
Christianity and Crisis 227
Christianity Today 228
Church and Society 216
Church History 115
Churchman (London) 15
Churchman (St. Petersburg, FL) 16
Cithara 17

Civiltà Cattolica 19
Commonweal 449
Cross Currents 255
Dansk Missionsblad 359
Dialogue and Alliance 427
Documentation Catholique 450
East Asian Pastoral Review 328
The Eastern Buddhist 469
Ecumenical Review 428
Encounter (Indianapolis, IN) 431
Etudes 231
Expository Times 181
Faith and Mission 35
Freiburger Rundbrief 432
Gregorianum 284
Harvard Theological Review 42
Heythrop Journal 285
Iliff Review 43
Indian Church History Review 118
Indian Journal of Theology 518
Inter-Religio 520
Japan Christian Quarterly 521
Japanese Journal of Religious Studies 522
Japanese Religions 523
Journal of Church and State 217
Journal of Religion 47
Journal of Religious History 120
Journal of Religious Studies 48
Journal of Religious Thought 49
Journal of the American Academy of Religion 50
Journal of Theology for Southern Africa 508
Lucerna 509
Lumen Vitae 385
Melita Theologica 58

24. ECUMENICS; MEETING OF TRADITIONS

423. ANIMA
Harry M. Buck, Executive Editor
1053 Wilson Ave.
Chambersburg, PA 17201

Subscription--2/yr.--$9.95; for 2 yrs.--$18.95. Anima cele-
brates the wholistic vision that emerges from thoughtful and imaginative encounters with the subject matter--the practice of ctice ofst,
yin and yang--anima and animus. Written largely by and about
women who are pondering new experiences of themselves and our
world, this equinoctial journal welcomes contributions, verbal and
visual, from the known and unknown. Publishes articles in Psychology
of Religion, Sociology of Religion, World Religions, Philosophy of Religion, Judaism, Islam, Hinduism, Buddhism, Eastern Religions. For:
Professors and laypersons Submissions must be in English. Accepts
unsolicited articles, dot-matrix printing; sometimes accepts unsolicited
reviews; does not accept simultaneous submissions; publishes research
notes and review-articles; accepts advertising--camera-ready copy.
Explores ideas in the areas of feminism, psychology, and religion.
Concentrates on the quest for wholeness through values traditionally
labeled "feminine." We seek scholarly articles in the above-mentioned
areas but also wish to encourage the expression of experience and
personal insight. Requires one copy of manuscript. Length require-
ments--maximum, 30 double-spaced pages; minimum, 10 pages. Selection process--Initial consideration by six editors. If an article
is not rejected at this point, it is forwarded to consulting editors
with a subject specialty for reactions and comments and returned for
a final decision. Responds in 3 months. Approximate proportion
of submissions accepted for publication--10 percent.

424. CHRISTIAN JEWISH RELATIONS
Rabbi Dr. Norman Solomon, Ed
Vivian Marr, Editorial Assistant
Institute of Jewish Affairs
11 Hertford St.
London W1Y 7DX, England

Subscription--4/yr.--$20. Description of subject matter--A
review of the more important developments, statements and publications

223

relevant to the Churches' new approach. Publishes articles in Scripture, Theology, Psychology of Religion, Sociology of Religion, Philosophy of Religion, Judaism, Interfaith Dialogue (Jewish-Christian). For: professors, students, laypersons, Christian & Jewish clergy. Submissions must be in French, German, English, or Hebrew. Accepts unsolicited articles, unsolicited reviews; does not accept dot-matrix printing, simultaneous submissions; publishes research notes and review-articles; accepts advertising--journals, books, conferences as paid exchange or leaflet advertising. Seeks articles on aspects of recent developments in or events pertaining to interfaith dialogue for inclusion as feature articles or brief reports in the "Reports from Around the World" section. Type of article especially looking for--an article focusing on new developments in Christian-Jewish dialogue. Style of journal--feature articles on one main theme followed by reports on conferences etc.; documentation; chronicle; reviews. Requires one copy of manuscript. Length requirements--maximum, 5000 words (articles); minimum, 150 words (reviews, reports). Selection process--The journal's main theme is selected according to topicality and quality of material available; reports on recent events are included as close as possible to actual event. Responds to submissions in 4-6 weeks. Approximate proportion of submissions that are accepted for publication--50 percent. (Co-sponsor--World Jewish Congress.) Indexed: Hist.Abstr.

425. CHRISTIAN ORIENT
Dr. Thomas Mannooramparampil, Ed.
P.B. 1 Vadavathoor
Kattayam--686 010
Kerala, India

Subject matter of journal--Church History, Sociology of Religion, World Religions, Philosophy of Religion, Islam, and Hinduism. Accepts unsolicited articles; sometimes accepts unsolicited reviews. Submissions must be in English.

426. COMMUNIO VIATORUM
Comenius Faculty of Protestant Theology
Jungmannova 9
110 00 Prague 1, Czechoslovakia

Subscription--3/yr.--19 francs. Subject matter of journal--Scripture, Ethics, Church History, Theology, Psychology of Religion, Sociology of Religion, Philosophy of Religion, and Ecumenical Studies. For: professors, students, and laypersons. Submissions must be in French, German, or English. Accepts unsolicited articles. Selection process--Editorial Board. Parent Organization--Ecumenical Institute. Indexed: New Test.Abstr., Rel.Per., Rel.Ind.One.

427. DIALOGUE AND ALLIANCE
Gene James, Ed.
JAF Box 1186
New York, New York 10116

Subscription--4/yr.--$19.95, individuals; $29.95, institutions.
Description of subject matter of journal--Dialogue and Alliance publishes scholarly articles, comments, reflections, poems, translations
of religious literature, book reviews, religious art, and other items
which enhance mutual understanding and respect across religious
tradition and culture. Publishes articles in Ethics, Church History,
Theology, Psychology of Religion, Sociology of Religion, World Religions, Philosophy of Religion, Judaism, Islam, Hinduism, Buddhism,
Eastern Religions, and World Peace. Accepts unsolicited articles and
unsolicited reviews; does not accept simultaneous submissions; publishes review-articles; accepts advertising--publications. Style of
journal--double-spaced, with notes placed at the end of the text.
Requires 2 copies of manuscript. Comments: articles should be accompanied by an abstract of approximately 100-200 words.

428. ECUMENICAL REVIEW
Emilio E. Castro, Ed.
World Council of Churches
150 Route de Ferney
1211 Geneva 20, Switzerland

Subscription--4/yr.--$19.95. Publishes articles that provide
an Ecumenical Perspective on Scripture, Ethics, Church History,
Theology, Evangelism, Sociology of Religion, World Religions, Philosophy of Religion, and Religious Education. For: professors and students. Submissions must be in French, German, Spanish, or English (preferably). Sometimes accepts unsolicited articles, unsolicited
reviews; does not accept dot-matrix printing, simultaneous submissions; does not publish research notes or review-articles; accepts
advertising--on books, theological courses, vacancy notices at sem-
inaries, etc. Requires one copy of manuscript. Length requirements--
maximum, 8000 words; minimum, 3000 words. Selection process-- publishes theme issues (requests articles that are needed); however,
there is room for other nonrelated articles. Responds in 3 months.
Approximate proportion of submissions accepted for publication--33
percent. Indexed: Curr.Cont., Hum.Ind., Rel.Per., Arts&Hum.
Cit.Ind., New Test.Abstr., Old Test.Abstr., Rel.Ind.One.

429. ECUMENISM
Thomas Ryan, Ed.
Canadian Centre for Ecumenism
2065 Sherbrooke St. W.
Montreal, Quebec H3II 1G6, Canada

Subscription--4/yr.--$15. Description of subject matter of
journal--Studies, witness, documentation, and news of ecumenical
significance in Canada and throughout the world. Ecumenism provides a forum in which Christians can dialogue among themselves and
with other believers or non-believers. For: students, laypersons.
Submissions must be in French or English. Accepts unsolicited articles. Issues are usually directed toward a specific theme. Indexed:
Rel.Ind.One.

430. ECUMENIST
Gregory Baum, Ed.
Rev. Kevin A. Lynch, Ed.
Paulist Press
997 MacArthur Blvd.
Mahwah, NJ   07430

Subscription--6/yr.--free. Description of subject matter--ma-
terial that promotes Christian unity and that deals with the problems,
hopes, outlooks, etc. of those working in this area. Publishes articles in Theology, Sociology of Religion, Ecumenical Theology, and
the Church of the World. For: professors, students, and laypersons. Articles appear in English. Accepts unsolicited articles and
unsolicited reviews; does not accept dot-matrix printing, simultaneous
submissions; does not publish research notes; publishes review-
articles; does not accept advertising. Seeks articles on new developments in theology especially as they impact on the ecumenical movement. Especially interested in articles dealing with the effort of the
churches to promote peace and justice in the world. Style of jour-
nal--middle-brow style with articles about 1500 words in length. Submit 1 copy of manuscript. Length requirements--maximum, 2000
words; minimum, 1000 words. Selection process--head editor makes
final decision--G. Baum. Responds in 2 weeks. Submissions accepted for publication--25 percent. Indexed: Cath.Ind., Old Test.
Abstr., New Test.Abstr.

431. ENCOUNTER
Clark M. Williamson, Ed.
Christian Theological Seminary
1000 W. 42nd St.
Indianapolis, IN   46208

Subscription--4/yr.--$12. Description of subject matter--seeks
to promote conversation among people of living faiths and diverse
traditions. Publishes articles in Scripture, Ethics, Theology, World
Religions, Philosophy of Religion. For: professors, students, and
ministers. Articles appear in English. Accepts unsolicited articles,
dot matrix-printing; sometimes accepts unsolicited reviews; does not
accept simultaneous submissions. Does not publish research notes or
review-articles. Accepts advertising--publishers. Seeks reflective

piece on a tradition (however broadly or narrowly defined) in relation to some other tradition or problem. Type of article journal is
especially looking for--no. Style journal follows--The Journal of
Religion. Submit one copy of manuscript. Length requirements--
maximum, 25 pages; minimum, 15 pages. Selection process--review
by Editorial Committee. Responds in one month. Approximately 30
percent of submissions accepted for publication. Indexed: Hum.Ind.,
Int.Z.Bibelwiss., New Test.Abstr., Old Test.Abstr., Rel.&Theol.
Abstr., Arts&Hum.Cit.Ind., G.Soc.Sci.&Rel.Per.Lit., Rel.Ind.One.

432. FREIBURGER RUNDBRIEF
    Postfach 420
    D-7800 Freiburg im Breisgau, West Germany (B.R.D.)

    Subject matter of journal--Scripture, Ethics, Theology, Soci-
ology of Religion, World Religions, Judaism, Jewish Christian Relations. Submissions must be in German.

433. INTERNATIONALE KIRCHLICHE ZEITSCHRIFT
    Hans Frei, Ed.
    Staempfli und Cie AG
    Postfach 2728
    30001 Berne, Switzerland

    Subscription--4/yr.--$26. Description of subject matter of
journal--Old-Catholicism, Ecumenical Movement, Orthodoxy, Interdenominational bilateral or multilateral dialogue. Publishes articles
in Church History, Theology, Psychology of Religion, Sociology of
Religion, Philosophy of Religion, Ecumenical Movement, Anglicanism,
Orthodox Churches. For: professors, students, laypersons, pastors,
and theologians. Submissions must be in German. Seeks articles
showing actual developments in the different Christian denominations.
Requires 1 copy of manuscript. Length requirements--maximum, 10-
15 pages; minimum, --. Selection process--in general, the editor
decides. Sometimes he corresponds with the two co-editors who live
in the Federal Republic of Germany and in Holland. Responds in
1-3 months. Comments--The quarterly was founded in order to promote the Old-Catholic and Ecumenical movement. Indexed: Old Test.
Abstr., New Test.Abstr.

434. IRENIKON
    Emmanuel Lanne, Ed.
    Monastère de Chevetogne
    5395 Chevetogne, Belgium

    Subscription--4/yr.--$30. Description of subject matter of
journal--matters concerning Christian Unity, Christian churches, and
Ecumenism. Publishes articles in Church History, Theology, Ecumenism, and Spirituality. For: professors, students, laypersons,

etc. Submissions must be in French. If submitted in another language, article will be translated into French. Sometimes accepts unsolicited articles and unsolicited reviews; does not accept dot-matrix printing or simultaneous submissions; publishes research notes and review-articles; does not accept advertising. Seeks articles concerning Church History, Eastern churches in the past; also seeks articles concerning the separation among Christians and endeavors for reunion. Especially looking for short articles about Christian Unity. Style of journal--scholarly but not too technical. Requires one copy of manuscript. Length requirements--maximum, 18 double-spaced pages; minimum, 10 pages or less. Selection process--Editorial Board. Responds in 3 months. Approximate proportion of submissions accepted for publication--50 percent. Indexed: Ind.Med., Rel.Per., New Test.Abstr., Rel.Ind.One.

435. JOURNAL OF ECUMENICAL STUDIES
Leonard Swidler, Ed.
Temple University (022-38)
Philadelphia, PA 19122

Subscription--4/yr.--$17.50, U.S.; $19.50, elsewhere. Description of subject matter--whatever fosters interreligious/inter-ideological dialogue. For: professors, students, laypersons, and clergy. Articles must be submitted in English (very occasionally a translation will be made from another language, if necessary). Seeks academically sound, properly footnoted articles dealing with the fostering of interreligious/ideological dialogue. Accepts unsolicited articles and dot-matrix printing; sometimes accepts unsolicited reviews; does not accept simultaneous submissions; publishes research notes; sometimes publishes review-articles; and accepts advertising--anything appropriate to interreligious dialogue. Style of journal--Primarily Univ. of Chicago. Length requirements--maximum, 35-40 pages (double space, elite); minimum, 15-20 pages for articles and shorter for explorations and responses. Selection process: Articles are sent to 3 evaluators. Their responses and the co-editor's own judgment together determine acceptance, acceptance if revised, or rejection. Respond in 1-6 months, depending on evaluator's response speed. Approximately 25 percent of the submissions are accepted for publication. Indexed: Cath.Ind., Curr.Cont., Hist.Abstr., Hum.Ind., Old Test.Abstr., Rel.Per., Arts&Hum.Cit.Ind., G.Soc. Sci.&Rel.Per.Lit., Int.Z.Bibelwiss., New Test.Abstr., Rel.&Theol. Abstr., Rel.Ind.One.

436. NORTHEAST ASIA JOURNAL OF THEOLOGY
Yoshinobu Kumazawa, Ed.
Northeast Asia Association of Theological Schools
c/o Japan Lutheran Theological Seminary
3-10-20 Osawa
Mitaka-shi Tokyo 181, Japan

Subscription--2/yr.--$10. Publishes articles in Scripture, Church History, Theology, Sociology of Religion, World Religions, Philosophy of Religion, Buddhism, Eastern Religions, and Religious Education. Submissions must be in English. Accepts unsolicited articles and unsolicited reviews. Seeks articles which promote theological dialogue and interchange among the countries of Northeast Asia and the rest of the world. Selection process--Editorial Board reaches a decision based on the recommendation of assigned readers. Indexed: Rel.Ind.One.

437. NOVA ET VETERA
     Georges Cottier, O.P.
     4, avenue Saint-Paul
     1208 Grange-Canal
     Geneva, Switzerland

Subscription--4/yr.--45 francs. Subject matter of journal-- Ecumenical Dialogue, Biblical Exegesis, and religious studies using scientific methodology. Publishes articles in Scripture, Ethics, Theology, and Philosophy of Religion. For: professors, students, and laypersons. Submissions must be in French. Accepts unsolicited articles and unsolicited reviews. Requires 2 copies of manuscript. Indexed: New Test.Abstr.

438. OEKUMENISCHE RUNDSCHAU
     Neue Schlesingergasse 24
     Postfach 101762
     6000 Frankfurt am Main, West Germany (B.R.D.)

Subscription--4/yr.--42 DM. Subject matter of journal--Church History, Theology, Sociology of Religion, Ecclesiology, and Ecumenism. Submissions must be in German.

439. ONE IN CHRIST
     Paschal M. Hardiment, Ed.
     Vita et Pax-Foundation for Unity
     Our Lady of Peace
     Turvey Abbey
     Turvey, Bedminster MK43 8DE, England

Subscription--4/yr.--15 pounds; $25--surface mail; $33 airmail. Description of subject matter--theology, history, practical application of ecumenism, documentation, spiritual ecumenism. Publishes articles in Ecumenism and the following subjects as related to it: Scripture, Ethics, Church History, Theology, Evangelism, Church Administration, Missions, Psychology of Religion, Sociology of Religion, and Religious Education. For: professors, students, laypersons, ecumenists at all levels. Submissions must be in English; they translate from French, German, and Dutch. Accepts unsolicited articles, dot-matrix printing; sometimes accepts unsolicited reviews; does not accept simultaneous submissions; does not publish research notes; publishes review-articles; does not accept advertising. Seeks articles that are helpful to progress in understanding between Christian churches, substantial, not "inspirational"! Style of journal--scholarly but accessible to general readers. Requires one copy of manuscript. Length requirements--maximum, 10,000 words; minimum, --. Selection process of an article--articles of an intrinsic interest or relevance to contemporary ecumenical happenings. Responds in about a month. Approximate proportion of submissions accepted for publication--75 percent. Indexed: Br.Hum.Ind., Cath.Ind., Old Test.Abstr., New Test.Abstr., Rel.Ind.One.

440. PROCHE-ORIENT CHRETIEN
Frans Bouwen, Ed.
Peres Blancs de Sainte-Anne de Jerusalem
B.P. 19079
Jerusalem, Israel

Subscription--4/yr.--$14. Subject matter of journal--Churches in the Middle East, especially ecumenical relations in the Middle East; Church History, Theology, and Islam. For: all levels. Submissions must be in French or English. Accepts unsolicited articles, dot-matrix printing; does not accept unsolicited reviews, simultaneous submissions; does not publish research notes; publishes review-articles; does not accept advertising. Requires one copy of manuscript. Length requirements--maximum/minimum--no fixed limit. Responds to a submission in 2 months. Approximate proportion of submissions accepted for publication--75 percent. Indexed: Bull.Signal, Rel.Ind.One.

441. RENOVATIO, ZEITSCHRIFT FUER DAS INTERDISZIPLINAERE GESPRAECH
Helmut-Josef Patt, Ed.
Venusbergweg
5300 Bonn 1, West Germany (B.R.D.)

Subscription--4/yr.--DM 20. Description of subject matter of journal--interdisciplinary issues. Publishes articles in Ethics, Theology, and Philosophy of Religion. For: professors, students, and laypersons. Submissions must be in German. Does not accept unsolicited articles, unsolicited reviews, dot-matrix printing; accepts simultaneous submissions; does not publish research notes; publishes review-articles; does not accept advertising. Reports on the situation of the Catholic Church in different countries and continents. Style of journal--scientific. Requires 1 copy of manuscript. Length requirements--maximum, 12 pages; minimum, 10 pages. Responds in 2-3 months. Indexed: New Test.Abstr.

OTHER JOURNALS THAT PUBLISH ARTICLES IN
ECUMENICS; MEETING OF TRADITIONS

25. CHRISTIANITY: PROTESTANT

442. BAPTIST PROGRAM
Reginald M. McDonough, Ed.
Southern Baptist Convention
Executive Committee
901 Commerce
Nashville, TN   37219

Subscription--11/yr.--$10. Description of subject matter of journal--articles about work of SBC agencies or of personal interest to church staff and denominational workers. Publishes articles in Evangelism; Church Administration; Pastoral Counseling; Missions; Information about Southern Baptist Convention Agencies, Institutions, Programs. For: church staff persons and denominational workers. Submissions must be in English. Seeks articles that are informative. Requires 1 copy of manuscript. Selection process--Subject matter must fit publication, writing of professional quality. Responds in 1-5 weeks. Approximate proportion of submissions accepted for publication--10 percent. Indexed: South.Bap.Per.Ind.

443. LUTHERAN FORUM
Rev. Glenn C. Stone, Ed.
American Lutheran Publicity Bureau
308 W. 46th St.
New York, NY   10036-3894

Subscription--4/yr.--$16. Description of subject matter of journal--articles in fields of ecumenism, worship, church and society, ecclesiology, church organization, and theological developments. Publishes articles in general issues and ideas relating to Lutheranism. For: clergy and educated laity. Submissions must be in English. Accepts unsolicited articles, dot-matrix printing, simultaneous submissions; sometimes accepts unsolicited reviews; does not publish research notes; publishes review-articles; accepts advertising--books, religious art, church supplies, classified. Seeks fairly brief articles (not more than 10 pages) relating to current concerns in the church. Style of journal--lively style, not heavily footnoted. Requires 1 copy of manuscript. Length requirements--maximum, 12 pages; minimum, 3 pages. Selection process--read by Editor. May be referred for second opinion to others. Responds to a submission in 2 months.

Approximate proportion of submissions accepted for publication--10 percent. Indexed: Rel.Ind.One.

444. LUTHERAN STANDARD
     Lowell G. Almen, Ed.
     Augsburg Publishing House
     426 S. Fifth St.
     Box 1209
     Minneapolis, MN 55440

     Subscription--20/yr.--$8. Description of subject matter--general articles relating to life and work of American Lutheran Church (ALC), to congregations and members, and entire Christian Church. For: laypersons. Submissions must be in English. Seeking personal experience stories with good description and quotation. Accepts unsolicited articles, dot-matrix printing, simultaneous submissions; does not accept unsolicited reviews; does not publish research notes or review-articles; does accept advertising. Requires 1 copy of manuscript. Length requirements--maximum, 1200 words. Selection process--manuscript is circulated among editorial staff, then it is discussed and voted on. Responds in 1 month. Approximately 5 percent of all submissions are accepted for publication. Parent Organization--American Lutheran Church. Indexed: G.Soc.Sci.&Rel. Per.Lit.

445. THE PRESBYTERIAN
     Hal Bray, Ed.
     920 Stemmons Frwy
     Denton, TX 76205

     Subscription 8/yr. Publishes articles in News, Resources, Mission Features, Opinion, News Format concerning the Presbyterian Church. For: laypersons. Submissions must be in English. Sometimes accepts unsolicited articles, unsolicited reviews; accepts dot-matrix printing; does not publish research notes, review-articles; accepts advertising--Presbyterian institutions/agencies. Seeks articles concerning mission features. Requires 1 copy of manuscript. Length requirements--maximum, 14 col. inches; minimum--none. Selection process--priority system--first is news of this region, Denton, Texas. Indexed: Old Test.Abstr., Chr.Per.Ind.

446. REFORMED JOURNAL
     Wm. B. Eerdmans Publishing Co.
     255 Jefferson Ave. S.E.
     Grand Rapids, MI 49503

     Subscription--12/yr.--$15. Description of subject matter--comments and opinions from a generally Calvinist perspective on theology

and on Christianity in its relation to society and the arts. For:
pastors and laypersons. Submissions must be in English. Accepts
unsolicited articles, unsolicited reviews, dot-matrix printing; does
not accept simultaneous submissions; does not publish research notes;
publishes review-articles; accepts advertising. Style of journal--
aim at the level of Harper's, The Atlantic, New Republic or Christian
Century. Length requirements--(maximum)--articles--10 pages, re-
views--6 pages; (minimum) articles--7 pages, reviews, 2 pages. Responds in 2 months normally. Approximately 10 percent of unsolicited
submissions are accepted for publication. Indexed: Rel.Ind.One.

447. WITTENBURG DOOR
     Mike Yaconelli, Ed.
     Youth Specialties
     1224 Greenfield Dr.
     El Cajon, CA 92021

     Subscription--6/yr.--$12. Nonfiction: Satirical articles on
church renewal, Christianity, and organized religion. Few book reviews. Accepts unsolicited articles; sometimes accepts unsolicited
reviews; accepts dot-matrix printing; does not publish research
notes; usually does not publish review-articles; does not accept advertising. For: professors, students, laypersons, others. Submissions must be in English. Buys about 30 mss. a year. 40 percent freelance written. Works with a small number of new/unpublished
writers each year. Bimonthly magazine for men and women connected
with the church. Circulation 19,000. Pays on publication. Publishes ms. an average of 1 year after acceptance. Buys all rights.
Reports in 3 months. Submit complete ms. Length--1000 words maximum, 500-750 preferred. Pays $25-$100. Sometimes pays expenses
of writers on assignments. Comments: We look for someone who is
clever, on our wave length, and has some savvy about the evangelical church. The writer has a better chance of breaking in with
short articles and fillers. Our material is funny/satirical. Indexed:
Chr.Per.Ind.

OTHER JOURNALS THAT PUBLISH ARTICLES IN
CHRISTIANITY: PROTESTANT

Africa Theological Journal 502
American Baptist Quarterly 1
American Presbyterians: Journal
  of Presbyterian History 110
American Scientific Affiliation
  Journal 249
Andrews University Seminary
  Studies 2

Anglican Theological Review 4
Banner 6
Baptist History and Heritage 111
Baptist Quarterly N.S. 112
Biblical Illustrator 173
Bibliotheca Sacra 8
Boletín Teológico 524
Buried History 177

26. CHRISTIANITY: ROMAN CATHOLIC

448. AMERICA
George W. Hunt, Ed.
America Press, Inc.
106 W. 56th St.
New York, NY 10019

Subscription--42-44/yr.--$23. Description of subject matter of journal--a Catholic journal (weekly) of opinion. Publishes articles in Scripture, Ethics, Church History, Theology, Evangelism, Church Administration, Pastoral Counseling, Missions, Psychology of Religion, Sociology of Religion, World Religions, Philosophy of Religion, Judaism, Islam, Hinduism, Buddhism, Eastern Religions, Religious Education. For: professors, students, laypersons, clergy. Submissions must be in English. Accepts unsolicited articles, dot-matrix printing; does not accept unsolicited reviews, simultaneous submissions; does not publish research notes; publishes review-articles; accepts advertising. Seeks articles concerning any topic of current interest--preferably from a moral or religious perspective. Style of journal--middle brow; popular, i.e. not slangy or academic. Requires one copy of manuscript. Length requirements--maximum, about 3000 words; minimum, about 500 words. Responds in 10 days. Approximate proportion of submissions accepted for publication--1 out of 20. Indexed: Cath.Ind., Old Test.Abstr., R.G., Abstrax, Biog.Ind., Bk.Rev.Dig., G.Soc.Sci.&Rel.Per.Lit., Mag.Ind., PMR.

449. COMMONWEAL
James Steinfel, Ed.
Commonweal Foundation
15 Dutch St.
New York, NY 10038

Subscription--biweekly--$28. Publishes articles in Public Affairs, Theology, Literature, the Arts, Contemporary Thought, Ethics, Sociology of Religion, World Religions, and Philosophy of Religion. For: laypersons. Submissions must be in English. Accepts unsolicited articles, dot-matrix printing; does not accept unsolicited reviews, simultaneous submissions; does not publish research notes; publishes review-articles; accepts advertising. Seeks essays, interpretive and with a clear point of view, 3000 words or less. Especially

looking for articles that are linked to current developments but go
beyond newspaper articles and reviews. Style of journal--Univ. of
Chicago. Requires one copy of manuscript. Length requirements--
maximum, 3500 words; minimum, 500 words. Selection process--
Editorial reading and discussion. Responds in 3-6 weeks. Approxi-
mate proportion of submissions accepted for publication--1 out of 20.
Comments: journal is edited by Roman Catholic lay people and gives
a priority to articles in some way reflecting Catholic perspectives and
experience. Indexed: Bk.Rev.Dig., Cath.Ind., Hist.Abstr., M.L.A.,
Old Test.Abstr., R.G., Amer.Bibl.Slavic&E.Eur.Stud., Abstrax,
A.I.P.P., Bk.Rev.Ind., Amer.Hist.&Life, CERDIC, Film Lit. Ind.,
G.Soc.Sci.&Rel.Per.Lit., Media Rev.Dig., Mag.Ind., PMR.

450. DOCUMENTATION CATHOLIQUE
     P. Francois Bernard, Ed.
     Bayard Presse
     5 Rue Bayard
     75393 Paris Cedex 08, France

     Subscription--22/yr.--(1 yr.): France, 328 F; USA, 436 F.
Description of subject matter--As a documentary publication, we pub-
lish official and not-so-official Church documents especially of the
Catholic Church around the world but also of the other Christian
churches and other faiths, particularly those in dialogue with Rome.
Publishes articles in Scripture, Ethics, Theology, Evangelism, Church
Administration, Missions, World Religions, Judaism, Islam, Religious
Education, Catholic Church, Ecumenism, Church and Politics, Science and Religion. For: professors, students, laypersons, clergy,
and scholars. Does not accept unsolicited articles, unsolicited reviews, dot-matrix printing, simultaneous submissions; does not publish research notes or review articles; very rarely accepts adver-
tising--books. Selection process for choice of articles in journal--
according to their ability to serve as documentary evidence of the
life of the church. Comments--In 1988 we hope to begin an English
edition to be entitled Catholic International. Indexed: Cath.Ind.

451. L'EGLISE CANADIENNE
     Jacques Barnard, Ed.
     Revue L'Eglise Canadienne Inc.
     1073 Blvd. St. Cyrille, W.
     Quebec P.Q. GIS 4R5, Canada

     Subscription--21/yr.--30.00 $ Canadian. Description of subject
matter of journal--documents, studies and information on the life of
the Roman Catholic Church in Canada. For: laypersons, religious,
clergy. Submissions must be in French. Sometimes accepts unsolicited articles, unsolicited reviews; does not accept dot-matrix
printing, simultaneous submissions; does not publish research notes
or review-articles; accepts advertising--any related to their objectives--

e.g., books, liturgy, retreats, etc. Requires 1 copy of manuscript. Length requirements--maximum, 10 pages; minimum, 6 pages. Selection process for publication of an article--selected according to the major events and trends in the life of the church. Responds to a submission in 1 week. Approximate proportion of submissions accepted for publication--few, since most manuscripts are solicited. Indexed: Pt.de Rep.

452. MAGNIFICAT
     Apostles of Infinite Love
     Sanctuary of the Magnificat
     Box 308
     St.-Jovite
     Quebec J0T 2H0, Canada

     Subscription--9-10/yr.--contributions. Publishes articles in Scripture, Church History, Theology, Evangelism, Missions, Lives of Saints, Accounts of Miracles. For: laypersons. Submissions must be in French or English. Does not accept unsolicited articles, unsolicited reviews, simultaneous submissions; does not publish research notes or review-articles; does not accept advertising. Indexed: Chem.Abstr., Eng.Ind.

453. NATIONAL CATHOLIC REPORTER
     Thomas Fox, Ed.
     National Catholic Reporter Publishing, Co., Inc.
     115 E. Armour Blvd.
     Box 281
     Kansas City, MO   64141

     Subscription--Weekly--$24. Description of subject matter--the church and social issues. Publishes articles in Scripture, Ethics, Theology, Church Administration, and Social Issues. For: clergy and laity. Submissions must be in English. Sometimes accepts unsolicited articles; does not accept unsolicited reviews, simultaneous submissions; accepts dot-matrix printing; does not publish research notes or review-articles; accepts advertising--church related. Requires 1 copy of manuscript to be submitted. Length requirements--maximum, 1000 words; minimum, 400. Responds in one week. Approximate proportion of submissions that are accepted for publication--one in eight. Indexed: Cath.Ind., Access, Mag.Ind.

454. TABLET
     John Wilkins, Ed.
     Tablet Publishing Co.
     48 Great Peter St.
     Westminster, London SW1P 2HB, England

Subscription--50/yr.-- 45.   Description of subject matter of journal--British and world news from Catholic angle; arts and religion. Publishes articles in Politics, Literature, Arts, Church News--Internationally.   For: socioeconomic AB generally.   Submissions must be in English.   Sometimes accepts unsolicited articles; does not accept unsolicited reviews, simultaneous submissions (not usually); accepts dot-matrix printing; does not publish research notes; publishes review-articles; accepts advertising--publishers, charities, classified, arts.   Requires 1 copy of manuscript.   Length requirements-- maximum, 1500 words; minimum, 500 words.   Responds in 1-6 weeks. Approximate proportion of submissions accepted for publication--N/A. Comments--the Tablet was founded in 1840 and is the oldest and most respected Roman Catholic journal of the English-speaking world.   Indexed: Cath.Ind., Rural Recreat.Tour.Abstr., World Agri.Econ.& Rural Sociol.Abstr.

OTHER JOURNALS THAT PUBLISH ARTICLES IN CHRISTIANITY: ROMAN CATHOLIC

27. CHRISTIANITY: OTHER DENOMINATIONS AND SECTS

455. BRETHREN LIFE AND THOUGHT
    Warren S. Kissinger, Ed.
    Brethren Press
    Butterfield and Meyers Roads
    Oak Brook, IL 60521

    Subscription--4/yr.--$12. Description of subject matter of
journal--Subjects of concern to the Church of the Brethren; often
issues are arranged around a general theme. Publishes articles in
Scripture, Ethics, Church History, Theology, Evangelism, and Missions. Submissions must be in English. Accepts unsolicited articles;
sometimes accepts unsolicited reviews; does not accept advertising.
Style of journal--typed, double-spaced. Length requirements for
submissions--maximum, 5000 words. Parent Organization--Brethren
Journal Association. Indexed: Rel.Pcr., Bk.Rev.Mo., Rel.Ind.One,
Rel.&Theol.Abstr.

456. THE MENNONITE
    Muriel T. Stackley, Ed.
    General Conference Mennonite Church
    722 Main St.
    Box 347
    Newton, KS 67114

    Subscription--24/yr.--$14. Description of subject matter--
Relates almost entirely to the concerns and activities of the General
Conference Mennonite Church. Publishes articles in Scripture, Ethics, Church History, Theology, Evangelism, Church Administration,
Pastoral Counseling, and Missions. For: the spectrum of our denomination. Submissions must be in English. Sometimes accepts unsolicited articles, reviews; does not accept dot-matrix printing,
simultaneous submissions; does not publish research notes; publishes
review-articles; accepts advertising--Mennonite related. Very little
free-lance material is accepted. Especially looking for articles that
concern the life and faith of General Conference Mennonites. Style
of journal--somewhat informal. Requires 1 copy to be submitted.
Length requirements--maximum, 1500 words; minimum, 650 words.
Responds in one month. Indexed: Rel.Per., G.Soc.Sci.&Rel.Per.
Lit.

457. MENNONITE HISTORICAL BULLETIN
     Leonard Gross, Ed.
     Mennonite Church
     Historical Committee
     1700 South Main St.
     Goshen, IN   46526

Subscription--4/yr.--$5. Publishes articles and news items
of interest to the Mennonite Church and its traditions. For: professors, students, and laypersons. Submissions must be in English.
Accepts unsolicited articles; sometimes accepts unsolicited reviews.
Seeks articles that shed light on the present by exploring Mennonite
history. Style of journal--popular. Indexed: Hist.Abstr.

458. MENNONITE LIFE
     David A. Haury, Ed.
     Bethel College
     North Newton, KS   67117

Subscription--4/yr.--$10; $18/2 years. Description of subject
matter--Mennonite history, culture, theology, missions. For: professors and laypersons. Submissions should be in English. Accepts
unsolicited articles, dot-matrix printing; sometimes accepts unsolicited
reviews; (usually) does not accept simultaneous submissions; publishes research notes and review-articles; does not accept advertising.
Seeks articles on popular topics as well as scholarly. Type of article particularly seeking--popular style with potential illustrations.
Style of journal--Chicago Manual. Requires 1 copy of manuscript.
Length requirements--maximum, 15 pages (double spaced); minimum,
5 pages (double spaced). Selection process--Editor and reviewers
decide. Responds in 1-4 weeks. Approximate proportion of submissions accepted for publication--75 percent. Indexed: Rel.Ind.One.

459. MENNONITE QUARTERLY REVIEW
     John S. Oyer, Ed.
     Mennonite Historical Society
     Goshen College and the Associated Mennonite Biblical Seminaries
     Goshen College
     Goshen, IN   46526

Subscription--4/yr.--$17. Description of subject matter--Rad-
ical Reformation studies (including Anabaptism especially); Mennonite,
Amish, Hutterite history, ethics, life, thought. Essays on peace;
sociological, economic, psychological, political, theological studies concerning Reformed groups. For: professors, students, laypersons.
Submissions must be in German, English, or Dutch. Style of journal--
University of Chicago Manual. Requires 2 copies of manuscript.
Length requirements--maximum, 30 double-spaced pages; minimum--
none. Selection process--Referees, anonymous. Responds in 1 to 3

months. Approximate proportion of submissions that are accepted for publication--50 percent. Indexed: Amer.Hist.&Life., Hist.Abstr., Rel.Per., Rel.Ind.One, Rel.&Theol.Abstr.

460. ORTHODOX TRADITION
     Hieromonk Auxentios, Ed.
     St. Gregory Palamas Monastery
     P.O. Box 398
     Etna, CA 96027

Subscription--3/yr.--$10.00; overseas--$22.00. Description of subject matter of journal--Orthodox Tradition publishes studies of the Orthodox Church, its history, and its spiritual traditions. Publishes articles in Church History, Theology, and Liturgy. Submissions must be in English.

461. OSTKIRCHLICHE STUDIEN
     Prof. H. M. Biedermann, Ed.
     Augustinus-Verlag
     Grabenberg 2
     8700 Wuerzburg, West Germany (B.R.D.)

Subscription--4/yr. (3 and 1 double copy)--DM 80. Subject matter of journal--Eastern Church History, Eastern Theology, Eastern Church Administration and Byzantine History. For: professors, students. Submissions must be in French, German, or English. Accepts unsolicited articles, unsolicited reviews; does not accept dot-matrix printing, simultaneous submissions; publishes research notes, review-articles; accepts advertising--of theological books only. Style of journal--scientific theological articles. Requires 1 copy of manuscript. Length requirements maximum, 30-50 pages; minimum, 3 pages. Responds in 3 months. Approximate proportion of submissions accepted for publication--60 percent. Parent Organization--Ostkirchliches Institut der Deutschen Augustiner. Indexed: New Test.Abstr., Rel. Ind.One.

462. PENNSYLVANIA MENNONITE HERITAGE
     Carolyn C. Wenger, Ed.
     Lancaster Mennonite Historical Society
     2215 Millstream Rd.
     Lancaster, PA 17602

Subscription--4/yr.--$20. Description of subject matter--Historical background, religious thought and expression, culture, and genealogy of Mennonite-related group originating in Pennsylvania. For: professors, students, laypersons. Submissions must be in English. Accepts unsolicited articles, dot-matrix printing; sometimes accepts unsolicited reviews; does not accept simultaneous submissions;

publishes research notes and review-articles; accepts advertising. Seeks articles concerning church history, documentary materials. Style of journal--Chicago Manual of Style. Requires 1 copy of manuscript. Length requirements--maximum, 50 pages elite type (double spaced); minimum, 10 pages elite type (double spaced). Selection process--three readers' recommendations, including editor's. Responds in 1 month. Approximately 75 percent of all submissions are accepted for publication. Indexed: Hist.Abstr., Amer.Hist.&Life, Geneal.Per.Ind.

463. QUAKER HISTORY
Arthur J. Mekeel, Ed.
Friends Historical Association
Haverford College Library
Haverford, PA 19041

Subscription--2/yr.--$10. Description of subject matter of journal--All aspects of the history of the Society of Friends, viewed internally as well as in its relationship to the world at large. Publishes articles in Church History, Psychology of Religion, Sociology of Religion, Philosophy of Religion--insofar as they apply to the Society of Friends. For: professors, laypersons. Submissions must be in English. Seeks articles that are the product of original research in primary as well as secondary sources. Requires 1 copy of manuscript. Length requirements--maximum, 10,000 words; minimum, 3500 words. Responds--from 2 weeks to 2 months. Approximate proportion of submissions that are accepted for publication--90 percent. Indexed: Rel.Per., Rel.Ind.One.

464. QUAKER YEOMEN
James E. Bellarts, Ed.
Brookside Business Consultants, Inc.
2330 S.E. Brookwood Ave.
Ste. 108
Hillsboro, OR 97123

Subscription--4/yr.--$15. Subject matter of journal--Genealogy of Quaker families in British Isles and America. For: Genealogists. Submissions must be in English. Accepts unsolicited articles, dot-matrix printing; does not accept unsolicited reviews, simultaneous submissions; does not publish research notes; publishes review-articles; does not accept advertising. Style of journal--newsletters 8 1/2" x 11"--offset--10 pages. Requires 2 copies of manuscript. Length requirements--depends on content. Approximate proportion of submissions accepted for publication--80 percent. Indexed: Geneal.Per.Ind.

465. SOBORNOST
Fr. Sergei Hackel, Ed.

Fellowship of St. Alban & St. Sergius
52 Ladbroke Grove
London W11 2PB, England

Subscription--2/yr.--$10. Description of subject matter of journal--material relating to tradition of Orthodox Churches, Western contacts with orthodoxy, comparison between Orthodox and Western (especially Anglican) traditions, etc. Publishes articles in Church History and Theology. For: professors, students, laypersons, clergy: people with general interest in Orthodox tradition. Submissions must be in English. Accepts unsolicited articles, dot-matrix printing; sometimes accepts unsolicited reviews; does not accept simultaneous submissions; does not publish research notes; publishes review-articles; accepts advertising. Seeks articles which provide sympathetic insight into the orthodox tradition. Requires one copy of manuscript. Length requirements--maximum, 10,000 words. Selection process--Editorial Committee decision. Approximate proportion of submissions accepted for publication--1/3 - 1/4. Indexed: Br. Hum.Ind., Cath.Ind., Curr.Cont., Rel.Per., Arts&Hum.Cit.Ind., New Test.Abstr., Rel.&Theol.Abstr., Rel.Ind.One.

OTHER JOURNALS THAT PUBLISH ARTICLES IN
CHRISTIANITY: OTHER DENOMINATIONS AND SECTS

Church Herald   14
Eternity   399
Global Church Growth   357
Greek Orthodox Theological Re-
    view   40
Gregorios Ho Palamas   41
Orthodox Word   348
Pendle Hill Pamphlets   336
Religious Humanism   73
St. Vladimir's Theological
    Quarterly   86
Second Century   132
Sojourners   268

28. EASTERN RELIGIONS

466. ANNALS OF THE BHANDARKAR ORIENTAL RESEARCH INSTI-
TUTE
R. N. Danderkar, Ed.
Bhandarkar Oriental Research Institute
Poona 411 004
India

Subject matter of journal--World Religions, Philosophy of
Religion, Islam, Hinduism, Buddhism, Eastern Religions. Submissions must be in English.

467. BULLETIN OF THE CHRISTIAN INSTITUTE OF SIKH STUDIES
Clarence O. McMullen, Ed.
Baring Union Christian College
Batala-143505, Punjab, India

Subscription--RS 10.00, India; $8, overseas. Subject matter
of journal--Church History, Philosophy of Religion, Missions, Islam,
Hinduism, Eastern Religions. Submissions must be in English. Accepts unsolicited articles; sometimes accepts unsolicited reviews.

468. CHING FENG
Peter K. H. Lee, Ed.
Christian Study Centre on Chinese Religion & Culture
P.O. Box 33
Shatin N.T., Hong Kong

Subscription--4/yr.--$14. Subject matter of journal--as the
name of our organization suggests, we are a Christian Centre concerned about Chinese (and also Asian) religions and cultural issues;
more and more we are engaged in contextualized theological thinking.
Publishes articles in Church History, Theology, Missions, World Religions, Buddhism, Eastern Religions, Contextual (Asian) Theology.
For: professors, students, and laypersons. Submissions must be
in English or Chinese. Accepts unsolicited articles, unsolicited reviews, dot-matrix printing, simultaneous submissions; publishes research notes and review-articles; accepts advertising. Manuscripts
should be scholarly but readable. Requires 1 copy of manuscript.

Length requirements--maximum, 25 double-spaced pages; minimum, 5 pages. Selection process--Editorial Committee. Responds in 1-2 months. Approximate proportion of submissions that are accepted for publication--50 percent. Editions in Chinese and English. Indexed: Rel.Ind.One.

469. EASTERN BUDDHIST
     Keiji Nishitani, Gadjin Nagao et al., Eds.
     Eastern Buddhist Society
     Otani University
     Koyama
     Kita-ku
     Kyoto, Japan

Subscription--2/yr.--$15. Description of subject matter of journal--A journal devoted to the open and critical study of Mahayana Buddhism. Publishes articles in Philosophy of Religion, Buddhism, Eastern Religions, and Mahayana Buddhism. For: professors, students, and laypersons. Submissions must be in English. Accepts unsolicited articles and dot-matrix printing; does not accept unsolicited reviews or simultaneous submissions; does not publish research notes; publishes review-articles (only when solicited); does not accept advertising--ads are carried but only on a strictly exchange basis with journals of a nature similar to that of Eastern Buddhist. Articles journal seeks--articles that are accessible to the informed reader but neither of purely scholarly interest nor propagational. Especially seeking articles of high quality on religious thought rather than on historical development. Requires 1 copy of manuscript. Length requirements--maximum, 30 double-spaced pages; minimum, 10 double-spaced pages. Selection process--reviewed by Editorial Board. Articles must have original content, should cite primary sources (not secondary ones), and be written from or sympathetic to a Buddhist standpoint. Responds in 6 months to 1 year. Approximate proportion of submissions accepted for publication--30 percent. Indexed: Curr.Cont., Rel.Per., Arts&Hum.Cit.Ind., Rel.Ind.One.

470. PARSIANA
     J. R. Patel, Ed. & Pub.
     c/o H. L. Rochat
     Navsari Chambers
     39 A. K. Nayak Marg Fort
     Bombay 400001, India

Subscription--12/yr.--Rs. 30. Description of subject matter of journal--activities and decisions concerning the welfare of Zoroastrians throughout the world. For: (mostly) laypersons, professors, students. Submissions must be in English. Sometimes accepts unsolicited articles, unsolicited reviews; accepts dot-matrix printing; occasionally accepts simultaneous submissions; publishes research

notes, review-articles; accepts advertising--commercial advertising.
Style of journal--Webster's English; Articles should be written for
the layperson. Requires 2 copies of manuscript. Length require-
ments--maximum, 2500 words. Selection process--Editorial Board
evaluates the article. Responds in 2 months. Approximate proportion of submissions accepted for publication--50 percent. Indexed:
Ind.India.

OTHER JOURNALS THAT PUBLISH ARTICLES IN
EASTERN RELIGIONS

America 448
Anima 423
Antonianum 271
Asian Issues 512
Bangalore Theological Forum
513
Buddhist-Christian Studies 411
The Bulletin of the Henry Mar-
tyn Institute of Islamic
Studies 471
China Study Project Journal
514
The Chinese Theological Review
515
Christian Century 224
Christian Orient 425
Christianity and Crisis 227
Church History 115
Civiltà Cattolica 19
Dansk Missionsblad 359
Dialogue and Alliance 427
Etudes 231
Faith and Mission 35
Focus 517
Haelan 346
Harvard Theological Review 42
Indian Church History Review
118
Indian Journal of Theology 518
Indian Theological Studies 519
Inter-Religio 520
Japan Christian Quarterly 521
Japanese Journal of Religious
Studies 522
Japanese Religions 523
Journal of Dharma 415
Journal of Religion 47

Journal of Religious Studies 48
Journal of Religious Thought
49
Journal of the American Academy
of Religion 50
Journal of Theology for Southern
Africa 508
Kairos 416
Mérleg 59
Missiology 365
Mission Studies 366
Nederlands Theologisch Tijdschrift
62
Northeast Asia Journal of The-
ology 436
Numen 417
Pendle Hill Pamphlets 336
Process Studies 145
Recherches de Science Reli-
gieuse 69
Reconciliation International 265
Religion 418
Religion in Communist Lands
245
Religion in Southern Africa 511
Religious Humanism 73
Religious Traditions 419
Revue de L'Histoire des Religions
420
Revue Theologique de Louvain
83
Studia Patavina, Rivista di Sci-
enze Religiose 90
Studies in Comparative Religion
421
Svensk Teologisk Kvartalskrift
93

29. ISLAM

471. THE BULLETIN OF THE HENRY MARTYN INSTITUTE OF
     ISLAMIC STUDIES
     P.O. Box 153
     Hyderabad-500 001
     A.P., India

     Subscription--4/yr.--$6.50. Subject matter of journal--Sociology of Religion, Islam, Hinduism, Buddhism, and Eastern Religions.
     Submissions must be in English. Accepts unsolicited articles and unsolicited reviews.

472. CENTRE FOR THE STUDY OF ISLAM AND CHRISTIAN MUSLIM
     RELATIONS NEWSLETTER
     Dr. Jorgen S. Nielsen, Ed.
     Selly Oak Colleges
     Centre for the Study of Islam and Christian-Muslim Relations
     Birmingham B29 6LE, England

     Subscription--4/yr.--$19. Subject matter of journal--Ethics,
     Church History, Theology, Pastoral Counseling, Missions, Psychology
     of Religion, Sociology of Religion, World Religions, Islam, Religious
     Education (if subject matter has relevancy to Muslims in Europe).
     For: professors, students, and laypersons. Submissions must be
     in English. Accepts unsolicited articles, dot-matrix printing, simultaneous submissions; does not accept unsolicited reviews; does not
     publish research notes or review-articles, does not accept advertising. Seeks articles which are usually experience-based and policy-
     oriented. One copy of manuscript required. Length requirements--
     maximum, 15,000 words; minimum 5000 words. Responds to a submission in one month. Indexed: Abstr.Musl.Rel.

473. HAMDARD ISLAMICUS
     Hakim Mohammed Said, Ed.
     H. M. Jafri, Co-editor
     Hamdard Foundation
     Nazimabad
     Karachi 8, Pakistan

Subscription--4/yr.--$15. Description of subject matter of journal--Islamic History, Culture, Law, Philosophy, Thought or other related aspects. For: professors, students. Submissions must be in English. Accepts unsolicited articles; sometimes accepts unsolicited reviews; does not accept dot-matrix printing, simultaneous submis-- sions; does not publish research notes; publishes review-articles; does not accept advertising. Seeks research articles that are inter- pretive, scholastic. Especially seeking original research in the field of Islamics. Style of journal--academic. Requires 2 copies of manu- script. Length requirements for a submission--not fixed. Selection process--a committee makes the final decision. Responds to a sub- mission in 4-6 months. Approximate proportion of submissions ac- cepted for publication--70 percent. Comments: Hamdard Islamicus is one of the most widely circulated academic journals of Islamic studies subscribed to by libraries and universities all over the world. Indexed: Abstr.Musl.Rel.

474. ISLAM AND THE MODERN AGE
Prof. M. S. Agwani, Ed.
Zakir Husain Institute of Islamic Studies
Jamia Nagar
New Delhi 110025, India

Subscription--4/yr.--$16. Description of subject matter of journal--all aspects of contact between Islam and modern society. For: professors, students, and laypersons. Submissions must be in English. Publishes articles in Muslim Scripture, Muslim Ethics, Muslim Theology, Sociology, Muslim Philosophy, Islam, Religious Edu- cation, Muslim Law, Muslim Astronomy, Medicine, Political Science, Economics, Government. Selection process--Editorial Board reaches a decision after consultation with members of an Advisory Board. Indexed: Abstr.Musl.Rel., Ind.Islam.

475. ISLAMIC STUDIES
Dr. Muhammad Khalid Masud, Ed.
Islamic Research Institute
Box 1035
Islamabad, Pakistan

Subscription--4/yr.--$15. Description of subject matter of journal--The journal publishes articles relating to Islamic History, Law, Jurisprudence, Political Science, Economics, Culture, Science, Religion, Philosophy, etc. For: professors, students, and layper- sons. Submissions must be in English or Arabic. Accepts unsolicited articles, unsolicited reviews; does not accept simultaneous submissions. Style of journal--a copy of guidelines for authors can be supplied on request. Requires 2 copies of manuscript. Selection process-- Editor reaches a decision in consultation with Editorial Committee. Indexed: Astr.Musl.Rel.

476. MINARET MONTHLY INTERNATIONAL
Muhammed Ja'Fer, Ed.
World Federation of Islamic Missions
Islamic Centre
B-Block
N. Nazimabad
Karachi 33, Pakistan

Subscription--12/yr.--$13.00. Subject matter of journal--Is-
lamic Ethics, Islamic Psychology of Religion, Islamic Sociology of Religion, Islamic Philosophy of Religion, Islamic Religious Education,
Comparative Religion, Sayings of the Prophet, Qur'an. Occasionally
accepts unsolicited articles, does not accept unsolicited reviews, dot-
matrix printing, simultaneous submissions; publishes research notes
(Islamic); does not publish review-articles; accepts advertising--
without human pictures concerning Islamically permitted goods. For:
professors, students, laypersons. Submissions must be in English.
Articles that are sought--Historical Seerah, Biography, Islamic Activity, Reports. Especially looking for articles concerning Qur'an,
Hadith, Figh (Islamic Jurisprudence, Islamic History, Islamic Think-
ers, Islamic Thought). Style of journal--educative, informative. Requires 2 copies of manuscript. Length requirements--maximum, 2000
words; minimum, 500 words. Responds--if accepted, 1 month; if
rejected, 1 week. Approximate proportion of submissions accepted
for publication--1 article per issue. Comments: There is no binding
on management for acceptance. No reason is recorded for rejection.
Indexed: Abstr.Musl.Rel.

477. THE MUSLIM WORLD
Willem A. Bijlefeld, Ed.
Hartford Seminary
77 Sherman St.
Hartford, CT 06105

Subscription--4/yr.--$15, individuals; $20, institutions. Description of subject matter--All topics related to Islam (although they
try to stay away from historical articles that stray too far from theology) and Christian-Muslim relations. For: professors and students.
Submissions in English. Accepts unsolicited articles and dot-matrix
printing; does not accept unsolicited reviews or simultaneous submissions; does not publish research notes or review-articles; accepts
advertising--half or full page only. Seeks original research or original thought on any area directly or indirectly related to Islam and/
or Christian-Muslim relations--the closer to Islam, the better, however. Style of journal--double spaced, Chicago manual, footnotes
double spaced at end of article; authors should write for rules of
transliteration. Length requirements--maximum, 40 ms. pages; minimum, 10 ms. pages. Selection process--All articles are read by the
three senior editors and often additional outside readers in the field
in which the article is written. Responds--length varies--from one

month to a year. Approximately 35 percent of all submissions are
accepted for publication. Indexed: Curr.Cont., Hist.Abstr., Hum.
Ind., Rel.Per., Rel.Ind.One, Rel.&Theol.Abstr.

478. STUDIES IN ISLAM
      Hakim A. Hameed, Ed.
      Indian Institute of Islamic Studies
      Panchkuin Rd.
      New Delhi 110001, India

      Subscription--4/yr.--$12. Subject matter of journal--Muslim
Scripture, History, Ethics, Theology, Philosophy, Political Science,
Economics, Art, etc. For: professors, students, and laypersons.
Submissions must be in English. Accepts unsolicited articles, un-
solicited reviews; does not accept simultaneous submissions. Selec-
tion process--Advisory Board makes recommendations to the Editor.
Indexed: Old Test.Abstr., Ind.Islam.

OTHER JOURNALS THAT PUBLISH
ARTICLES IN ISLAM

Afroasiatic Linguistics 208
America 448
Anima 423
Annals Magazine 222
Annals of the Bhandarkar Ori-
   ental Research Institute 466
Antonianum 271
Bangalore Theological Forum
   513
Bibbia e Oriente 163
Bibel und Kirche 164
Bulletin of the Christian Insti-
   tute of Sikh Studies 467
Burgense 10
China Study Project Journal
   514
The Chinese Theological Review
   515
Christian Century 224
Christian Orient 425
Christianity and Crisis 227
Church History 115
Civiltà Cattolica 19
Dansalan Quarterly 516
Dansk Missionsblad 359
Dialogue and Alliance 427

Documentation Catholique 450
Faith and Mission 35
Focus 517
Haelan 346
Harvard Theological Review 42
Indian Church History Review
   118
Indian Journal of Theology 518
Indian Theological Studies 519
Journal of Dharma 415
Journal of Religion 47
Journal of Religion in Africa/
   Religion en Afrique 507
Journal of Religious Studies 48
Journal of Religious Thought 49
Journal of Theology for Southern
   Africa 508
Kairos 416
Mérleg 59
Missiology 365
Mission Studies 366
Nederlands Theologisch Tijdschrift
   62
The Nigerian Journal of Theology
   291
Numen 417

30. JUDAISM

479. **AJS REVIEW**
Prof. Robert Chazan, Ed.
Queens College
Department of History
Flushing, NY   11367

Subscription--2/yr.--$15. Publishes articles in Scripture,
Ethics, History, Theology, Jewish Psychology, Philosophy, Judaism,
Jewish Studies, Jewish Mysticism. Submissions must be in English
or Hebrew. Accepts unsolicited articles, unsolicited reviews; publishes review-articles. Seeks significant studies that make a lasting
contribution to Jewish studies. Length requirements--maximum, 40
pages. Selection process--Editorial review. The journal is supported
by a grant from the National Foundation for Jewish Culture. Parent
Organization--Association for Jewish Studies. Indexed: Hist.Abstr.,
Amer.Bibl.Slavic&E.Eur.Stud., Amer.Hist.&Life.

480. **AMERICAN JEWISH ARCHIVES**
Jacob R. Marcus, Ed.
Abraham J. Peck, Ed.
American Jewish Archives
3101 Clifton Ave.
Cincinnati, OH   45220

Subscription--2/yr.--Free to qualified personnel. Description
of subject matter of journal--Western Hemispheric Jews and Judaism.
Publishes articles in Judaism, Ethics, Psychology of Religion and
Sociology of Religion. For: professors and laypersons. Submissions
must be in English. Accepts unsolicited articles, dot-matrix printing,
simultaneous submissions; sometimes accepts unsolicited reviews; publishes research notes and review articles; does not accept advertising.
Seeks well-written, scholarly articles. Style of journal--Univ. of
Chicago; we have our own author's style sheet. Requires 2 copies
of manuscript. Length requirements--maximum, 50 pages; minimum,
20-25 pages. Selection process--Editorial Committee. Responds in
1-2 months. Approximate proportion of submissions accepted for pub-
lication--50 percent. Indexed: Curr.Cont., Hist.Abstr., Amer.Bibl.
Slavic&E.Eur.Stud., Arts&Hum.Cit.Ind., Amer.Hist.&Life, Ind.Jew.
Per., Rel.Ind.One.

481. ARCHIVES JUIVES
Bernhard Blumenkranz, Ed.
Commission Francaise des Archives Juives
3 rue des Prouvaires
75001 Paris, France

Subscription--4/yr.--80 francs. Description of subject matter
of journal--History of Jews in France through the ages. For: professors, students, historians. Submissions must be in French, but
sometimes accepts articles in German and English to be translated
into French. Requires one copy of manuscript. Accepts unsolicited
articles; does not accept unsolicited reviews, dot-matrix printing,
publishes research notes; does not publish review-articles; does not
accept advertising. Length requirements--maximum, 4500 words;
minimum, 450 words. Selection process--scientific. Responds to a
submission--Immediate acknowledgment; publication in 6 months.
Approximate proportion of submissions accepted for publication--50
percent. Indexed: Bull.Signal.

482. CONGRESS MONTHLY
Maier Deshell, Ed.
American Jewish Congress
15 E. 14th St.
New York, NY 10028

Subscription--7/yr.--$7.50. Description of subject matter of
journal--Political, Social, Economic, and Cultural Issues of Concern
to the Jewish Community. For: professors, students, and laypersons. Submissions must be in English. Sometimes accepts unsolicited
articles, unsolicited reviews; accepts dot-matrix printing; does not
accept simultaneous submissions; does not publish research notes;
publishes review-articles; accepts advertising--all within bounds of
good taste. Seeks informed, insightful criticism. Requires 1 copy
of manuscript. Length requirements for submission--maximum, 1500
words--articles; 1000, reviews. Selection process--Editorial choice.
Responds to a submission--as soon as possible. Indexed: Ind.Jew.
Per.

483. CONSERVATIVE JUDAISM
David Wolf Silverman, Ed.
Rebecca Jacobs Handler, Mng. Ed.
Rabbinical Assembly
3080 Broadway
New York, NY 10027

Subscription--4/yr.--$20/yr. and $50/3 yrs., individuals; $15/
yr., students. Description of subject matter--articles which express
a serious, critical inquiry of Jewish texts and traditions, legacy, and
law; which further the quest for a Conservative theology and ideology;

and which explore today's changing Jewish community. Subject matter of journal--Scripture, Ethics, Theology, Pastoral Counseling, Psychology of Religion, Sociology of Religion, Philosophy of Religion, Judaism, Jewish texts, Israel, Contemporary issues that have an affect on Judaism and Jewish life. For: professors, students, laypersons, and rabbis (primary audience). Submissions must be in English or Hebrew. Seeks articles that articulate our subject matter with insight and intelligence. Style of journal--semi-scholarly; write Managing Editor at above address for stylistic information. Requires 3 copies of manuscript--1 original and 2 photocopies. Length requirements--maximum, 20 ms. pages; minimum, 5 ms. pages. Selection process--articles are read by managing editor and editor. If necessary, they are circulated to editorial board. Responds in 2-12 weeks. Approximately 30-50 percent of all submissions are accepted for publication. Indexed: Ind.Jew.Per.

484. EUROPEAN JUDAISM
Albert Friedlander, Ed.
Foundation for European Judaism
Kent House
Rutland Gardens
London S.W.7, England

Subscription--2/yr.--$9. Description of subject matter of journal--Jewish life and thought. Publishes articles in Judaism, Philosophy of Religion--Jewish. For: professors, students, laypersons (mixture of all). Submissions must be in English. Accepts unsolicited articles; sometimes accepts unsolicited reviews; does not accept dot-matrix printing, simultaneous submissions; does not publish research notes; publishes review-articles; does not accept advertising. Style of journal--scholarly as well as popular. Requires one copy of manuscript. Length requirements--maximum, 3000-4000 words; minimum, none. Selection process--Editorial decision. Responds--variable, but rarely fast. Approximate proportion of submissions accepted for publication--1/4-1/2. Indexed: Ind.Jew.Per.

485. GESHER
Shlomo Shafir, Ed.
World Jewish Congress
4 Rotenberg St.
Jerusalem, Israel

Subscription--2/yr.--IS.12. Description of subject matter of journal--Judaism, Jewish Affairs, the Jewish People and Israel. For: professors, students, laypersons. Submissions must be in English. Sometimes accepts unsolicited articles, unsolicited reviews; accepts simultaneous submissions; publishes research notes, review-articles; does not accept advertising. Seeks scholarly articles, fit also for a broader public. Requires 2 copies of manuscript. Length requirements--maximum, 5000 words; minimum, 1000 words. Selection process--some are chosen by the editor; some are reviewed by members of the Board. Responds to a submission in 2-3 months. Approximate proportion of submissions accepted for publication--50 percent. Indexed: Ind.Heb.Per.

486. HUMANISTIC JUDAISM
     M. Bonnie Cousens, Ed.
     Ruth Duskin Feldman, Ed.
     Society for Humanistic Judaism
     28611 W. 12 Mile Rd.
     Farmington Hills, MI   48018

Subscription--4/yr.--$15 in U.S.; $17, Canada; $20, overseas. Description of subject matter of journal--journal is an international voice for secular and humanistic Judaism, whose purpose is to share creative work, discuss relevant issues, and provide celebrational materials. Publishes articles in Ethics, Philosophy of Religion, Judaism, Humanism. For: laypersons. Submissions must be in English. Accepts unsolicited articles, unsolicited reviews, simultaneous submissions; does not publish research notes; publishes review-articles; advertising--exchange only from like-minded organizations or publications. Humanistic Judaism is the voice of the fourth Jewish alternative. This movement embraces all Jews who value their Jewish identity, but who find no place in the three traditions of conventional Judaism. Humanistic Judaism is the philosophy of those who affirm their Jewish identity, their independence of supernatural authority, and their right to determine the purpose and course of their own lives. This is a journal for people who seek to participate in the secular, cultural, and creative aspects of the Jewish experience. Humanistic Judaism publishes articles, book reviews, short fiction, poetry, and essays consistent with this philosophy. Each issue has a theme; however, not all the contents need relate to the theme. Requires 3 copies of manuscript. Length requirements--maximum, 12 typed double-spaced pages; minimum, 300 words. Selection process--Selection by Editorial Board based on relevance to upcoming themes and Humanistic Judaism. Responds in 6 months to 1 year. Approximate proportion of submissions accepted for publication--50 percent. Indexed: Ind.Jew.Per.

487. JEWISH QUARTERLY REVIEW
     Dropsie University
     Broad and York Sts.
     Philadelphia, PA   19132

Subscription--4/yr.--$35. Description of subject matter of journal--Judaic and Near Eastern studies. For: professors, students, laypersons. Submissions must be in English (preferred); any modern language--including Hebrew--accepted. Sometimes accepts unsolicited articles, unsolicited reviews; accepts dot-matrix printing; does not accept simultaneous submissions; publishes research notes, review articles; accepts advertising--relevant to the focus of the journal--scholarly study of Judaism and the Near East. Style of journal--Chicago, generally. Requires 2 copies of manuscript. Selection process--article submitted anonymously to expert referees. Responds in 1 month. Approximate proportion of submissions accepted for publication--50 percent. Indexed: Curr.Cont., Old Test.Abstr., Rel. Per., Arts&Hum.Cit.Ind., Ind. Jew.Per., New Test.Abstr., Rel.& Theol.Abstr., Rel.Ind.One.

488. JEWISH SOCIAL STUDIES
    Toby B. Gitelle, Managing Ed.
    Conference on Jewish Social Studies, Inc.
    2112 Broadway, Rm. 206
    New York, NY 10023

Subscription--4/yr.--$30. Description of subject matter of journal--journal is devoted to contemporary and historical aspects of Jewish life. Publishes articles in Judaism, Sociology of Religion, and any articles of contemporary relevance to the Jewish community. For: professors, students, and laypersons. Submissions must be in English. Accepts unsolicited articles, dot-matrix printing (but not happily); sometimes accepts unsolicited reviews; does not publish research notes; publishes review-articles; does not accept advertising. Seeks fully-documented scholarly articles pertaining to Jewish interest. Style of journal--Chicago Style Manual and MLA. Requires 3 copies of manuscript. Length requirements--maximum, 16,000 words; minimum, 4,200 words. Selection process--refereed by 2 or more scholars. Responds in 1 year. Approximate proportion of submissions accepted for publication--30 percent. Indexed: Curr.Cont., Hist.Abstr., P.A.I.S., SSCI, Soc.Sci.Ind., Amer.Bibl. Slavic&E.Eur.Stud., Adol.Ment.Hlth.Abstr., Arts&Hum.Cit.Ind., Abstr.Anthropol., Bk.Rev.Ind., Amer.Hist.&Life, Ind.Jew.Per., Lang.&Lang.Behav.Abstr.

489. JOURNAL FOR THE STUDY OF JUDAISM IN THE PERSIAN, HELLENISTIC, & ROMAN PERIOD
    E. J. Brill
    Plantÿnstraat 2
    2321 JC Leiden, Netherlands

Subscription--2/yr.--88 fl. Description of subject matter of journal--Judaism in the Persian, Hellenistic, and Roman Periods. For: professors and students. Submissions must be in French, German, or English. Accepts unsolicited articles; sometimes accepts unsolicited reviews; does not accept dot-matrix printing, simultaneous submissions; publishes research notes and review-articles; accepts advertising--scholarly publications. Requires 1 copy of manuscript.

Length requirements--maximum, 30 pages; minimum, no minimum. Selection process--Articles are selected by the Editorial Board. Indexed: Old Test.Abstr., Rel.Per., New Test.Abstr., Rel.Ind.One, Rel.&Theol.Abstr.

490. JOURNAL OF REFORM JUDAISM
Samuel M. Stahl, Ed.
Central Conference of American Rabbis
21 E. 40th St.
14th Fl.
New York, NY 10016

Subscription--4/yr.--$12. Description of subject matter--Jewish thought. For: professors, students, and rabbis. Accepts unsolicited articles; sometimes accepts unsolicited reviews; does not accept simultaneous submissions; does not publish research notes; publishes review-articles; accepts advertising--primarily from publishers. Style of journal--thoughtful, nonfiction, not pedantic pure scholarship, some poetry. Requires 2 copies of manuscript. Selection process--Editorial Board. Responds--quick acknowledgment, 1-2 months for acceptance. Indexed: Ind.Jew.Per., Rel.&Theol.Abstr.

491. JUDAICA
Kurt Hruby, Ed.
Martin Cunz, Ed.
Judaica Verlag
Etzelstrasse 19
CH-8038 Zurich, Switzerland

Subscription--4/yr.--$13. Publishes articles in Scripture, Theology, Judaism, and Jewish-Christian Dialogue. For: professors, students, laypersons, pastors, and rabbis. Submissions must be in German. Accepts unsolicited articles and unsolicited reviews; does not accept dot-matrix printing; publishes research notes and review-articles; accepts advertising. Seeks articles--research, ground information, texts. Style of journal--a special subject for each issue. Requires 1 copy of manuscript. Length requirements--maximum, 15 pages; minimum, 5 pages. Selection process--Committee. Responds in one month. Parent Organization--Stiftung fuer Kirche und Judentum. Indexed: Old Test.Abstr.

492. JUDAISM
Robert Gordis, Ed.
American Jewish Congress
15 E. 84th St.
New York, NY 10028

Subscription--4/yr.--$12. Description of subject matter--

religious, moral, and ethical concepts of Judaism. Accepts unsolicited articles, dot-matrix printing; does not accept unsolicited reviews, simultaneous submissions; does not publish research notes; publishes review-articles; accepts advertising--books. For: professors, students, laypersons. Submissions must be in English. Style of journal--University of Chicago handbook. Length requirements--maximum, 5000 words. Selection process--Editorial staff reads and decides. Responds in less than a month. Approximate proportion of submissions accepted for publication--30-40 percent. Indexed: Curr.Cont., Rel.Per., SSCI, Arts&Hum.Cit.Ind., G.Soc.Sci.&Rel.Per. Lit., New Test.Abstr., Rel.Ind.One, Rel.&Theol.Abstr.

493. KEEPING POSTED
     Aron Hirt-Manheimer, Ed.
     Union of American Hebrew Congregations
     838 Fifth Ave.
     New York, NY 10021

Subscription--6/yr.--$6.25; teacher's edition, $15.25. Subject matter of journal--Each issue deals with a different topic relevant to Reform Judaism. For: professors, students, laypersons, religious schools, adult studies. Submissions must be in English. Sometimes accepts unsolicited articles; does not accept unsolicited reviews; accepts dot-matrix printing, simultaneous submissions; does not publish research notes, review-articles; does not accept advertising. Type of article the journal seeks--depends on subject matter; thus, it is a matter of real chance if an unsolicited article would meet our needs. Style of journal--magazine format. Length requirements--maximum, 2000 words; minimum, 750 words. Responds in 2-3 weeks. Approximate proportion of submissions accepted for publication--2 percent. Indexed: Ind.Jew.Per.

494. MODERN JUDAISM
     Steven T. Katz, Ed.
     Johns Hopkins University Press
     701 W. 40th St.
     Ste. 275
     Baltimore, MD 21211

Subscription--3/yr.--$17, individuals; $31, institutions. Description of subject matter of journal--high level of material on all aspects of modern Jewish life and thought. Publishes articles in Ethics, Theology, Sociology of Religion, and Philosophy of Religion as they are related to modern Judaism. For: professors, students, laypersons, rabbis, and Jewish communal workers. Submissions must be in English. Accepts unsolicited articles, unsolicited reviews, dot-matrix printing, simultaneous submissions; does not publish research notes; publishes review-articles; accepts advertising. Requires 2 copies of manuscript. Length requirements--maximum, 30 pages;

minimum, 10 pages. Selection process--readers and editor. Responds
in 3-5 months (usually). Approximate proportion of submissions accepted for publication--1/15. Indexed: Curr.Cont., Arts&Hum.Cit.
Ind., Ind.Jew.Per., Rel.Ind.One.

495. PROOFTEXTS
     Alan Mintz, Ed.
     David G. Roskies, Ed.
     Johns Hopkins University Press
     701 W. 40th St.
     Ste. 275
     Baltimore, MD 21211

Subscription--3/yr.--$18, individuals; $32, institutions. Description of subject matter--Jewish literary history from ancient to
modern times. For: professors, students, laypersons. Submissions should be in English. Accepts unsolicited articles, dot-matrix
printing; does not accept unsolicited reviews, simultaneous submissions; publishes research notes, review-articles; accepts advertising--
books, academic conferences. Seek articles of literary essays in the
Anglo-Saxon tradition--i.e., stating a general thesis and fleshing it
out with textual evidence. Articles especially seeking--articles that
have a broad frame of reference. Style of journal--essayistic, devoid
of jargon. Requires 4 copies of manuscript. Length requirements--
maximum, 30 pages; minimum, 6 pages. Selection process--articles
are prescreened by the editors-in-chief, then sent to 2 more readers
on the Editorial Board for written evaluations; a majority then decides.
Responds in 2-3 months. Approximate proportion of submissions accepted for publication--one out of 8. Indexed: Curr.Cont., Old
Test.Abstr., Arts&Hum.Cit.Ind., Ind.Jew.Per., Rel.&Theol.Abstr.,
Rel.Ind.One.

496. REVUE DES ETUDES JUIVES
     Nahon and Tohati, Eds.
     Editions Peeters s.p.r.l.
     Bondgenotenlaan 153
     B-3000 Louvein, Belgium

Subscription--4/yr.--2500 francs. Publishes articles in Judaism.
For: professors and libraries. Submissions must be in French, German, or English. Sometimes accepts unsolicited articles, unsolicited
reviews; accepts dot-matrix printing; does not accept simultaneous
submissions; publishes research notes and review-articles; accepts
advertising. Requires 1 copy of manuscript. Length requirements--
maximum, 20 pages; minimum, 5 pages. Responds to a submission in
3 months. Indexed: Bull.Signal, Lang.&Lang.Behav.Abstr., New
Test.Abstr.

497. SOVIET JEWISH AFFAIRS
      Dr. L. Hirszowicz, Ed.
      Institute of Jewish Affairs
      11 Hertford St.
      London W1Y 7DX, England

Subscription--3/yr.--$20. Description of subject matter of journal--Jewish problems in the USSR and Eastern Europe within the context of general developments in the region. Publishes articles in Sociology of Religion, Judaism, Religious Education, and Policies on Religion and Nationality. For: professors, students, and laypersons. Submissions must be in English. Accepts unsolicited articles, unsolicited reviews; does not accept simultaneous submissions; publishes research notes, review-articles; accepts advertising--of other publications in related fields. Seeks articles pertaining to all aspects of Jewish life since the 1917 revolution in the USSR and on the post-1945 development in other countries of Eastern Europe; articles on the historical background are not excluded. Especially seeking articles on Jewish religious life in the USSR. Requires 2 copies of manuscript. Length requirements--maximum, 7000 words; minimum, 2000 words. Selection process--Articles are read by members of the Editorial Board. Articles on contemporary affairs or with topical complications have priority. Academic standards are the decisive criterion. Responds to a submission--6 months or before. Approximate proportion of submissions that are accepted for publication--about 50 percent of the unsolicited submissions. Co-sponsor--World Jewish Congress. Indexed: Hist.Abstr.

498. TRADITION
      Rabbi Shalom Carmy, Ed.
      Human Sciences Press, Inc.
      275 Seventh Ave.
      New York, NY 10001

Subscription--4/yr.--$20, individuals; $25, libraries. Description of subject matter of journal--Subjects of interest to Orthodox Jews. Publishes articles in Scripture, Ethics, Theology, Psychology of Religion, Sociology of Religion, Judaism, Orthodox Jewish Thought. For: professors, students. Accepts unsolicited articles; sometimes accepts unsolicited reviews; publishes research notes and review-articles. Style of journal--MLA. Biblical verses and Talmudic passages should be included in the text, surrounded by parentheses, rather than in the notes. Transliteration of the Hebrew should follow Encyclopaedia Judaica. Requires 3 copies of manuscript. Selection process--Editorial Committee. Parent Organization--Rabbinical Council of America. Indexed: Old Test.Abstr., Arts&Hum.Cit.Ind., Ind.Jew.Per., Rel.&Theol.Abstr., Rel.Ind.One.

499. WESTERN STATES JEWISH HISTORY
      Dr. Norton B. Stern, Ed.

Western States Jewish History Association
2429 23rd St.
Santa Monica, CA   90405

Subscription--4/yr.--$15. Description of subject matter of jour-
nal--Jewish history of United States west of Mississippi, including
Alaska, Hawaii, Western Canada, Mexico and Pacific Islands. Publishes articles in Synagogue History, Sociology of Judaism, Judaism,
and Jewish Religious Education. For: professors and laypersons.
Submissions must be in English. Accepts unsolicited articles, simultaneous submissions; sometimes accepts unsolicited reviews; does not
accept dot-matrix printing; does not publish research notes; publishes review-articles; does not accept advertising. Seeks scholarly,
documented articles. Especially seeking articles of 19th century Jewish history in the West. Style of journal--standard scholarly style
and documentation. Requires one copy of manuscript. Length re-
quirements--maximum, 100 pages; minimum, 3-4 pages. Selection pro-
cess--Chosen by Editor and Associate Editor. Responds in 7-10 days.
Approximate proportion of submissions accepted for publication--75
percent. Indexed: Hist.Abstr., Amer.Hist.&Life, Ind.Jew.Per.

500. ZION
      Editorial Board
      Historical Society of Israel
      Box 4179
      Jerusalem, Israel

Subscription--4/yr.--$30. Publishes articles in Jewish History
(in all countries and all periods). For: professors, students, and
laypersons. Articles are in Hebrew with English summaries. Does
not accept simultaneous submissions; publishes research notes and
review-articles; accepts advertising--history books only. Seeks
historical research. Requires one copy of manuscript. Length re-
quirements--maximum, 30 pages; minimum, 5 pages. Selection pro-
cess--articles are given to outside readers; editorial board makes a
decision. Responds to a submission in 4-6 weeks. Indexed: Curr.
Cont., Hist.Abstr., Ind.Heb.Per., Arts&Hum.Cit.Ind., Int.Z.Bibel-
wiss., Rel.&Theol.Abstr.

OTHER JOURNALS THAT PUBLISH
ARTICLES IN JUDAISM

31. RELIGION IN AFRICA

501. AFER (AFRICAN ECCLESIAL REVIEW)
Felician N. Rwehikiza, Director
Gaba Publications
P.O. Box 4002
Eldoret, Kenya

Subscription--6/yr.--$17.60. Description of subject matter of journal--AFER offers a platform for the exchange of views and experiences to all who are involved in the apostolate in Africa; to make Christ's message relevant for Africa today. Publishes articles in Scripture, Theology, Development, Ethics, and Church History. For: professors, students, laypersons, and clergy. Submissions must be in English. Sometimes accepts unsolicited articles; does not accept dot-matrix printing; accepts simultaneous submissions; publishes research notes and review-articles; does not accept advertising. Requires one copy of manuscript. The orientation of AFER is practical and pastoral. Length requirements--maximum, 3,500 words; minimum, 700 words--double-spaced typing. Responds to a submission--3-6 months from date of receipt. Indexed: Cath.Ind., Canon Law Abstr., New Test.Abstr., Rel.Ind.One.

502. AFRICA THEOLOGICAL JOURNAL
Dr. Howard S. Olson, Ed.
Lutheran Theological College, Makumira
P.O. Box 55
Uso River, Tanzania

Subscription--3/yr.--$27. Description of subject matter of journal--subjects that concern Lutheran Christians in Africa. Publishes articles in Scripture, Ethics, Church History, Theology, Evangelism, Missions, Sociology of Religion, Ecumenism, and the Relationship between Christianity and African Traditional Religions. Accepts unsolicited articles and unsolicited reviews. For: professors, students, laypersons, and clergy. Submissions must be in English. Length requirements--maximum, 6,000 words. Selection process--Editorial Board reviews submissions. Co-sponsor--Lutheran World Federation. Indexed: New Test.Abstr., Rel.Ind.One.

503. ANNALES AEQUATORIA
Centre Aequatoria de Bamanya
Mbandaka, Zaire

Subscription--1/yr.--$15.00. Description of subject matter of journal--Annales Aequatoria publishes results of research into Central African cultures, history, and languages. Submissions must be in French.

504. CAMEROON PANORAMA
Sr. Mercy Horgan, Ed.
P.O. Box 46, Buea
South West Province
Republic of Cameroon, West Africa

Subscription--12/yr.--1000 CFA; 4000 CFA, overseas. Subject matter of journal--Scripture, Church History, and Theology. Submissions must be in English.

505. DIALOGUE
Yvon Pomerleau, Ed.
Joseph Ntamahungiro, Ed.
B.P. 572
Kigali, Rwanda

Subject matter of journal--Missions, Sociology of Religion, and Religious Education. Accepts unsolicited articles. Submissions must be in French.

506. EAST AFRICA JOURNAL OF EVANGELICAL THEOLOGY
Rev. Isaac Simbiri, Ed.
Box 49
Machakos, Kenya

Subscription--2/yr.--Kshs. 100.00; $20.00, overseas. Subject matter of journal--Scripture, Ethics, Church History, Theology, Evangelism, Sociology of Religion, Religion and Literature. Accepts unsolicited articles and unsolicited book reviews. Submissions must be in English. Indexed: Rel.Ind.One: Periodicals.

507. JOURNAL OF RELIGION IN AFRICA/RELIGION EN AFRIQUE
E. J. Brill
Oude Rijn 33a-35
2312 HB Leiden, Netherlands

Subscription--3/yr.--72 fl. Description of subject matter of journal--all aspects of the history, sociology and spirituality of the

religions of Africa, especially traditional religions, Christianity and
Islam. For: professors, students. Submissions must be in French
or English. Accepts unsolicited articles; does not accept unsolicited
reviews, dot-matrix printing, simultaneous submissions; does not publish research notes; publishes review-articles; does not accept advertising. Seeks specialized articles breaking new ground based on
original research (whether field research or archival), or original
theoretical studies. Especially seeking studies of either past or contemporary religious developments in Africa hitherto ignored or little
considered. Style of journal--fully academic and scholarly. It is
not a journal of theology nor of evangelism. Length requirements--
maximum, 12,000 words; minimum, 4000 words. Selection process--
articles that are considered appropriate by the Editor are sent out
to other members of the Editorial Board for a second or third opinion. Responds to a submission--Acknowledgment given at once; acceptance or rejection normally within 1 month. Approximate proportion of submissions accepted for publication--30 percent. Indexed:
Cur.Cont., Rel.Per., Arts&Hum.Cit.Ind., Rel.Ind.One.

508. JOURNAL OF THEOLOGY FOR SOUTHERN AFRICA
     J. W. de Gruchy, Ed.
     c/o University of Cape Town
     Dept. of Religious Studies
     7700 Rodebosch
     Cape Town, South Africa

Subscription--4/yr.--R10,00, Southern Africa; R15,00, Libraries;
Elsewhere R15,00 (in SA currency only) or $15.00 US; institutions,
R25,00 (in SA currency only) or $25.00 US; single copies, R3,00.
Description of subject matter of journal--broadly theological, academic,
contextual, ecumenical. The journal's purpose is to encourage theo-
logical reflection and dialogue within the Southern African context.
Publishes articles in Scripture, Ethics, Church History, Theology,
Evangelism, Church Administration, Pastoral Counseling, Missions,
Psychology of Religion, Sociology of Religion, World Religions,
Philosophy of Religion, Judaism, Islam, Hinduism, Buddhism, Eastern
Religions, African Traditional Religions, Religious Education. Especially seeking articles of contextual theology relating to Southern
Africa. Accepts unsolicited articles, unsolicited reviews, dot-matrix
printing, simultaneous submissions; publishes research notes and
review-articles; accepts advertising. For: professors, students, laypersons, others. Submissions must be in English. Requires 1 copy
of manuscript. Length requirements--maximum, 7500 words (typed,
double-spaced according to Univ. of Chicago Press Manual of Style);
minimum, (same specifications) 4000 words. Selection process--arti-
cles are refereed. The reception of manuscripts will be acknowledged
as soon as possible after they have been received, but the decision
to publish is normally made only after the receipt of a referee's report. Approximate proportion of submissions accepted for publication--
60 percent. Indexed: Old Test.Abstr., New Test.Abstr., Rel.Ind.
One.

509. LUCERNA
Rev. Msgr. Cyriac S. Mba, Ed.
Bigard Memorial Seminary
P.O. Box 327
Enugu, Nigeria

Subject matter of journal--Theology, Sociology of Religion,
and World Religions. Submissions must be in English. Accepts unsolicited articles.

510. ORITA
J. Kenny, Ed.
University of Ibadan
Dept. of Religious Studies
Ibadan, Nigeria

Subscription--2/yr.--$16. The aim of the journal is to promote
the study and understanding of "the phenomenon and the social implications of religion in general and religion in Africa in particular."
This involves more specifically "the field of history and phenomenology
of religions, theology and philosophy, aiming at an interpretation and
understanding of African Traditional Religion, Christianity and Islam,
separately and insofar as there has been cross-fertilization between
them." Every effort will be made to give an equal amount of space
to articles and reviews dealing with each of the three Faiths; and
to encourage articles which treat their interaction. The phenomenon
of secularization, which represents a common problem for them all
will also not be neglected. Orita is a Yoruba word meaning "where
the ways meet." Subject matter of journal--Scripture, Ethics, Church
History, Theology, Psychology of Religion, Sociology of Religion,
Philosophy of Religion, Islam, and African Traditional Religion. For:
professors, students, and laypersons. Submissions must be in English. Accepts unsolicited articles, unsolicited reviews, dot-matrix
printing, simultaneous submissions; publishes research notes, review-
articles; accepts advertising--any legitimate. Requires 2 copies of
manuscript. Length requirements--maximum, 30 pages double-spaced;
minimum, 10 pages. Selection process--two assessors must give a
positive report. Responds to a submission in 6 mos. Approximate
proportion of submissions accepted for publication--15 percent. Indexed: Afr.Abstr.

511. RELIGION IN SOUTHERN AFRICA
M. H. Prozesky, Ed.
Association for the Study of Religion (Southern Africa)
Box 375
Pietermaritzburg 3200, South Africa

Subscription--2/yr.--$12. Description of subject matter of jour-
nal--Academic studies of the religions of Southern Africa and elsewhere

by means of the methods associated with Religious Studies/Science of Religion. Publishes articles in Psychology of Religion, Sociology of Religion, World Religions, Philosophy of Religion, Judaism, Islam, Hinduism, Buddhism, Eastern Religions, and Methodology in Religious Studies. For: professors. Submissions must be in English. Accepts unsolicited articles, unsolicited reviews, dot-matrix printing; does not accept simultaneous submissions; publishes research notes and review-articles; accepts advertising--academic and book-related. Seeks articles that are research based dealing with the religions of Southern Africa and more general studies of religion. Especially looking for studies of religion and apartheid in South Africa and articles on the contemporary philosophy of religion. Style of journal--Harvard reference system, endnotes. Requires 2 copies of manuscript. Length requirements--maximum, 7000 words; minimum, 2000 words. Selection process--Submission to at least two independent referees from or nominated by an International Editorial Advisory Board followed by Editorial Board decision. Receipt of manuscript is acknowledged immediately; a verdict takes approximately 4-5 weeks. Approximate proportion of submissions accepted for publication--50 percent. Indexed: Ind.S.A.Per., Rel.Ind.One.

OTHER JOURNALS THAT PUBLISH ARTICLES ON RELIGION IN AFRICA

Journal of Religion 47
Journal of Religious Studies 48
Journal of Religious Thought 49
Leadership 331
Maryknoll 364
Le Monde Copte 237
Neotestamentica 203
The Nigerian Journal of Philosophy 144
The Nigerian Journal of Theology 291
Orientation 389
Pro Mundi Vita Bulletin 241
Pro Mundi Vita Dossiers 242
Reconciliation International 265
Religion in Communist Lands 245
Religious Studies Review 75
Revue Africaine de Theologie 79
Revue Zairoise de Theologie Protestante 84

Sojourners 268
Telema 156
Theologia Evangelica 301
Witness 269
Zeitschrift fuer Religions und Geistesgeschichte 107

32. RELIGION IN ASIA

512. ASIAN ISSUES
International Affairs
57, Peking Road
41F Kowloon, Hong Kong

Subscription--2/yr. Subject matter of journal--Church History, Sociology of Religion, World Religions, Philosophy of Religion, Buddhism, Eastern Religions. Submissions must be in English.

513. BANGALORE THEOLOGICAL FORUM
The Rev. Dr. Eric J. Lott, Ed.
United Theological College
17 Miller's Rd.
Bangalore 560 046, S. India

Subscription--4/yr.--$10. Description of subject matter of journal--Indian Theology, Worship and Folk-Religion; Islamic Hermeneutics; Spirituality. Publishes articles in Philosophy of Religion. For: professors, students, laypersons, and alumni. Submissions must be in English. Sometimes accepts unsolicited articles and unsolicited reviews. Selection process--contributions are primarily by the staff, students, and alumni of the United Theological College. Indexed: Rel.Ind.One.

514. CHINA STUDY PROJECT JOURNAL
British Council of Churches
Edinburgh House
2 Eaton Gate
London SW1W 9BL, England

Subject matter of journal--Missions, Sociology of religion, Islam, Buddhism, and Eastern Religions. Accepts unsolicited articles. Submissions must be in English. Seeking articles that extend our knowledge of the history of the major religions of China where these provide insights of relevance to understanding the contemporary religious situation. Selection process--Editorial Board.

515. THE CHINESE THEOLOGICAL REVIEW
     86 East 12th Street
     Holland, MI   49423

Subscription--1/yr. Subject matter of journal--Church History, Theology, Sociology of Religion, World Religions, Philosophy of Religion, Islam, Buddhism, Eastern Religions, Religious Education. Does not accept unsolicited articles or unsolicited reviews. Submissions must be in English. Presents translations of previously published Chinese articles, stories and sermons. Parent Organization--Foundation for Theological Education in Southeast Asia.

516. DANSALAN QUARTERLY
     Michael J. Diamond, Ed.
     P.O. Box 5430
     Lligan City 8801, Philippines

Subject matter of journal--Sociology of Religion and Islam. Submissions must be in English.

517. FOCUS
     Pastoral Institute
     P.O. Box 288
     Multan, Pakistan

Subscription--RS 50; $15.00, overseas. Subject matter of journal--Theology, Sociology of Religion, Philosophy of Religion, Islam, Hinduism, and Eastern Religions. Accepts unsolicited articles. Parent Organization--The Conference of Major Superiors in Pakistan.

518. INDIAN JOURNAL OF THEOLOGY
     Editor
     c/o Bishop's College
     224 Acharya Jagadish Bose Road
     Calcutta 700 017, India

Subscription--4/yr.--$8. Description of subject matter of journal--all aspects of theology that are of special interest to theological students in India. For: professors, students, laypersons. Submissions must be in English. Publishes articles in Scripture, Ethics, Church History, Theology, Evangelism, World Religions, Philosophy of Religion, Islam, and Hinduism. Accepts unsolicited articles and unsolicited reviews. Selection process--Editorial Board. Indexed: Old Test.Abstr., New Test.Abstr., Rel.Per., Rel.Ind.One, Rel.&Theol.Abstr.

519. INDIAN THEOLOGICAL STUDIES
     St. Peter's Pontifical Seminary

Mallescuaram West P.O.
Bangalore - 560 055, India

Subscription--4/yr.--RS. 30, India; $12.00, overseas. De-
scription of subject matter of journal--Indian Theological Studies
provides a forum for theological research either conducted in India
or relevant to India. Publishes articles in Church History, Church
Administration, Sociology of Religion, Islam, Hinduism, and Eastern
Religions.

520. INTER-RELIGIO
Nanzan Institute for Religion and Culture
18 Yamazato-cho, Showa-ku
Nagoya 466, Japan

Subscription--2/yr.--free. Description of subject matter of
journal--Inter-Religio serves as a clearing house for ideas on interreligious encounter in Eastern Asia. Subject matter of journal--
Evangelism, Sociology of Religion, Buddhism, Eastern Religions, and
Ecumenism. Submissions must be in English.

521. JAPAN CHRISTIAN QUARTERLY
George L. Olson
Kyo Bun Kwan
4-5-1 Ginza, Chuo-Ku
Tokyo 104, Japan

Subscription--4/yr.--$28. Description of subject matter of
journal--Christian thought, opinion, and action in Japan (or related
to Japanese people). Publishes articles in Theology, Evangelism,
Pastoral Counseling, Missions, Sociology of Religion, World Religions,
Buddhism, Eastern Religions, Religious Education as topics relate to
Japanese Christianity. For: professors, students, laypersons, missionaries, mission executives. Submissions must be in English. Sometimes accepts unsolicited articles, unsolicited reviews; accepts dot-
matrix printing, simultaneous submissions; publishes research notes
(but encourages incorporating material into articles); publishes review-
articles; accepts advertising--travel, medical, publishing, education,
etc. Seeks articles that deal with pertinent issues and/or activities
in or about Japanese Christianity. Especially seeking historical articles that have significant meaning for contemporary Japanese Christianity. Style of journal--Chicago; style sheets available on request.
Requires one copy of manuscript. Length requirements--maximum,
30 double-spaced pages; minimum--8 double-spaced pages. Selection
process--largely determined by the editor. He may seek advice from
editorial staff. Usually tries to fit submissions into themes of issues.
Responds in 3 months. Approximate proportion of submissions accepted for publication--50 percent. Comments: Japan Christian
Quarterly's history goes back to 1893. Parent Organization--Fellow-
ship of Christian Missionaries. Indexed: Rel.Per., Rel.Ind.One.

522. JAPANESE JOURNAL OF RELIGIOUS STUDIES
      Jan Swyngedouw, Ed.
      Nanzan Institute for Religion and Culture
      18 Yamazato-cho
      Showa-ku
      Nagoya 466, Japan

Subscription--3/yr. (one in double issue--usually nos. 2-3)--
$20, individuals; $25, institutions. Description of subject matter of
journal--Japanese religiosity from a non-sectarian viewpoint (also
more general issues in the scientific study of religion but preferably
related to Japan or East). Publishes articles in Japanese Christianity,
Psychology of Religion, Sociology of Religion, World Religions, Philosophy of Religion, Buddhism, Eastern Religions, and above. For: professors, students, and others who are interested in Japanese religiosity. Submissions must be in English. Accepts unsolicited articles,
dot-matrix printing; does not accept unsolicited reviews, simultaneous
submissions; publishes research notes, review-articles; does not accept advertising. Seeks articles by young scholars who have just
finished a doctoral thesis on a subject connected with Japanese religiosity. Requires one copy of manuscript. Length requirements--
maximum, 30-35 pages; minimum 10-15 pages. Selection process--a
small committee of advisors, familiar with the subject, decides on the
acceptance. Responds in about a month. Approximate proportion of
submissions accepted for publication--50 percent. Indexed: Curr.
Cont., Arts&Hum.Cit.Ind., Rel.Ind.One.

523. JAPANESE RELIGIONS
      Hideo Yuki, Ed.
      National Christian Council of Japan
      NCC Center for the Study of Japanese Religions
      Karasuma-Shimotachiuri
      Kamikyo-ku
      Kyoto 602, Japan

Subscription--2/yr.--$16. Subject matter of journal--Japanese
Religions--particularly encounter between Christianity/Buddhism,
Shinto, New Religions. For: professors, students. Submissions
must be in English. Accepts unsolicited articles, unsolicited reviews;
does not accept dot-matrix printing; sometimes publishes research
notes; publishes review-articles; does not accept advertising. Style
of journal--scholarly, but not for the sake of scholarship; also pastoral. Requires 1 copy of manuscript. Length requirements--maxi-
mum, 25 pages; minimum, 10 pages. Selection process--Editor and
Editorial Committee. Responds in about two weeks. Approximate
proportion of submissions accepted for publication--25-30 percent.
Indexed: Rel.&Theol.Abstr., Rel.Ind.One.

OTHER JOURNALS THAT PUBLISH ARTICLES
ON RELIGION IN ASIA

524. BOLETIN TEOLOGICO
Oficina de la FTL
José-Mármol 1734
(1602) Florida, Buenos Aires
Argentina

Subscription--4/yr.--$7.00; $12,00, overseas. Subject matter of journal--Scripture, Evangelism, and Sociology of Religion. Parent Organization--Fraternidad Teologica Latinoamericana.

525. CARIBBEAN JOURNAL OF RELIGIOUS STUDIES
Rev. Ashley Smith, Ed.
United Theological College of the West Indies
Golding Ave.
P.O. Box 136
Mona, Kingston 7, Jamaica, W.I.

Subscription--Sept.-April-- $10. Description of subject matter of journal--all matters related to religion with special reference to Third World concerns. Publishes articles in Scripture, Ethics, Church History, Theology, Church Administration, Pastoral Counseling, Missions, Psychology of Religion, Sociology of Religion, World Religions, Philosophy of Religion, Islam, Hinduism, Eastern Religions, Religious Education, Theology and Personality. For: professors, students, laypersons. Submissions must be in English. Seeks articles dealing with the interaction between religion and society; communication of the Gospel; interpretation of Scripture. Especially looking for articles aimed at clarifying issues related to Scripture and traditional theology. Requires 3 copies of manuscript. Length requirements-- maximum, 3000 words; minimum, 1500 words. Selection process-- articles need to conform to a theme or an issue under consideration. Responds in about a month. Comments: we appreciate contributions from persons who have visited or lived in the Caribbean region. Indexed: Rel.Ind.One.

526. CRISTIANISMO Y SOCIEDAD
Jean Pierre Poastian, Director
Apartado postal 20-656

Col. San Angel
Mexico 01000, D. F. Mexico

Subscription--4/yr.--$12. Description of subject matter of journal--A platform for interdisciplinary study of religious phenomena in Latin America. Interested in interpreting the religious reality of Latin America by using the tools of history, sociology, political science, anthropology, theology, and philosophy. Publishes articles in Scripture, Ethics, Church History, Theology, Evangelism, Psychology of Religion, Sociology of Religion, Philosophy of Religion, Religious Education, and Ecumenical Studies. Accepts unsolicited articles. Selection process--Editorial Board and outside referees. Indexed: Rel.Ind.One.

527. CULTURA POPULAR
José Maria Serra, Dir.
CELADEC
General Garzón 2267
Lima 11, Peru

Subscription--4/yr.--$15, individuals; $20, institutions; $24, overseas. Subject matter of journal--Sociology of Religion and Religious Education. Accepts unsolicited articles and advertising. Submissions must be in Spanish.

528. KEYHOLE
Richard Renshaw, Ed.
Ladoc
Apartado 5594
Lima 100, Peru

Subscription--6/yr.--$7.00, Peru; $18.00, overseas. Description of subject matter of journal--each issue of the Keyhole Series explores one theme essential to understanding the Church in Latin America. Publishes articles in Scripture, Ethics, Church History, Theology, Evangelism, Sociology of Religion and Religious Education. Submissions must be in English.

529. LATIN AMERICA PRESS
Noticias Aliadas
Apartado 5594
Lima 100, Peru

Subscription--48/yr.--$40, individuals; $60, institutions. Description of subject matter of journal--Latin American news analysis from the point of view of church and human rights. Publishes articles in Church History, Politics, Human Rights, Economics, and Socio-Cultural News. For: laypersons. Submissions must be in

French, Spanish, or English. Sometimes accepts unsolicited articles; does not accept unsolicited reviews, accepts dot-matrix printing, simultaneous submissions; does not publish research notes or review-articles; does not accept advertising. Seeks news stories with some church angle that reflect the daily lives and struggles of Latin American peoples. Style of journal--interpretative journalism. Requires 2 copies of manuscript. Length requirements--maximum, 1500 words; minimum, 1000 words. Selection process--weekly Editorial Staff Meetings. Responds in 3-5 weeks. Approximate proportion of submissions accepted for publication--60 percent. Indexed: I.C.U.I.S.Abstr.

530. MENSAJE
Renato Hevia, Ed.
Compania de Jesus
Provincia Chilena
Residencia San Roberto Bellarmino
Almirante Barroso 24
Casilla 10445
Santiago, Chile

Subscription--10/yr.--$35. Description of subject matter of journal--national and international affairs from a Christian viewpoint. Publishes articles in Ethics, Theology, Evangelism, and Pastoral Counseling. For: professors, students, laypersons, bishops, clergy. Submissions must be in Spanish. Accepts unsolicited articles; sometimes accepts unsolicited reviews; does not publish research notes; publishes review-articles; accepts advertising. Seeks articles telling how Christianity helps shape a better society. Especially seeking articles on how to be a Christian in a wealthy society such as the U.S. Requires 1 copy of manuscript. Length requirements--maximum, 3000 words; minimum, 1000 words. Indexed: Biol.Abstr.

OTHER JOURNALS THAT PUBLISH ARTICLES ON RELIGION IN LATIN AMERICA

CEHILA 114
Christus 252
Cuadernos de Derechos Humanos 256
Cuestiones Teológicas Medellin 278
Grande Sinal 345
Journal of Religion 47
Journal of Religious Studies 48
Lucha/Struggle 259

Maryknoll 364
Perspectiva Teologica 292
Pro Mundi Vita Bulletin 241
Pro Mundi Vita Dossiers 242
Puebla 264
Reconciliation International 265
Religion in Communist Lands 245
Religious Studies Review 75
Revista Biblica 188
Revista Eclesiástica Brasileira 78

APPENDIX: LIST OF STYLE MANUALS

1. AP. French, Christopher W., Eileen Alt Powell, and Howard Angione, eds. The Associated Press Stylebook and Libel Manual. Reading, MA: Addison-Wesley Publishing Company, Inc., 1980.

2. APA. American Psychological Association. Publication Manual of the American Psychological Association. 3rd ed. Washington, D.C.: American Psychological Association, 1983.

3. CBQ. "Instructions for Contributors," Catholic Biblical Quarterly 46 (1984): 393-408.

4. CAMPBELL'S. Campbell, William Giles, Stephen Vaughan Ballou, and Carole Slade. Form and Style: theses, reports, term papers. 7th ed. Boston: Houghton Mifflin, 1986.

5. CHICAGO or CHICAGO MANUAL OF STYLE. University of Chicago Press. The Chicago Manual of Style. 13th ed. of A Manual of Style Revised and Expanded. Chicago: University of Chicago Press, 1982.

6. HTR or HARVARD. "Instructions for Contributors," Harvard Theological Review 80 (1987): 243-260.

7. JBL. "Instructions for Contributors," Journal of Biblical Literature 95 (1976): 311-46.

8. MLA. Achtert, Walter S., and Joseph Gibaldi, eds. The MLA Style Manual. New York: Modern Language Association of America, 1985.

9. NEW YORK TIMES. Jordan, Lewis, ed. The New York Times Manual of Style and Usage. New York: The New York Times Company, 1976.

10. SBL. Society of Biblical Literature. SBL Member's Handbook. Chico, CA: Scholars Press, 1980.

11. TURABIAN or KATE TURABIAN. Turabian, Kate L. A Manual for Writers of Term Papers, Theses, and Dissertations. 5th ed. revised and expanded by Bonnie Birtwistle Honigsblum. Chicago and London: The University of Chicago Press, 1987.

12. WEBSTER'S or WEBSTER'S THIRD DICTIONARY. Merriam-
     Webster Inc. Webster's Third New International Dictionary of
     the English Language Unabridged. Springfield, MA: Merriam-
     Webster Inc., 1981.

13. WEBSTER'S NINTH COLLEGIATE DICTIONARY. Merriam-
     Webster Inc. Webster's Ninth New Collegiate Dictionary.
     Springfield, MA: Merriam-Webster Inc., 1984.

INDEX OF JOURNALS